RUSI DEFENCE STUDIES SERIES

General Editor David Bolton, Director, Royal United Services Institute for Defence Studies

Questions on defence give rise to emotion, sometimes to the detriment of balanced judgement. Since 1831 the Royal United Services Institute for Defence Studies has been noted for its objectivity, independence and initiative, the views of its members sharpened by responsibility and experience. In continuance of the Institute's aims, the *RUSI Defence Studies Series* seeks to provide a wider understanding and better informed debate of defence and national security issues. However, the views expressed in the books are those of the authors alone.

Published

Richard Clutterbuck
THE FUTURE OF POLITICAL VIOLENCE: Destabilization, Disorder
   and Terrorism

Christopher Coker
NATO, THE WARSAW PACT AND AFRICA
THE FUTURE OF THE ATLANTIC ALLIANCE
THE UNITED STATES, WESTERN EUROPE AND MILITARY
   INTERVENTION OVERSEAS
US MILITARY POWER IN THE 1980s

John Hemsley
THE SOVIET BIOCHEMICAL THREAT TO NATO: The Neglected
   Issue

Michael Hobkirk
THE POLITICS OF DEFENCE BUDGETING: A Study of Organisation
   and Resource Allocation in the UK and USA

Michael Leifer (editor)
THE BALANCE OF POWER IN EAST ASIA

K. G. Robertson (editor)
BRITISH AND AMERICAN APPROACHES TO INTELLIGENCE

Clive Rose
CAMPAIGNS AGAINST WESTERN DEFENCE: NATO's Adversaries
   and Critics

James Sherr
SOVIET POWER: The Continuing Challenge

E. S. Williams
THE SOVIET MILITARY: Political Education, Training and Morale

Forthcoming

Ewen Broadbent
THE MILITARY AND GOVERNMENT FROM MACMILLAN TO
    HESELTINE

Christopher Coker
US MILITARY POWER IN THE 1990s

Anthony H. Cordesman
FROM LEBANON TO THE FALKLANDS: The Lessons of Five Wars

Jonathan Eyal
THE BALKANS: The Soviet Union's Soft Underbelly?

Michael Hobkirk
DEFENCE DECISIONS: A Survey of Inter-Service Rivalry

THE UNITED STATES, WESTERN EUROPE AND MILITARY INTERVENTION OVERSEAS

Edited by

Christopher Coker

Lecturer in International Relations
The London School of Economics

MACMILLAN
PRESS

First published 1987

Published by
THE MACMILLAN PRESS LTD
Houndmills, Basingstoke, Hampshire RG21 2XS
and London
Companies and representatives
throughout the world

Typeset by Wessex Typesetters
(Division of The Eastern Press Ltd)
Frome, Somerset

Printed and bound in Great Britain at
The Camelot Press Ltd, Southampton

British Library Cataloguing in Publication Data
The United States, Western Europe and military
intervention overseas.—(RUSI defence
studies series)
1. Developing countries—Foreign relations
2. Developing countries—History, Military
3. Intervention (International law)—History
I. Coker, Christopher   II. Series
341.5′8   D887
ISBN 0–333–40554–4

Contents

Notes on the Contributors

John Chipman is Assistant Director for Regional Security Studies at the International Institute for Strategic Studies in London. He was formerly Research Associate at the Atlantic Institute for International Affairs in Paris. He is author of *French Military Policy and African Security*, Adelphi Paper 201 (1985), from which parts of this chapter have been drawn. He has also edited books on NATO's southern region and NATO institutions.

Christopher Coker is a Lecturer in International Relations at the London School of Economics, and was previously a Junior Research Fellow at Wolfson College, Oxford. He is the author of *US Military Power in the 1980s*, *The Future of the Atlantic Alliance*, *NATO*, *The Warsaw Pact and Africa* and *Constructive Engagement and its Critics: The United States and South Africa 1968–84* as well as numerous articles on African politics and related issues.

Paul E. Gallis is an analyst in West European affairs at the Congressional Research Service in Washington DC. He received an AB degree from Davidson College in North Carolina. He holds an MA and a PhD in history from Brown University, and has studied at the University of Montpellier and the Ecole des Hautes Etudes en Sciences Sociales in France. He has worked at the State Department and as a speechwriter for a US Senator.

Andrew Hurrell is Assistant Professor of International Relations at the Johns Hopkins University's School of Advanced International Studies in Bologna, Italy, and was formerly a Research Lecturer at Christ Church, Oxford. He is the author of *The Quest for Autonomy: Brazil's Changing Role in the International System* and various articles on Latin American foreign policies.

Douglas T. Stuart is Director of the International Studies Program at Dickinson College, Carlisle, Pennsylvania. He is the author (with

William T. Tow) of *The Limits of Alliance: NATO Out of Area Problems since 1949*; editor of *Politics and Security in the Southern Region of the Atlantic Alliance* and *Security within the Pacific Rim*; and co-editor of *China, the Soviet Union and the West*. His articles have appeared in *Atlantic Quarterly*, *China Quarterly*, *International Affairs*, *NATO Review*, *ORBIS*, *Third World Affairs* and *World Today*.

Bernhard Weimer has been a research staff member at the Research Institute for International Affairs (Africa Desk) of the Stiftung Wissenschaft und Politik in Ebenhausen, West Germany, since 1980. Educated at the Universities of Hamburg and Munich (Diplom Volkswirt, 1973), he served as Research Fellow at the National Institute of Development Research and Documentation, University of Botswana (1975–8). His publications include monographs on Botswana and Mozambique as well as articles which have appeared in *Atlantic Quarterly*, *Afrika Spectrum* and *Informationsdienst Südliches Afrika*.

Phil Williams is Lecturer in International Relations at the University of Southampton. He is author of *Crisis Management* and *The Senate and US Troops in Europe*, co-author of *Contemporary Strategy* and co-editor of *The Carter Years*. He has also contributed articles to many journals and is the author of a Chatham House paper on *US Troops in Europe*.

Introduction

Those familiar with the Atlantic Alliance's 40-year history will not fail to be impressed by the unremitting tension between the national interests of its members and those of the Alliance as a whole. Nor will they have been able to ignore the endemic tension between interests defined by treaty and those that fall outside the strict treaty area, in regions beyond the Tropic of Cancer. Apart from the United States, which has always seen itself as a power with interests outside the Alliance, most of its European members have remained for the most part heavily dependent upon non-European lines of communication and even more on non-European sources of fuel and non-fuel raw materials, especially in Southern Africa and the Middle East. Whether those interests are best defended by NATO or, indeed, whether NATO is the best forum in which to discuss their defence, has been a persistent, and frequently divisive, theme in the Alliance since its earliest years.

This book is not a study of NATO out-of-area operations as such, nor is it specifically about NATO. It represents a collection of essays on a variety of themes within a single analytical framework: the extent to which Western Europe, acting either on its own account or in association with the United States, can intervene out-of-area and contribute to the defence of Western interests defined somewhat more broadly than at present in the Atlantic Charter.

Recently the perceptions of international interests have extended to take account of West of Suez issues as well, especially in the South Atlantic, a subject treated at length by one of the seven authors. All of the contributors, whether writing of Africa or the Middle East, whether looking historically at the subject in order to draw lessons for the future, or focussing on NATO as an organisation, are pre-occupied by a question that has come to tax the imagination and energies of both Europeans and Americans alike. No other subject, except for the management of *détente* and arms control, has proved more divisive or more fraught with difficulties in the enduring relationship between the United States and its European allies.

Despite the unity of the theme, not all the authors are agreed on the importance which should be attached to out-of-area problems or the way in which they are best tackled. None of them, however, would dispute the fact that the overall subject is either eccentric or marginal. Whether these essays contain valid interpretations or reasonable hypotheses, they express the reactions and sentiments of a group of writers confronting problems common to all the NATO countries but to the West Europeans most of all. It is they who will have to confront the problem of adjusting to a diminishing role in the Third World, and a diminishing US presence in Western Europe. How they do so will depend on the importance they attach to non-European security issues. To this extent, the essays represent not theory but testimony, testimony to a phenomenon which has yet to be lived through: European military intervention in areas of the world from which the Europeans have been absent for many years. Some of the authors suggest that there are opportunities still to be created, others, such as the Editor, that those opportunities are merely ways of escape from the intractable dilemmas of the defence of Western Europe. The reader, as always, will draw his own conclusions.

In the making of such a work, a number of debts should be acknowledged. I am particularly grateful to the Royal United Services Institute for the occasion to publish this collection of essays in their *Defence Studies Series*. Special thanks are due to Caroline Bolton and Brian Holden Reid for their encouragement throughout and for the production of the final manuscript. The book itself, of course, would not have been possible without the active cooperation of the authors and the enthusiasm with which they set to their task. The editor's task was the easiest one of all.

CHRISTOPHER COKER

1 East of Suez Revisited: The Strategic Recoupling of Western Europe and the Third World

CHRISTOPHER COKER

The retreat of European military power east of Suez has been a persistent theme of international politics since the mid-1970s – captured on film of flags lowering ceremonies in the British colonies, and peacekeeping operations in Aden and Cyprus, until the retreat seemed to come full circle with the troubles in Ulster after 1969. For the French the break was less dramatic, but still real. In the early 1970s a spate of successful coups which swept French clients out of Niger, the Central African Republic and finally Chad prompted many to question whether the presence of French troops elsewhere served any useful purpose. The evacuation of 2000 troops from Chad was followed closely by the evacuation of French forces from Madagascar (1973). By 1974 only one company of marines remained in Gabon, and about 1000 troops in the whole of central Africa.

The retreat from east of Suez was marked by a clear faltering of purpose. This was perhaps its most distinctive feature. There were occasional Anglo-Dutch and Anglo-French naval exercises off the Cape in 1972 and 1974 respectively, and occasional manoeuvres like the Ber Satu exercise in the Far East in 1971 during which 2500 men and 200 vehicles were airlifted from the United Kingdom in the space of ten days. But for all this investment of men and resources it served only to parade a commitment the Europeans preferred to observe in the breach rather than the observance. Europe's retreat left a vacuum of purpose rather than power; its military exercises represented

1

commitments which could not be cashed, promissory notes which
could never be drawn. Britain's emphasis on strategic mobility rather
than fixed bases, and the importance which the French attached to the
metropolitan *force d'intervention*, marked a clear policy of
retrenchment, or strategic contraction.

In the mid-1960s Britain's defence secretary, Denis Healey, had told
a meeting in Canberra that Britain intended to remain 'in the military
sense, a world power' for many years to come.[1] As Chancellor of the
Exchequer, however, in the next labour government in 1974 he could
not even find the money for a *west* of Suez role, for a fleet in the
Mediterranean, or a naval base in Malta, or the permanent
deployment of frigates in the Caribbean, much less the maintenance in
Simonstown of the South Atlantic station. By 1977 Britain's non-
NATO expenditure was less than 1.5 per cent compared with 20 per
cent in the mid-1960s. The 1966–8 review process had turned on the cost
of overseas intervention which the government had merely wished to
contain, or scale down; the 1975 review turned on the implicit
understanding that the European theatre was the only sphere of
operations in which British forces 'can best contribute', a clear
repudiation of Wilson's claim seven years earlier that a thousand men
in the Persian Gulf were a far more valuable investment than another
thousand men on the Rhine.

The second factor which influenced the Europeans in the retreat
into fortress Europe was the confidence in which their overseas allies
or former dependencies clearly felt they could dispense with external
support. Such previously stalwart allies of France as Benin and
Congo-Brazaville terminated their defence agreements while Senegal
and Cameroon insisted on defining the clauses more precisely.
Although the retreat was marked by great diversities of approach and
differences of attitude, although it was more protracted in some parts of
the world than others, strategic decoupling followed on from
independence within ten years. Britain concluded a treaty with only
one Commonwealth state, Malaysia, and agreements with two others,
the Maldives and Mauritius. The rest felt they could dispense with
British protection altogether.[2] When the Heath government tried to
reverse the withdrawal from the Gulf in 1971 the Gulf sheikdoms made
it clear that they were in no hurry to have the British back. Inevitably,
in these circumstances the retreat gave a spurious plausibility to the
theme of coming to terms with history, of abdicating a role which
seemed more relevant in the context of imperialism than the cold war.

It also gave a special importance to the European theatre at a time when the British were once again seeking admission to the European Community. For the government of Edward Heath, less prone to imperial nostalgia than its predecessors, the retreat fitted well into its own construct of Britain's future.

Finally, the recall of the legions tended to reinforce a belief which became increasingly popular in European circles, coloured by the Nye and Keohane school of international relations in the United States, that military power was no longer cost-effective, a business term which rapidly found its way into the academic discipline – strategic studies. In Britain economists, not military strategists, were elected in the early 1970s to head institutes devoted to the study of conflict, notably Andrew Shonfield at Chatham House, and François Duchene at the IISS, a man who went on to coin the phrase 'civilian power' to describe a continent that had become convinced that military force no longer held out much political utility. In the 1960s and 1970s civilian status even appeared to have transformed Europe's military weakness into a political asset which offered it a unique chance to ride out the apparent tide of history, to escape inevitable relegation to the second league of powers.

In the wake of the Vietnam war many Americans were inclined to believe this too. In the Reith lectures of 1973 Schonfield quoted with approval an article in *Foreign Affairs* by a senior American economic official who, starting from the doubtful premise that 'commercial and financial issues are starting to replace traditional diplomatic and security questions as the main stuff of foreign policy' had gone on to argue that the United States itself would have to adjust to the 'changing framework of international politics'.[3] It was because the European community had become such a significant part of that international framework, not least in the Third World through such economic arrangements as the Lomé Convention, that Schonfield expected that the problem of adjustment for the United States would be particularly acute.

There was not much political or academic support for military operations overseas in a period when so many authorities who could agree on little else, were none the less unanimous in devaluing military power and writing off the United States and the Soviet Union as declining powers attempting to prop up their crumbling 'imperial systems'. This conclusion was so pervasive that the Europeans could not even resist involvement in their own political eclipse by devaluing what military strength of their own still remained. Many of the more civilian-minded European countries, principally the Benelux and

Scandinavian states, would have agreed with Hammarskjöld's analysis of France's position in Africa 'France provides the gin, the UN the angostura',[4] an analogy which revealed that he knew almost as little about mixing martinis as he did about the politics of a continent which ended in claiming his life.

European support for such American operations as there were in this period became increasingly selective, even muted. The further their own history of intervention began to recede into folk memory the more they began to question the morality as well as the wisdom of the use of force. As Europe's military resources contracted still further, the two communities found they were living in separate mental worlds, a world in which American 'imperialism', because it was more readily 'accessible' than its Soviet equivalent, became more real, a world that would have been intellectually foreign to de Gaulle, or even Adenauer.

Taking these three features together, it can be said that the retreat east of Suez happened to fit a historical pattern. It may have been a longer stretch from the Suez débâcle of 1956 to the British defence review of 1975 than writers describing the post-Bandung era found historically convenient, the pattern may have been ragged at the edges, but it seemed to fit recent events. In fact, it proved deceptive, if not necessarily false.

What happened to change European perceptions about their interest in the Middle East and the need to re-couple strategically was the apparent breakdown of the political order which had formed the framework in which disengagement had taken place. A European presence after the OPEC embargo of 1973 might no more be necessary to guarantee the flow of oil than it had before, but there was a perceived need to support moderate Arab regimes: to send peacekeeping forces to the Sinai in November 1981, to preserve central government in the Lebanon from enemies internal and external alike, to discourage a more militant Iranian foreign policy by patrolling the Gulf, and an equally threatening Libyan challenge by guaranteeing the freedom of passage in the Red Sea.

These were new factors in the political equation; they were also new arguments for revamping military commitments, and dusting off old contingency plans – not only furnishing the Americans with recently discarded maps of the region for their mission to rescue their own hostages in Iran, but also pre-positioning French tanks in Saudi Arabia after the siege of the Great Mosque (1979), relaxing the rules on

German arms shipments to the Gulf, despatching a German naval squadron into the Indian Ocean for the first time since the war.

Under the pressure of events which had been neither predicted nor foreshadowed before 1973 historical memories began to be revived; in the face of new challenges more unpalatable memories of the past were conveniently forgotten. The Italians, exorcising the spirit of Mussolini, once again contemplaced a *mare nostrum* of sorts; some Germans even wished to change a constitution which still forbids the deployment of German forces beyond Europe, although in this case with much less success.

Is the retreat from east of Suez, therefore, a passing phase, one of history's false trails? If it is still very much entrenched in academic scholarship, if European public opinion is still resolutely introspective and even solipsistic, has the retreat as a concept become confusing for understanding recent events?

THE END OF THE POST-WAR ERA

The world after 1973 was never to be the same after the OPEC embargo; not the first embargo, of course (there had been two others during two previous Arab–Israeli wars) but by far the most serious in its impact.

What changed after 1973 was a perceived shift in the *geo-strategic* balance, and more worrying for the Europeans in the *geo-political* importance of the Middle East and Africa. In the case of the former, Soviet intervention between 1974 and 1978 led to the emergence of Marxist–Leninist regimes in Southern Africa and the Horn, the two regions considered most vital to Western security. The invasion of Afghanistan in 1979 also appeared to bring the Soviet Union within striking distance of the Gulf, to present the first real military threat to the West's supply of oil since the appearance in the Caucasus of Field Marshal Kleist's First Panzer Group in 1942.

The emergence of the Soviet Union as a regional threat beyond its own frontiers and that of its immediate satellites made NATO's security dilemmas particularly intractable. Strategy as Michael Howard reminds us works within an interdependent global system;[5] security is largely indivisible. Try though it might NATO found it increasingly difficult to compartmentalise areas of immediate geographical concern from those beyond the Tropic of Cancer. The disappearance in the 1970s of such NATO-style treaty organisations as SEATO and CENTO, the fossilised offspring of Dulles' conception of containment, did not make this dilemma any the less intractable; indeed, it concentrated the minds of its respective members all the more on out-of-area issues, a response which ranged from SACLANT's contingency planning for the Cape route, commissioned in 1972 but not completed until 1981, to the discussion of out-of-area problems by bodies such as the Atlantic Policy Advisory Group.[6]

For the United States, the strategic challenge fitted into the long and debilitating history of proxy wars, and the containment of Soviet ambitions. For the Europeans, however, the challenge was quite new; the context in which their re-coupling to the Third World took place in the 1970s was quite different from the context of strategic decoupling in the 1950s, a period which had been characterised by the absence of a Soviet geo-strategic threat.

The imperial recessional[7] was brought about in the case of Britain itself by a collapsing pound, in the case of France by the collapse of the Fourth Republic, in the case of both countries by a nationalist challenge that was successfully outflanked by translating formal control into the much older patterns of informal influence, not by the type of external threats which had almost brought down the British position in the Far East between the wars. Neither the British nor the French were forced to rethink their positions after the Second World War by the Soviet Union – indeed in Africa where they were most strongly entrenched they faced a situation, where in the words of one State Department official in the 1950s, 'in the broadest sense of the word – no crisis exists'.[8]

It was the Western powers themselves who competed against one another – it was the British who drove the French out of the Levant in the 1940s, only to be displaced in Egypt and Iran by the United States at much higher cost. If anyone was to blame for bringing to an end what Elizabeth Monroe calls 'the British moment' in the Middle East it was not the Soviet Union but General Nasser and the Baathist party in Iraq. Outside Europe the United Kingdom had to contend only with the possibility of war with Iraq (1961) and Indonesia (1963–6). One of the facts which sweetened the bitter pill of eventual disengagement was that none of Britain's former dependencies faced a Soviet threat.

If the absence of the Soviet Union played a part, albeit a minor one, in determining Europe's strategic decoupling from the Third World, its re-coupling was given a definite geo-strategic colouring. At the very time that Britain completed its east of Suez pull-out the appearance for the first time of Soviet warships in the Indian Ocean, gave rise to new French concern first given expression in a speech delivered by Michel Debré, France's Minister of Defence, before the French Defence College in 1970;[9] later still in Debré's insistence during a visit to the Malagassy Republic that France was now quite unable to protect its own sea-lanes, or those of its allies;[10] in Giscard's admission in 1976 that in a world which had witnessed a 'general destabilisation of security' the Western powers must act together because they could no longer act alone.[11] For the first time since de Gaulle's insistence in 1958 in excluding the United States from the discussion of French security policy outside Europe, the French began to insist on the need to work together, a development which was given operational reality in 1978 when the American and French navies in the Indian Ocean embarked on joint contingency planning.

This change of perspective derived added force from events in Africa and the Middle East which appeared to alter fundamentally the *geo-political* relationship between Europe and its former dependencies. Indeed the influence of geo-politics was to prove more decisive in shaping Europe's view of the world.

In the Middle East the oil embargo of 1973–4 not only trebled the price of oil, it also served as a major catalyst in reducing economic growth and pushing up inflation to 10 per cent in the major European economies. In seven leading Western nations the annual shift in GNP dropped to 60–80 per cent of the growth projected in their national budgets.

At first the Europeans responded to the new challenge not by trying to establish a new relationship with the Arabs, but by trying to dispense with that relationship as far as possible. As an exemplary civilian power Europe acted its part, putting its trust not in keeping its powder dry, but in reducing its energy consumption, seeking alternative non-OPEC suppliers, and developing its own reserves, principally in the North Sea.

By the late 1970s, however, the Europeans had to face the reality that the demand for OPEC oil would rise, that the trend towards lower energy consumption would soon become recessionary rather than efficient, that non-OPEC production would soon peak, and that the Gulf would become an increasingly important market, providing 89 per cent of OPEC production by the mid-1990s, as compared with 50 per cent or less prior to 1973.[12]

Clearly, these considerations influenced military thinking. The comforting illusions which had determined Healey's thinking in 1968 gave way to less comforting speculations about the future; the insouciant opposition of the Gulf Sheikdoms to Heath's attempted re-entry in the area from 1971 to 1973 gave way to greater interest in external support after the outbreak of the Iran–Iraq war, the first serious threat to Western access since the Second World War. Even if Europe survived the fighting, attacks on several oil tankers, and a rise of over 300 per cent in insurance premiums, what is tolerable today may prove intolerable tomorrow. As Shahram Chubin notes, in a period of glut attitudes towards local wars and revolutions may be the confident one of the containment, not termination of hostilities; in a period of renewed dependence indifference may not be possible.[13] After 1979 European warships slipped quietly into place on their foreign stations, the big ships of the RN returning for the first time since they slipped anchor for the North Sea in the Fisher era. For the Germans memories of the *Seekriegsleitung* (German naval command) poring over their maps may not have been rekindled, but even the Germans returned in a fashion, when in 1981 they tried to negotiate an arms deal with Saudi Arabia in return for a guaranteed supply of oil, a deal which challenged their own rigid guidelines against selling arms to countries in 'areas of tension'.[14]

There were several other reasons why Europe found itself condemned to live in a military rather than civilian world after 1973 much as it might imagine it had just escaped it. Its financial circumstances changed permanently as the 1970s progressed, creating a totally new interest in political stability, an interest that had hardly figured in the strategic calculations of Curzon, Leo Amery or Glubb Pasha. The Arab investment in the European banking system made Europe an extension of the Middle East, much though the French might continue to treat the Near East as a geographical extension of Europe.

Between 1974 and 1980 Kuwait invested $5.2bn in British banks and other financial concerns. Kuwait was merely one among many. The massive construction projects in Saudi Arabia and its neighbours which helped to fuel Europe's recovery from the mini-recession of 1973–5 substantially increased the number of European expatriates in the Middle East, itself a reason for offering them limited military protection, President Mitterand's publicly stated defence for sending French forces to the Lebanon in 1983.[15]

The oil crisis also precipitated a shift from the Affluent Society to the more traumatic Age of Uncertainty. If the mid-1960s had been 'good and confident years, a good time to be an economist' (a time when economists, Galbraith might have added, helped to reshape Europe's perception of its own civilian status) the following decade demonstrated once more 'the disarming complexity of the problems mankind now faces'.[16] At the very time that economic growth in Western Europe became more uncertain, economic development in the Third World became a questionable panacea for its security ills. Development economics no longer seemed either the only answer, or the most viable, as under the stress of the oil price increases in many Third World countries income distribution became more unequal, not less; and the process or pace of modernisation unseated the Shah, and threatened the stability of other dynasties in the region. As a result, European politicians lost much of their confidence in economic solutions to problems which the superpowers, rightly or wrongly, still believed susceptible to military force.

Finally, the oil increases of the 1970s encouraged massive debt borrowing by the Less Developed Countries (LDCs), leaving them nearly $300bn in arrears by 1982. In no time at all the West was presented with an intriguing dilemma. In 1973 the United States, preoccupied as always with the *geo-strategic* balance in the Near East, had connived at Iran's role in jacking up the price of oil so that its government could afford even more massive US arms purchases, and thus discharge the role of regional *gendarme* recently abdicated by the British. Ten years later the Europeans were forced to recognise a new *geo-political* reality at a time when geo-politics was once again back in fashion: that attractive as further cuts in oil prices might seem, the stability of international lending relied heavily on stable oil prices, even high ones.[17] An increase in world borrowing particularly by the LDCs made it so difficult for financial institutions in Europe to cope with rapid shifts of income in the developing world that it was forced to admit what had long been suspected, that major cuts in the price of oil would pose a serious risk to Europe's economic recovery.[18]

In taking into account, therefore, the new financial/investment environment which the politics of oil brought into being in the 1970s the Europeans were not operating within a narrow strategic framework as they had before 1973 but within a much broader and complex economic one, but it was a framework which in laying so much emphasis on political stability conveyed its own strategic logic.

The upshot of all this was that the Middle East was once again seen as a geo-political appendage of Europe. From time to time the French might find it convenient to deny the fact, 'being exterior to the region'. Claude Cheysson remarked in November 1981 apropos the Arab–

Israeli conflict, 'we know that we have neither a project nor an initiative to propose'[19] yet it was that conflict among others and the threat that the oil price might once again be coupled to the dispute that encouraged France to become in the words of Charles Hernu the region's 'most indispensable Western power',[20] a role it had not claimed even at the time of the Sykes-Picot pact, and which it had probably last played in 1860 when it had intervened in Syria on behalf of the Maronite Christians.

Another development which gave additional weight to the geo-political perspective was the rise of international terrorism against Europe's principal ally, first at the time of the Iranian hostage crisis, and then in 1983–5 in the Shi'ite assault on American 'imperialism'. Perhaps the critical date, if only for its symbolic importance, was October 1983 when American battleships bombarded Druze positions in the Chouf mountains, in a vain attempt to show that the United States could use force against 'terrorist' forces in a Third World context, and that military intervention could bring order to the 'anarchical society' the state of Lebanon had become.[21]

These developments did not escape America's European allies who had largely relied on the United States to defend their interests since 1973 when US aircraft carriers had visited the Gulf for the first time in 25 years. The terrorist assault on the United States was very different from the PLO campaign in the early 1970s which had no other objective than the traditional territorial claim for a separate and secular Palestinian state. The rise of Islamic fundamentalism and its implicit rejection of Western influence seemed an echo of the Islamic revolt which had almost brought the British 'moment' in the Middle East to an end between 1919 and 1922. Some Europeans saw it as part of a pattern in which the OPEC embargo had pointed the way, a presentiment of a future *jihad* against the international economic order, an order which hitherto had been challenged only by a Hindu ethic of revolt, *satyagraha*, of self-denial,[22] a challenge which presented much less of a threat to Western economic 'imperialism' than it had to the British Raj.

All this lay in the future. By 1983 most Europeans recognised that the secular state system which they themselves had played a role in creating out of the détritus of Ottoman rule, made it difficult to wait upon events. The imminent collapse of the Lebanon brought the Europeans back to the Levant, the British for the first time since 1948, the French since 1946. As it happened, history repeated itself in the same fashion. The clear intractability of the Lebanese problem, the demonstrable despair of the Europeans in attempting to create order out of disorder, offered at times and particularly at the end, a distant but distinct refrain of Churchill's despair over Palestine. 'Simply such a hell disaster,' he had told Weizmann in 1948 'that I cannot take it up again – and must, as far as I can, put it out of my mind.'[23] The Europeans may have returned, but they lacked their earlier confidence, certainly their *panache*.

Africa presented fewer problems, even though here too was a region of the world where under the pressure of events European thoughts turned to geo-political speculations. In the 1970s Africa began to face new dangers of a kind which appeared to differ both in scope and importance from the threats it had faced and surmounted in the 1960s. In West Africa the rise of Islamic fundamentalism which had once haunted British and French administrators in the 1890s threatened the political balance in countries such as Nigeria and Senegal, and the foundations of British influence in one and French influence in the other. In the Horn the last of Africa's imperial systems which Haile Selassie had struggled for 50 years to defend found itself on the brink of dissolution, beset by five separate movements of national liberaticn.

Elsewhere in the continent the state system itself came under challenge. The great majority of countries lapsed under the increase in oil prices into an unrelenting cycle of poverty. By 1980 seven out of every ten states were underdeveloping, not undeveloped, actually poorer in real terms than they had been at independence.[24] Presenting a parody of the future predicted in Waugh's *Black Mischief*, some moved out of the market economy altogether. By then:

> it had become apparent that the great bulk of the continent had become and would remain politically unstable and incapable of self-sustained economic growth . . . Africa (has) simply become a place for proxy wars like Spain in the 1930s.[25]

In such circumstances, it is hardly surprising that the Europeans were invited back. An unabashed Leopold Senghor informed the United States that since it had applied the Monroe Doctrine to the Western hemisphere it could hardly object to France following suit in West Africa.[26] Houphouet-Boigny looked forward to the day when there would be 100 000 Frenchmen in his country, a larger ex-patriate force than in the days of empire.[27]

French military operations in Chad (1968–84), the Western Sahara (1977) and Zaire were on a much greater scale than its activities in the

1980s. British military missions once again appeared in Uganda, and for the first time in Zimbabwe. At one point the French even floated the idea of replacing Cuban troops when they eventually left Angola.[28] Beset by an escalating cycle of South African military intervention, a policy of pre-emptive raids, or 'pro-active action', the Front Line States even dreamed of a European military presence in Southern Africa to guard key installations and mines and the rail lines which carried their exports to the coast, a request that the Finance Minister of Botswana carried to the European Parliament itself in November 1983.[29]

Behind much of the European concern there was certainly an element of strategic calculation. An Italian official described Soviet policy in the Horn as 'one of the Soviet pincers' designed to cut off the Middle East region, and thus 'the most important energy sources necessary for the West European countries'.[30] The German defence minister Georg Leber described the Soviet transport fleet as a 'new strategic element' in the East–West balance to which the West had no immediate answer.[31]

But in the most active European country of all, geo-political calculations figured much more prominently. It was not entirely coincidental, perhaps, that it was a French geographer who described Africa in 1656 as 'a peninsula so large that it comprises the third part and this the most southerly of our continent'.[32] In the 1950s the French had divided the continent into two *zones strategiques*, in the 1960s into four *zones d'outre mer*, bounded by three key bases at Dakar, Fort Lamy and Diego Suarez in Madagascar. In the 1980s a socialist administration that had promised when in opposition to turn its back on 25 years of French policy in Africa found itself giving new meaning to the concept of *Eurafrique*.

Speaking at the Institut des Hauts Etudes in 1981 Charles Hernu described France's relationship with Africa as one of the spokes of the two great axes around which contemporary international relations revolved: the North/South and East/West struggles. As a result, France was 'inevitably concerned with the conflicts and contests which are played out in the Third World'.[33] Returning to this theme the following year Hernu again pointed to the numerous externally fuelled conflicts in Africa which he saw as justification for a continued French military presence:

the privileged relations between France and the numerous African countries and the great vulnerability of the continent as a whole are the two essential realities on the basis of which any French role in Western security must be considered.[34]

Contemporaries viewing the continent through jaundiced eyes might have felt justified in thinking in 1983 that a second scramble for Africa was in progress, a contest in which some of the countries involved in the first were once again leading participants. The Lomé Conventions could be said to have created an economic regime which excited as much controversy as the regime which had been sanctioned by the Berlin congress (1884–5), an economic order which seemed to confirm Johann Galtung's prediction of the rise of a *pax Bruxellana* deriving its fixity of purpose, however, from Paris rather than Brussels.[35]

At other times the recoupling of Europe and Africa seemed more like the era of partition than the brief era of open access to which the Berlin Congress had looked forward. And like the first partition there has been a distinctively surreal quality to French endeavours. Today's dreams of a French-built canal from the Saharan desert to the Mediterranean passing through Quadaffi's Libya recalls to mind the survey parties which were despatched in 1879 to map possible routes for a trans-Saharan railway linking Algeria with the Western Sudan, an endeavour which finally ended with three separate expeditions setting out for Lake Chad in 1900 to mark the new empire's symbolic creation. In the 1870s the French had accepted the financial burden of expansion and political control as the essential precondition of economic development. In the 1980s they seemed to accept economic development as a political investment in a region from which they continued to import important reserves of uranium and liquified natural gas.

For many Europeans the effort is questionable, the context surreal. In the 1890s Lord Salisbury seeking to explain one of those innumerable agreements which led to the drawing up of frontiers in West Africa, observed with cynical detachment:

Anyone who merely looks at a map and measures distances may think that France has gained a great deal of land. But land must be measured not by its extent, but its value. What France has gained is what agriculturalists call 'very high land', that is to say the Saharan desert.

It probably never crossed Salisbury's mind that one day there would arise another dispute in the region, this time between Libya and France, in the area from which the state of Chad eventually emerged. But he would certainly have recognised the considerations which have led three French governments to concern themselves with the fate of the world's second poorest country. Great powers have a horror of power vacuums being occupied by others, even if the space itself is quite worthless.

A second and more telling reminder of the first scramble was the competition for mineral resources, especially in Southern Africa where the race had provoked a political crisis in the 1890s. Seventy years later the considerations which led the British to challenge the independence of the Boer republics came back to haunt the very European countries which had supported the Boer cause. It was they who insisted that the region's mineral potential should be placed on NATO's agenda in 1976; and appropriately it was Britain who persuaded the Secretariat to carry out the first survey of the Continent's non-fuel resources in 1980 (see Table 1.1).

TABLE 1.1

Mineral	Country	Main mineral exports as a % of total exports (1972–9 average)	EEC share of exports (as average %)
Copper	Zaire	55	91
Phosphates	Togo	59	92
	Senegal	18	54
Bauxite	Guinea	90	34
Manganese	Gabon	15	32
Iron Ore	Liberia	69	74
	Mauretania	71	75

SOURCE　Oye Ogunbadejo, *The International Politics of Africa's Strategic Minerals* (London: Frances Pinter, 1985) p. 53.

By then most of the European countries had come to recognise their critical vulnerability to embargoes or disruptions in supply. The fear first arose during the Angolan civil war when the closure of the Benguella railway which linked Zaire to the coast reduced Zaire's cobalt exports by 90 per cent and discouraged major banking houses including Chase Manhattan and Standard Bank from investing in the next phase of mineral development.[36]

The second threat came during the escalating conflict in Zimbabwe from nationalist movements, armed and supported by the Soviet Union. By 1976 it was widely predicted that if the production of chrome was suspended the mines on the Great Dyke might flood within six months, those in Selukwe within two. In the four years it might take to reopen them, 25 per cent of the world's supply of metallurgical ore might be lost.[37]

Hostilities came to an end before this could happen but the threat almost came true in Zaire in 1978 when FNLC guerillas, former members of Tshombe's Katanganese *gendarmerie*, invaded the province of Shaba and successfully cut back the world's production of copper by closing a single mine. In the immediate aftermath of the invasion, the African Metals Corporation, the sole distributor of Zairean cobalt, was also forced to cut back on delivery to its customers, by nearly 30 per cent. For a time Zaire was only to operate the Kolwezi mines at 25 per cent capacity.

The threat of further disruption on a much larger scale in South Africa still remains. This is the real measure of Southern Africa's geo-political importance to Western Europe – not the threat that the Soviet Union might embargo mineral supplies to the West by military action, but the threat that Europe might face a bleak future if it remains on the sidelines and allows events to take their own course. As the English historian John Morley once observed, governments may stop short, history never does; a lesson which from time to time even a civilian power must take to heart.

FROM CIVILIAN POWER TO MILITARY POWER EUROPE?

In the light of such events even some of the smaller European powers have been forced to reconsider their civilian status. The Netherlands and Belgium too have responded to the same set of events – indeed, at the time of the oil boycott and the Shaba emergency (1978) both countries found themselves much more at risk, much more evidently in the front line than Britain or France, or for that matter West Germany.

Because public attitudes to military intervention, however, have not changed radically in either country, their governments have been forced to act with circumspection, even stealth. In contrast to the self-professed forward policy of France Leo Tindermans (Belgium's Prime Minister) went out of his way to assure the Belgian people in

1978 that in sending paratroopers to Zaire the government had 'only envisaged a rescue operation for its own citizens'.

Humanitarian intervention was the constant refuge of reluctant imperialists throughout the nineteenth century just as it was the excuse for American operations in central America and the Caribbean in the 1920s and 1930s. It is even more ironic that in Zaire itself the Stanleyville drop in 1964 came to represent for a whole generation of African leaders the first signs of an incipient new imperialism – that of Uncle Sam.

Once the Belgians arrived, reality soon intruded. They also found as the British had often found before them that retreats are more problematic than interventions. Clearly aware of its limited options, clearly reluctant to see its own interests in the country entirely subsumed within *Francophonie*, Belgium proposed that an inter-African force be despatched to replace French forces with its logistics costs picked up by the European Community. When this failed it found itself despatching its own force nine months later to deal with a further outbreak of hostilities at Kimona.

Direct experience of the harsh world of the late 1970s made even the Dutch more interested in a global role for the EEC, an objective which Belgium tried to promote during the first half of 1982 when it found itself President of the Community. In February 1981 the second chamber of the Netherlands Parliament adopted almost unanimously a motion calling for the government to advance the discussion of 'the international political dimension' of European security within the framework of European Political Cooperation, a significant reversal of the attitude the Dutch negotiators had shown in drafting the Document of European Identity (December 1973) when they had insisted that Europe should refrain from any attempt to pursue a military role in the world at large.

Although the Europeans may have returned to the Third World, however, their military power is not what it was 25 years ago. In arguing for a more extensive European role its strategists have still not come to terms with the fact that its geographical pretensions and actual resources are ridiculously at variance.

British forces may be stationed across the globe from Hong Kong to the Caribbean but they are engaged for the most part in parading paper commitments which in many cases are hardly worth defending. In the Far East the British have resolved none of the insoluble strategic problems which bedevilled defence planning between the wars. During a naval exercise with Malaysia in 1978 one of the most powerful squadrons ever seen in local waters was 'sunk' in a few hours by the Malaysian airforce, as decisively as were the *Prince of Wales* and *Repulse* by Japanese bombers in 1941.

Quite clearly, the RN is under-equipped to engage in offensive operations outside European waters without the massive application of force which was used in the South Atlantic in 1982. The relentless cutback in escort vessels has also rendered questionable the commitment to deploy a task force in the Indian Ocean every two years, as too has the shortage of depots and spare parts, a problem which was graphically highlighted by *HMS Invincible*'s troubled tour of the Far East in 1983/4.

In the early 1960s the Singapore base was able to support 70 000 men and half the surface ships of a navy that was three times its present size. Today no government would be able to find the money for pre-positioning stores and equipment to sustain even medium-term naval operations, largely because it would mean locking up valuable resources already in short supply at home; one reason why most of the destroyers and frigates which are sent overseas are not due for re-fit for at least eight or nine months.

Indeed Britain's 'recoupling' to areas like the Caribbean and the Middle East must be looked for not in the navy but in talk of a new rapid deployment force, the first mention of which appeared in 1981 when the Defence Secretary, John Nott, spoke of a 'modest use of force to protect the interests of friendly local states', an interesting concept but a modest one in view of the fact that he envisaged a 'company size intervention, a battalion at most'. Since then plans have been drawn up for a force of 10 000 men, without their own tanks or heavy equipment, an obvious operational constraint.

There has also been some improvement of airlift capability, although this too has fallen far short of dramatically improving Britain's strategic mobility along the lines proposed by Denis Healey in 1966. Existing units may have been given an out of area capability: 5 Infantry Brigade has been transformed into 5 Airborne Brigade, half RAF Hercules has been modified to carry nearly 50 per cent more paratroopers; and finally the range and speed of deployment has been greatly increased by significant advances in air-to-air refuelling.

Yet even these limited improvements have only marginally improved Britain's military position. The British have re-entered the Middle East, for example, not on their own account, but as allies of the Americans, a fact not without historical continuity for those who recall that the British base at Jufair (Bahrein) was the very first which the

USN took over in 1974 on the long road to the Rapid Deployment Force. Indeed, were it not for their new role as a client of the United States, a role quite different by the way from that of 1958 when the two countries last intervened together in their respective 'spheres of influence' Jordan and the Lebanon – our interest might be with the mirrored reflection of an historical phenomenon rather than with the phenomenon itself.

Of necessity, therefore, the British role has been restricted to areas where the United States can provide protection, or reinforcement or the promise of future assistance – in the Sinai, as part of a diplomatic effort to underwrite the Camp David process; in the Levant as part of a five power peacekeeping force in Beirut protected by the 16 inch guns of the *USS Jersey*; in the 'gulf and the Red Sea as part of a joint naval operation from which France and Italy chose to distance, if not disassociate themselves, in order to maintain a semblance of independent action.

In that respect, Britain's dependence on Washington has changed very little since Suez when it was expressed in the form of a US veto and a run on sterling which brought that particular operation to an end. To that extent Britain can be described as a surrogate of the United States not a truly independent Middle East actor. This is not just an exercise in typological description, an example of 'butterfly collecting' as Edward Leach called it in a different context. Labelling is at least useful in understanding the extent to which the Europeans deceive themselves if they imagine that their geo-political ambitions could be pursued but for the fact that they frequently fit into the *geo-strategic* designs of the United States. To reverse Chou en lai's remark about *détente*, Britain and America may be dreaming different dreams, but the British have no choice of sleeping partners.

More surprising still than the United Kingdom's return to the Middle East, has been that of Italy after a 40 year absence. Although the re-orientation of Italian security policy to what is now popularly called its 'Mediterranean vocation' began with the oil crises of the 1970s official government disquiet was not publicly expressed until 1981 when the Defence Minister first described the situation in the Mediterranean as 'unstable' and at risk from local 'confrontational issues'.[38]

Although its new policy has been neither dynamic nor revolutionary, in so far as the country has managed to break with a 40-year moratorium on out-of-area operations it does represent a political *caesura* of sorts, a response to the exigencies of the moment.

As the Italian defence minister concluded in 1982 his country's interests could no longer be met in the Alliance. 'There is a vast area outside NATO in which our country has many reasons and opportunities to make its own independent and autonomous voice heard.'[39]

As a European state, Italy has tended to see its position in geo-political rather than strategic terms. To borrow a figure from geometry we may say that its approach to the Middle East has been eccentric. A strategic perspective, of course, has not been entirely absent. In its decision to set up its own RDF to meet what its chief of staff described in November 1984 as 'a change in the geo-strategic situation of the whole Mediterranean'[40] we can see a NATO-centric circle of Italian policy making varying intersections with circles centred on the enduring continuities of Italy's geographical position in the Near East and the Mediterranean. But its strategic re-coupling to the Middle East has not been an exclusive function of either circle.

The various crises in the region which have evoked an Italian response have essentially been the result of autonomous changes rather than external forces. At times the Italians have been anxious to down play the larger East–West context and emphasise the European dimension of their policy, agreeing to send minesweepers into the Red Sea only on the strict understanding that the request came from Egypt, not the United States; and refusing to have any contact with the Anglo-American control group responsible for coordinating the operation.

In a similar vein Italian politicians have consistently spoken of a 'European mandate' to resolve the problem of Malta's neutrality, even though at Valetta's request Europe was not mentioned at all in the text of its treaty with Italy. Indeed, to make the link more explicit the Italian government went on to claim in 1981 that the treaty represented a 'bridge' between Malta and Western Europe.[41]

But in reality the Italians are no more independent of the United States than the British. Like the British they have been closely associated with Washington, participating in the Sinai peacekeeping force even before the Europeans had had a chance to reach a common position on the issue, and contributing to a 5-power Task Force which was despatched to the Horn of Africa at the height of the Ogaden war (1978). Even though of all the European powers Italy was historically most closely associated with both protagonists, its military aid to Somalia in the form of 100 M47 tanks originally the property of the US army clearly represented an example of two NATO allies working closely together.[42] As usual it was the French who broke rank and tried to act on their own account by selling arms to Somalia in defiance of American wishes.[43]

On the evidence since 1981 it can be argued that re-coupling has been essentially a pre-emptive exercise. That the change of perspective has largely gone unchallenged illustrates how far civilian power in Italy has travelled since 1973; that its actual military role has been relatively modest, however, illustrates how dependent it still is on its Superpower patron.

France's role East of Suez, by contrast, has been the most persistent expression of European intervention for the last ten years. There are now 20 000 French troops scattered throughout the world from the Middle East to the South Pacific. French capabilities tend to be much greater than the British because their East of Suez role has assumed a much higher defence profile. In 1976 the navy transferred its aircraft carriers from Brest to Toulon so that they could be redeployed in areas like Cape Verde in less than a week. Its new *force d'action rapide*, although mostly committed to the defence of Western Europe has an out-of-area role, and exercised for the first time in the Mediterranean in the summer of 1985. Only two years earlier the logistics for the force were almost entirely accounted for by operations in Chad and the Lebanon, a development which did not pass without comment from the members of the Western European Assembly.

Finally, their navy has also been the main beneficiary of increases in defence spending, with its budget for 1984–8 projected to rise faster than for the other two services and with continued interest in new landing craft which are due to become operational by 1993.

It is in the arc of crisis which Brezinzki sketched from Iran to the Horn of Africa and then through the Levant that the French have now become an important regional actor. Behind their return lies the memory of Suez (1956), an event which has been exorcised only recently, and which played an important part in discouraging France and Britain from intervening again in 1967, when both countries discussed forcing the straits of Aquaba to break Nasser's blockade.

At the time Suez had a profound effect on French political society. Not only did it seem that the loss of French influence in the Middle East had preceded the loss of Western influence in general it also seemed that it had prepared the way for it, leaving European interests entirely beholden to the United States, a view which was forcefully expressed by Ferdinand de Miksche, de Gaulle's old companion in exile, speaking at a colloquium in Hamburg in 1980:

The Franco-British expedition to Suez in 1956 was, had it succeeded, the last chance to channel the evolution of the Third World and especially of Africa into a path favourable to the West. In obliging Paris and London to withdraw their expeditionary corps, the U.S. committed one of its most catastrophic blunders. Since the dramatic scuttling Western prestige has fallen into the *oubliettes* of history. The Third World has escaped all control.[44]

Significantly, de Miksche's point was not that the Suez debacle had opened the Middle East to Soviet penetration; such an argument would be difficult to square with the Soviet Union's effective exclusion from the Middle East since 1973. De Miksche was far more concerned about the loss of control over events which he attributed (rather simplistically perhaps) to the foreclosure of the European option: the rise of Arab nationalism and the OPEC embargo; the challenge of Islamic fundamentalism in the bazaars of Tehran; and the appearance of a terrorist threat aimed principally, though not exclusively, against the United States.

In trying to restore some control over events (rather than governments) Europe may now have to intervene on behalf of, rather than against, Arab regimes. De Miksche's analysis derives its force as much from first principles, as it does from empirical observation, from ideas about the nature of Third World society which make it imperative that France once again becomes a world power. As Giscard's former defence minister Yves Bourges has observed more modestly, the country's ability to control its own destiny now depends more than ever on 'its role in the world'.[45]

If the French, however, are now committed to a forward policy of a sort, *faux de mieux* they now cannot contemplate acting in the world without the tacit approval, or cooperation of the United States. Ironically for so confirmed a gaullist as de Miksche the return to geo-politics presupposes 'solidarity on the part of the Atlantic world'.[46] Despite memories of Suez the American connection is very much to the fore. National interests have been narrowly defined; allied interests defined more broadly.

To be sure ambiguity remains. The need to be seen acting on its own behalf entirely independently of the United States dictated that France did not request aerial or naval protection in the Lebanon, that it did not join the British or Americans in the Gulf although it undertook to patrol the area on its own, and that it disassociated itself from the attempts of both countries to clear the Red Sea of mines even though it was invited by the Saudis to keep open the important ports of Jidda and Vanbu in the same period.[47]

In substance, however, French policy in the Lebanon and the Gulf reveals a deep pessimism about an independent European role, manifested most clearly perhaps, in its indifference to the Euro-Arab dialogue. In Africa American policy may, to quote one American official have acquired a French accent,[48] in the Middle East 'to speak of a European role . . . is largely to discuss the French contribution to American strategy'.[49] Although American troops did not die in the Suez operation, it was symbolic perhaps that American and French marines both died in the streets of Beirut 27 years later. During Mitterand's state visit to Washington in 1984 Reagan publicly referred to a Franco-American brotherhood in arms spanning the centuries from Yorktown to the Lebanon.[50]

In the quarter century since Suez however very little has actually changed. The French are no more independent now than they were in 1956; it is the Americans who have become a little less sanguine about Arab politicians. The French role is flawed by the fatal paradox that to be listened to by the Arabs, the Europeans must disassociate themselves from the United States; to exert any influence however, they must adopt policies complementary to those of their main ally.[51] The Europeans may have returned, but their limited resources in an era when the building of the RDF alone has exceeded America's annual foreign aid budget has foreclosed the type of independent operations the French and British tried to mount at Suez.

Despite de Miksche, 1956 taught two lessons, not one – that the West had not only relinquished control over events, but had also lost the last opportunity for independent action. To become a prisoner of the past is a particularly ironic fate for a country which so evidently wishes to escape it. In that respect France's fate is testimony to the very reality it is trying to transcend.

In Africa the situation has certain parallels. France's military role is now so established that America felt no embarrassment in 1983 in referring to Chad as a country in the French 'sphere of influence'.[52] For the United States which has shied away from direct military intervention in Africa since its depressing experience in the Congo French operation have an undoubted attraction. As James Goldsborough explained 'French paratroopers jumping into Shaba are not the same as US paratroopers jumping into Shaba – even if the French are wearing US parachutes',[53] a not entirely accurate picture as it later turned out. It was largely because so many of the parachutes used by the French were borrowed from the Zairean army that many failed to open, with the result that the paratroopers suffered more casualties in the air than on the ground.

But if the French are Africa's policemen, as Goldsborough suggests, their police duties are becoming increasingly onerous and open-ended. The second scramble for Africa, like the first, may not have been marked by conflicts on the ground between the participants. But the parties in the game are no longer members of the Concert of Europe, dividing the continent at an international conference, and respecting each other's ambitions. There are now new actors including East Germany pursuing often irreconcilable ends for whom the avoidance of conflict is merely an interest, not a duty.

During Shaba 2 French forces were also only committed on the strict understanding that the United States would intervene if East German or Cuban forces supported the FNLC guerillas directly. At the height of the crisis the 82nd Airborne Division was put on 24 hour alert ready to be airlifted to Zaire if the French had got into difficulties.[54]

In Chad (1983–4), however, where the French had to rely heavily on American satellite reports – having no satellites of its own – for once reality intruded; geo-politics eventually had to take a back seat. Following insistent Chadian demands for military aid when Libyan planes bombed government forces the French government at first envisaged a lightning air attack on Libyan air bases in the Aouzou strip, a plan that was discarded as too hazardous in favour of Operation MANTA. The French army imagined it was going in as an offensive force to fight the Libyans; instead it found itself acting as a dissuasive force intent on not firing a shot, whose policy of keeping the two sides apart effectively partitioned the country and prevented Habré's force from recapturing lost territory in the north.

It is quite possible that Operation MANTA was carried out in collusion with the Libyans from the start. They certainly appear *de facto* the new 'imperial' power, given Mitterrand's ambiguous statements on the need to find a new Chadian leader acceptable to both Libya and France, given also the fact that Operation SILURE – the French withdrawal from Chad in the autumn of 1984 was clearly carried out in the knowledge that Quadaffi had no intention of honouring his own promises.[55] No wonder that the Americans were furious. Fighting Quadaffi on contract to Washington, however, was not what the French had in mind; the stakes were larger, the reality more sobering. Both protagonists might have imperial ambitions, but both found themselves living in the same Mediterranean world. Trade in the form of oil and liquefied natural gas are more important stakes, gains to be won, not lost through geo-political posturing in the heart of the Sahara.

These concerns mark the limit to how far American policy can have a 'French accent', even if the myths on which French policy is based, of course, are not peculiarly French. The Americans are prey to the same delusions. Fear of losing Africa to the Soviet Union gained wide currency in the late 1950s long before Quadaffi's brand of Islamic socialism posed an entirely new challenge. Back in the days of the Greenbrier conferences (1959) the British and Americans were planning Africa's future with the cold war very much in the foreground of their thinking. Today the Americans are doing so again, this time in conversation with the French.

This time, however, there is one crucial difference. The absurdity of French policy in Chad is matched only by the seriousness of America's purpose. If the French are playing games, indulging themselves in a century old *folie africaine*, the Americans are clearly not. If in the neurotic world of the 1980s the rational calculations of policymakers seem to have given way to irrational obsessions about power vacuums and geo-political threats, for America those obsessions are still very real. In that respect Europe's role can only take the form of a historical rally before its forces finally depart, leaving the stage to other players who have the power to write the script themselves, unless of course Africa degenerates into greater disorder, confronting even the Superpowers with a Samuel Beckett world where the players will have to make up the script as best they can.

CHANGING THE GUARD

Herein lies the most disturbing feature of Europe's strategic re-coupling to the Third World – it is largely unreal. Despite the changing post-1973 environment, Europe is still a civilian power whether it wishes to be or not, still unable to shape the world in which it lives, if its power to respond to the unexpected is still considerable.

By contrast, America's increasing interest in out of area issues is perfectly consistent with its history. Possibly the post-war order which NATO represents rests on a deceptive foundation. Possibly the threat of Soviet aggression in Europe is less real or immediate than it is in the Middle East. Possibly the United States will look increasingly to the Middle East and the Pacific; possibly, it may have to if its global interests and commitments are not to out-run its capacity to defend them.

But the Europeans do not have this option. For them the defence of Europe must still be their primary concern, even more so if the American commitment is to be reduced. Julius Nyerere had a point when he questioned what European troops were doing in Africa when the overwhelming mass of Soviet divisions were positioned in Eastern Europe.[56]

In recent years Europe's out of area posture has become an alibi for the demonstrably unconvincing nature of its contribution to its own defence, a special problem at a time when defence spending may have doubled (1971–80) but manpower has actually halved.

In this connection, we should be aware of the historical parallels with Britain in the 1930s during the long and often acrimonious debate about the continental commitment. The parallels are not exact, of course, but they provide a cautionary reminder of how countries can fall into the error of strategic misperception. In 1938 the British general staff finally convinced itself that it was cheaper to re-garrison Egypt and the Middle East than to re-enter the continent in time of war. As the 'last European war' loomed on the horizon the British world position was revived as its position in Europe crumbled, a strategy which at its most absurd led Churchill to despatch tanks to the desert in 1940 as Britain itself awaited a German invasion. Given the lessons of history it is somewhat disconcerting to find Yves Bouges arguing that the French presence overseas provides an alternative to 'falling back on Europe'.[57]

The present debate in France is whether French forces are still capable of defending Western Europe, whether they have enough tanks, destroyers and tactical aircraft; whether the FAR can achieve what it is intended to, or whether the build-up and modernisation of the *force de frappe* has tied up such an enormous part of the national resources as to seriously hamper the maintenance and modernisation of the country's conventional forces and thus make more attractive the idea of retreating behind a nuclear maginot line.

The same question must be asked about the United Kingdom, as it faces a future in which the RN may be reduced to less than 40 surface ships. In October 1979 a quarter of the RN's front line ships and nearly half its support vessls were to be found outside NATO waters, at a time when the North Atlantic Assembly found it necessary to remind its own members that they would do well to remember that SACLANT's assets were already below requirement.[58] Keeping warships on distant stations seems a high price to pay for political influence in areas of the world where the British moment has long since come to an end.

I do not wish to labour points that have long been made – though familiarity is no excuse for indifference. My purpose here is not to argue against the wisdom of 're-coupling' so much as to question whether it can be anything more than a historical rally in an otherwise long retreat, and whether re-coupling itself is not another 'alibi' for not confronting the real problems of European defence cooperation.

What has happened in the last ten years stands testimony to the strength of the historical baggage which Europe's politicians still carry like an albatross around them. French Presidents, socialist and conservative alike, still seem to derive prestige from hosting ever larger Franco-African summits; British Prime Ministers from travelling to summit meetings, like James Callaghan, with maps in their briefcases showing the global disposition of British warships. It is an eloquent commentary on the role that historical myths still play in political life, but it is not an accurate index of Europe's real military standing. Like poor Macbeth, Europe may have 'over vaulting ambition', but in a crisis it will probably find it lacks 'the spur to prick the sides' of its intent. It is no longer living in the world of the 1950s.

2 The United States, Britain and Out-of-Area Problems

PHIL WILLIAMS

The idea that the period since 1945 saw the replacement of the Pax Britannica by Pax Americana is seductive. There is a correlation between the contraction of British (as well as other European states) obligations outside Europe and the expanding commitments of the United States. In some instances – such as Greece in 1947 – the United States moved almost immediately to fill the vacuum left by British withdrawal. In other cases such as the Persian Gulf after 1971 there were attempts to find a surrogate for the British role. The downfall of the Shah of Iran, however, showed the bankruptcy of this policy and led the United States into developing contingency plans and capabilities for direct intervention in the region. In a sense, therefore, the creation of the Rapid Deployment Joint Task Force can be seen as the belated successor to the British military presence East of Suez.

Attractive as this interpretation appears, however, it should not be pushed too far. Correlation is not the same as causation, and although British withdrawal might, at times, have provided the occasion for the United States to shoulder new and unprecedented responsibilities, the direction of American policy was determined in a more fundamental sense by the bipolar structure of the international system, by the perception of the Soviet/Communist threat, and by a predisposition, once the Cold War was underway, to treat regional conflicts as part of a global struggle in which any loss to the West represented a commensurate gain for the Soviet Union and in which commitments were interdependent.

This somewhat rigid approach led Washington to reverse its traditional hostility towards European imperialism. The French in Indochina, for example, were transformed during the Korean War from old fashioned imperialists resisting legitimate aspirations for national self determination to free world allies in the struggle against communism. The American attitude towards the British Empire was similarly transformed. Although the United States disliked some of the economic arrangements associated with the British Empire and Commonwealth, the importance of friendly control over regions of the world rich in raw material sources was explicitly acknowledged. Western Europe was valued as an ally not only for its own sake but also because it would provide the United States with access to bases and resources elsewhere. The American approach to the East–West conflict was in large part ideological, but few important American policy-makers were oblivious to geo-political considerations.

Although this gave the United States and its European allies an apparent identity of interests in the Third World, the underlying rationales for their respective policies were very different. This was true even in the case of the two closest allies, Britain and the United States. As one analyst has pointed out

> The language of British overseas policy was less effusive but in similar vein to the American. The Atlantic charge was taken to be the defence of international order, the promotion of regional stability, the maintenance of the peace. The realities, however, were different. Beneath the rhetoric, anti-Communism was the drawstring of United States policy. Despite the phraseology, the principles that informed Britain's action east of Suez arose from her imperial past.[1]

The European and especially the British preference was often to obscure or, at the very least, to minimise these differences. To some extent this reflected the nature of the initial 'transatlantic bargain'.[2] Although the Truman Administration explicitly acknowledged the importance of Western Europe to American security, this judgement was not shared to anything like the same extent either by critics who believed in 'Fortress America' or by those who wanted an 'Asia first' approach. In order to make the American commitment to Europe more palatable, therefore, it was made conditional upon European efforts at 'self-help' in rebuilding its military strength.[3] There was also an expectation of reciprocity: if the United States helped to contain Soviet military power in Europe, the allies should and would help to contain the Soviet Union and its allies elsewhere. The first major test of this was in the Korean War during which, with the exception of the

Turks and the British, the allies were found wanting. There were many complaints in Congress that 90 per cent of the effort and 90 per cent of the casualties in Korea were American.

To some extent this reflected the fact that the Europeans were still recovering from the ravages of world war and had neither the resources nor the inclination to become engaged in further hostilities – especially when the conflict could be dismisssed as a feint intended to divert attention from the much more direct threat in Europe itself. But it was also symptomatic of what was to prove a more enduring problem. Because the Europeans and the Americans were operating on different principles outside the NATO area, it was inevitable that they would have different perceptions and priorities. On no occasion was this more evident than in the Suez crisis of 1956. As Richard Neustadt has pointed out, for the United States 'the Canal was neither life line nor symbol, nor was Nasser public enemy number one'.[4] With Eisenhower campaigning for re-election on a peace platform the military intervention of Britain and France was politically embarrassing for the US President. Not surprisingly, therefore, it was American pressure which brought the action to a halt and fully revealed the growing disparity in the relative power positions of the NATO allies.

In the aftermath of Suez, British and French attitudes towards the United States diverged significantly. France opted for independence and opposition to American designs for Western Europe while the United Kingdom emphasised Anglo-American interdependence – a term which unkind critics could dismiss as a euphemism for dependence. The attempt to overcome the damage to the 'special relationship' caused by Suez was particularly evident in the pattern of nuclear collaboration which developed in the late 1950s. This was not the only cooperative venture between Britain and the United States however. In 1958 the American intervention in Lebanon was accompanied by a parallel British intervention in Jordan. Indeed, the two operations were 'characterised by a high degree of coordination in both planning and execution'.[5]

If British and American interests coincided at least temporarily in the Middle East in 1958, they complemented each other far less in other regions. During the 1960s the United Kingdom was unwilling to provide even symbolic military support for the American intervention in Vietnam. At the same time, Britain, in contrast to some of the other European members of NATO, was muted in its criticism of American policy. The indifference or hostility of many Europeans to the

Vietnam war, however, underlined the divergence between American and European conceptions of the Alliance. For the United States, NATO was part of its global strategy of containment; for the Europeans it was a way of correcting an imbalance of power on the European continent. It is not surprising that in such circumstances the United States Congress began to emphasise once more the conditional nature of the American commitment and to demand reductions in the US military presence in Western Europe. In response, the Europeans accepted the need to shoulder a greater share of the burden, at least in Europe. Britain played a key role in the process of re-establishing a consensus. The formation of the Eurogroup was in large part a British initiative, while the withdrawal from East of Suez made additional military resources available to NATO.

If Britain remained acutely aware of the need to satisfy American demands for greater burden-sharing, it was far less willing to go along with the United States during the Middle East Crisis of 1973. Indeed, in 1973 there was a reversal of roles from 1956. This time it was American support for Israel which put the Alliance under strain. And what was most striking about the British position is that it did not differ significantly from that of the major European allies. For the United States the primary threat was that directed against Israel by the client states of the Soviet Union; for the Europeans the major threat was that oil supplies would be cut off. These divergent concerns came to a head with the American alert of conventional and nuclear forces in response to indications of a possible Soviet intervention. The aftermath of this episode was one of mutual recrimination: American complaints about the lack of support were matched by European allegations about a lack of advance consultation. Although this 'intra-mural crisis' had eased by the middle of 1974 it was significant for a number of reasons.

In the first place it accentuated the differing vulnerabilities, interests and attitudes of the Europeans on the one side and the US on the other. Second, the crisis helped to shape a closer European identity – if only in opposition to Washington. The Middle East crisis was also important because of its impact on Superpower *détente*. Although it did not put an end to the *détente* of the 1970s it gave it a blow from which it was never able to recover – the degree of domestic support in the United States for Superpower accommodation declined significantly after 1973. Finally, it provided a foretaste of the problems that were to develop in the late 1970s as Washington became less concerned about maintaining *détente* and more concerned about countering Soviet advances in the Third World. In these circumstances, it was inevitable that tensions which had been inherent in the differing conceptions of the Alliance from the outset should come to the fore. The United States was increasingly resentful of allies who were perceived as being extremely selective in their support. For their part most European governments were reluctant to sacrifice *détente* on the continent because of what they regarded as relatively marginal gains for the Soviet Union in the Third World. These differences emerged most strongly in response to the Soviet intervention in Afghanistan in December 1979 but had been lurking beneath the surface for some time.

At the root of the differences over Afghanistan were two very different models of the world. On the one side the Europeans, for the most part, approached out of area issues with a concept of pragmatic pluralism. Aware of the difficulties of maintaining control over emergent nations, they tended to dismiss Soviet gains in Africa, for example, as ephemeral. Although the military incursions of the Soviet Union and Cuba could not be ignored, they did not require immediate or large-scale counter-measures. Local forces would prove resistant to domination from Moscow just as they had proved resistant to continued domination by the old imperial powers of Western Europe.

The United States, in contrast, had a conception which was both ideological and bipolar. Regional variations were less important than the East–West dimensions of instability in the Third World. Even in those cases where Moscow did not create such instabilities, it was ruthless in exploiting them – despite all its protestations about the importance of Superpower *détente*. During the early years of the Carter Administration there was an attempt to replace this approach with one which acknowledged complexity and diversity, tried to look beyond Superpower rivalry, and attempted to treat problems in the Third World in their own terms rather than within the framework of East–West competition. This approach, however, failed to command unanimity among Carter's advisers, and with the Soviet invasion of Afghanistan was completely abandoned. Inevitably, this change created tensions with allies in Western Europe – tensions which became even more pronounced under the Reagan Administration.

As well as differences over the nature of the threats to NATO's security arising outside the area there were also differences over the most appropriate response. These became especially marked in the early 1980s during discussions over the Rapid Deployment Force. Although the Weinberger Doctrine enunciated in November 1984 established the preconditions for the use of American military force and thereby went some way to dispelling the notion that the United States is excessively reliant on military power in its approach to Third World problems, differences of emphasis remained. The European allies tend to stress 'maximum assistance and minimum presence' as the key to Western success in the Third World.[6] The Conservative Government's 1980 White Paper on British defence policy summed up this approach in its claim that the most suitable response to security challenges in the Third World was

> to try to remove the sources of regional instability which create opportunities for outside intervention. In some circumstances military measures will not be appropriate at all; in others they form only one component of the total response. Diplomacy, development aid, and trade policies will usually have a greater contribution to make.[7]

These differences also became apparent in transatlantic arguments over how best to respond to the problems of international terrorism. In 1986 the United States launched an air-strike against Libya in retaliation for acts of terrorism carried out against American nationals in Europe. The raids on Tripoli and Benghazi were roundly condemned by many European governments, who differed with Washington over the nature of the problem and its solution. Libya was seen as a target of convenience for the United States rather than the major source of international terrorism, and concerns were expressed that military reprisals would simply exacerbate the situation. The British government, however, set itself apart from the other European allies by granting permission for the operational use of American planes deployed in south-east England. Not only was this in marked contrast to France, which denied the American planes overflying rights, but it also aroused considerable controversy within Britain itself. The action of the Thatcher Government was roundly condemned by opposition parties, not least because it appeared to put the United Kingdom out of step with the European allies.

At first sight, the Thatcher government's support for the Reagan Administration seemed to contravene the philosophy of preventive diplomacy as propounded in the 1980 White Paper. Yet the issue is one of emphasis and nuance rather than fundamental principle. Even those who are anxious that military force should play a minimal role in the Western response to regional instability in the Third World, may nevertheless acknowledge that there are circumstances in which its use cannot be avoided. Indeed, the British response to Argentina's invasion of the Falklands in 1982, and a series of French interventions in Africa during the late 1970s suggest that the differences between American and European approaches, although real and enduring, should not be exaggerated. On these occasions not only was there a convergence of views but, in some instances, the United States even provided practical help. American assistance proved of considerable importance to the British during the war in the South Atlantic, while American logistic support greatly facilitated the French intervention in Zaire in 1978.

There has, of course, been an element of reciprocity in all this. Although the Europeans are often accused of ignoring out-of-area problems they have made a larger contribution than is generally acknowledged in the United States. France in particular has maintained a significant naval presence in the Indian Ocean. The British presence in the Indian Ocean and the Persian Gulf has been smaller but far from negligible. Furthermore, Britain has made Diego Garcia available to the United States as a forward base to assist American power projection in the Indian Ocean and the Gulf. Even so there have been demands that the Europeans do more. There is a widespread belief in the United States that in attempting to prevent the Iran–Iraq War from disrupting the flow of oil through the Gulf, the United States is contributing primarily to the security and prosperity of its allies rather than to its own security and prosperity. Because American dependence on imported oil is much lower than that of its allies, it is sometimes suggested that the United States should play a limited role and that the Europeans should have a larger naval presence in the region. The Europeans, however, remain cautious, contending that a very visible presence of external military forces increases tension in the region.

It is clear from these divergent assessments that the out-of-area issue could prove a highly mischievous element in the Atlantic relationship. The potential for this is increased by the growing trend towards globalism and unilateralism in American foreign policy. This trend suggests that Western Europe is in danger of losing its position as the priority area of American foreign policy. At the very least, Washington may be less sensitive to European views and concerns than it has been throughout much of the postwar period – something that was evident in the lack of consultation with Britain prior to the invasion of Grenada. Once again the dangers should not be over-estimated. The United States has always been a Pacific as well as an

Atlantic power and has fought two large wars in Asia without any weakening of its commitment to Western Europe. Nevertheless, the growing prosperity of the Pacific basin, the preoccupation with Central America, and the continuing concern over the Persian Gulf suggest that the focus of American foreign policy is changing and that Western Europe will increasingly have to adjust to such change.

One probable result is that burden-sharing arguments in NATO will become more intense as the United States finds itself squeezed between global commitments and finite defence budgets. American demands for greater 'compensation, facilitation and participation' by the allies when American forces are used outside the NATO area, represent more than another phase in the traditional arguments over burden-sharing. They highlight the issue which has been present since the Korean War but which was partially obscured in the 1950s by the residual imperial obligations of the European allies, namely, what is the Alliance for and what is it directed against? This question manifests itself in various forms. In the late 1970s and early 1980s it was the implicit problem underlying the controversy about the divisibility or indivisibility of *détente*. Consequently, the out-of-area issue cannot simply be dismissed or ignored. In one form or another it is a major item on NATO's agenda and will almost certainly become even more salient in the future. The only question, therefore, is whether it is handled well or handled badly.

OUT-OF-AREA OPERATIONS IN THE FUTURE

There are two major ways in which the out-of-area problem might be approached. It could be argued that the members need to revise the initial 'transatlantic bargain' in ways which give the Europeans a greater share of both the burden and the responsibility for their own defence in Europe. This would be accompanied by a tacit division of labour in which the United States accepts the responsibility for Western security elsewhere. The problem with an approach based on specialisation and a division of labour between Western Europe and the United States, however, is that it presumes an identity of outlook and an indivisibility of interest among the members which may not always be present. For a division of labour to be acceptable, certain minimum requirements have to be met. The first is that there must be a widespread agreement within the Alliance on the severity of threats which emanate from outside the NATO area. The second is that there has to be a workable consensus on how such threats might best be handled. Neither of these conditions can be taken for granted. Because of a belief that the United States all too often superimposes a framework of East–West rivalry on problems which are essentially local or regional in nature, the European allies – who frequently disagree among themselves – will be reluctant to give Washington total discretion in dealing with out-of-area contingencies. This reluctance is strengthened by concerns over what is seen as an American propensity to respond to political problems with military 'solutions'. Another difficulty with the division of labour approach is that it could all too easily become an excuse for American unilateralism and European parochialism and irresponsibility. Opportunities for the European allies to temper or moderate American policies would be reduced. Indeed, in circumstances where Washington alone was bearing the burden in response to out-of-area contingencies, advice from the Europeans would probably be dismissed as irrelevant and gratuitous.

The second, and more compelling, alternative is to opt for incremental rather than radical change and attempt to improve the capacity of the Alliance to deal with out-of-area challenges without major alterations or reductions in national roles and missions. In this connection, measures to improve the monitoring and alert procedures of the Alliance, and to strengthen the machinery for crisis management are crucial. The establishment of an out-of-area consultative group with both permanent and revolving membership could be a particularly valuable step towards both these objectives and help to minimise frictions in the Alliance in much the same way that the Nuclear Planning Group did in the 1960s. By institutionalising early diplomatic exchanges on issues which are not formally a matter of Alliance responsibility but which, if mishandled, could undermine cohesion, an out-of-area consultative group could prove extremely helpful. At its best, such a step could assist the development of concerted policies towards flashpoints in the Third World. At the very least, it would help to limit the political damage to the Alliance that inevitably results from divergent or competing responses to crises outside Europe. Indeed, the deliberations of such a group would often be no more than an exercise in damage limitation. But this should not be denigrated. Differences on extra-regional issues could become sufficiently acute to jeopardise existing patterns of cooperation in Europe. Consequently, damage-limitation is vital. If an out-of-area group can encourage common awareness of the differences of approach which exist, and thereby help to prevent issues becoming tests of European loyalty on the one side and American wisdom and restraint on the other, it will render a considerable service. In the absence of early consultations of this kind, the Alliance will suffer once again from what might be termed the politics of symbolism, a development that can only lead to increased recrimination and resentment.

In attempting to prevent this, it would also be helpful if the group could identify ways in which the European allies might play a more positive role and meet American demands for compensation, facilitation, and where possible participation in responding to extra-alliance contingencies. Much, of course, has already been done in this area, but it is increasingly important to highlight the European contribution and thereby challenge the 'free rider' allegations that are frequently voiced in the American Congress.

If the European contribution is greater than is often suggested, however, there is no room for complacency. Europeans clearly need to think about their security in global rather than regional terms, and to recognise that they have to shoulder more of the responsibility for dealing with challenges which arise in the Third World. To recommend such a course is not to recommend deference to the United States. On the contrary, it is precisely because European assessments of the problem and appropriate responses diverge from those in Washington that the Europeans have to take a more active role in devising those responses.

There is something of an irony in all this, especially for the United Kingdom. In the 1940s British policymakers believed an American commitment to Europe, by restoring the balance of power on the continent, would allow the UK to continue in its global role. In the decades that followed, that global role was replaced by a much narrower regional focus. Maintaining the American commitment in the latter half of the 1980s and through the 1990s, however, requires that Britain and the other European allies broaden their horizons once again. In other words, what was once only possible as a by-product of the Atlantic Alliance has, in a much amended form, become a prerequisite for its continued health and vitality.

3 The NATO Allies and the Persian Gulf

PAUL E. GALLIS

INTRODUCTION

Various potential threats to the sources of oil in the Persian Gulf endanger the interests of the United States and of its NATO allies. Several of the allied nations have developed extensive trade contacts with Iran or Iraq, as well as with other states in the region. In addition Japan imports a significant amount of its petroleum from the Gulf. A disruption of the flow of oil from the Persian Gulf could pose a serious economic and strategic threat to members of the alliance and to Japan. The United States and its allies, however, differ in important ways over how to respond to such a threat.

Continuous attacks upon oil tankers in the Persian Gulf and the mining of the Red Sea in the late summer and autumn of 1984 have underscored the petroleum importers' vulnerabilities in the region. This chapter begins with an analysis of the general strategic and economic interests of NATO in the region of the Persian Gulf. The depth of dependency of most of the NATO states upon petroleum from the Gulf means that they remain potentially open to future economic and political pressures from nations in an unstable region of the world. However, the United States, Great Britain, and France hold conflicting perceptions for resolving a potential disruption of the flow of oil. These conflicting perceptions arise primarily from competition among the allies for markets and for access to resources in the Gulf, and from differing views over the proper methods to resolve outstanding issues between the Arab world and Israel. Several grades of possible military action are examined, with an emphasis upon the impediments to a concerted allied operation.

INTERESTS OF THE UNITED STATES AND ITS ALLIES

Though the United States now imports little oil from the Persian Gulf (approximately 3 per cent of its total need), petroleum is a world-wide commodity the price of which is sensitive to any change in supply. Most of the European allies, and Japan, rely more heavily than does the United States on petroleum imports. Should the current conflict in the Gulf cause the supply of oil to diminish appreciably and for an indefinite period of time, certain oil-importing nations might bid for petroleum from other regions, driving up the price for all importing states. The potential therefore exists for a serious threat to the economies of the United States and its allies.[1]

The ultimate concern of the NATO Alliance is to prevent a Soviet political foothold in the region. Any effort by NATO states to secure their supply of oil that, in the view of Moscow, menaces Soviet interests in the region could lead to a US–Soviet confrontation.

THE QUESTION OF OUT-OF-AREA RESPONSIBILITIES OF THE NATO STATES

Article VI of the North Atlantic Treaty confines joint NATO actions to the boundaries of the Alliance, defined as the territory of the member states and 'the islands under the jurisdiction of any Party [to the Treaty] in the North Atlantic area north of the Tropic of Cancer'.[2] So-called out-of-area challenges to the security of member states require coordination between concerned states. Subsequent positions taken by the Alliance as a whole acknowledge the possibilities and the potential need for out-of-area action by NATO states. In the wake of the initial attacks against tanker traffic in the Gulf, the North Atlantic Council – NATO's governing body – addressed the issue of out-of-area engagements in May 1984:

> The Allies recognize that events outside the Treaty area may affect their common interests as members of the Alliance. They will engage in timely consultation on such events, if it is established that their common interests are involved. Sufficient military capabilities must be assured in the Treaty area to maintain an adequate defence posture. Allies who are in a position to do so will endeavor to support those sovereign states who request assistance in countering threats to their security and independence. Those Allies in a

position to facilitate the deployment of forces outside the Treaty area may do so, on the basis of national decision.[3]

The leadership of NATO has never moved beyond this point. While recognising that a crisis outside the Alliance boundaries may threaten NATO's interests, any action taken to deal with such a crisis will be arranged independently by individual member states and not as a function of the Alliance as a whole.

THE NATO ALLIES AND JAPAN IN THE PERSIAN GULF

Only Great Britain and Norway among NATO states are self-sufficient in their supply of petroleum. The member states of the European Community agreed on a coordinated programme in the mid-1970s to reduce their reliance on imported oil. In 1973, 62 per cent of the EC member states' total energy needs was supplied through imports of petroleum. Through conservation, the increased use of nuclear power, and the development of the North Sea oilfields, that figure had fallen to 32 per cent by 1983 (see tables). However, only marginal reductions are estimated for the rest of the decade. By 1990 the European Community as a whole will depend on imports for one-third of its energy needs, with Persian Gulf states supplying more, and not less, of its petroleum. Some states are appreciably more vulnerable to the need for imported oil than others: Greece, Turkey, Portugal, Italy, the Netherlands, Denmark, and Ireland will each rely

TABLE 3.1   Selected countries: September 1973 crude oil imports from Persian Gulf

	Thousand b/d	*Percentage of total imports*
US	994	29%
Canada	303	32%
Japan	3701	76%
FRG	1283	56%
Italy	1585	63%
UK	1308	68%
France	1585	63%

SOURCE   See Table 3.2.

TABLE 3.2   Imports of crude oil (estimated), third quarter of 1984; thousand b/d (percentage of total petroleum imports)

	From Gulf States excluding Iraq and Iran	Iraq	Iran
US	443 (13%)	29 (negl.)	6 (negl.)
Canada	... (negl.)	9 (3%)	25 (10%)
Japan	2038 (58%)	19 (negl.)	156 (4%)
FRG	200 (16%)	39 (3%)	75 (6%)
France	242 (22.5%)	33 (3%)	86 (8%)
UK	60 (12%)	11 (2%)	31 (6%)
Italy	215 (16%)	107 (8%)	186 (13.5%)

SOURCE   Central Intelligence Agency, *International Energy Statistical Review* (Washington, DC, CIA, 26 March 1985).

on oil for at least 50 per cent of their energy needs by 1990.[4] The enduring need for petroleum from the Gulf has played an important role in moving several NATO states to prepare to assume military responsibilities in the region.

Great Britain

Great Britain has progressed from producing virtually no petroleum in 1975 to self-sufficiency in 1980. Though North Sea oil production will most likely begin to diminish by 1990, Britain should not need to import petroleum – except small amounts for purposes of blending – until early in the next century.

   Great Britain's immediate interests in the Persian Gulf stem from its historic ties to many countries in the region and to its flourishing trade with and investments in the area. From the late nineteenth century London controlled the foreign policy of the Gulf sheikdoms and the South Arabian principalities. Great Britain assumed protection for much of the Arabian Peninsula in the First World War, and was influential in the region through the presence of its armed forces and petroleum companies well into the 1960s. In Oman, the British supported Sultan Qaboos' successful coup against his father in 1970, and seconded British officers lead the Omani land and air forces. Small numbers of Britons act as trainers within the armed forces of Saudi Arabia, Kuwait, and the United Arab Emirates.

Great Britain's links to the region range beyond trade and security assistance. Several Gulf states – in particular Saudi Arabia and Kuwait – have invested heavily in the United Kingdom. These developing financial relationships contribute to the already existing mutual interests between the Gulf's western littoral states and Great Britain.[5] For these reasons, Great Britain increased its naval presence in the Gulf and the Indian Ocean in 1980 after the Soviet invasion of Afghanistan and the outbreak of the Iran–Iraq war.[6]

France

It is France, of all the European allies, that has greatest economic interests in the region. France has longstanding political links with many nations in the Middle East, as evinced by its willingness to play a major role in the MNF in Lebanon, and by its decision to send naval detachments into the region of the Gulf from 1980 to the present. In part because France is no longer a major power, the Iraqis and others have been less cautious about inviting the French into the region to supply arms and military training as well as to undertake ambitious construction projects. The former French Minister of Defence, Charles Hernu, has said: 'In the Near East, France is the indispensable Western power', enjoying access that few other nations can hope to match.[7]

France has sought to diversify the sources that supply its energy needs. In addition to a growing nuclear power industry, France has contracted with the Soviet Union to double its purchases of natural gas from the Soviet Union's new pipeline to Western Europe. Currently, 20 per cent of French needs for natural gas are supplied by the Soviet Union. By 1990, France will depend upon Soviet supplies for approximately 30 per cent of its natural gas consumption.[8]

In the Middle East, French dependency on oil is closely linked to a programme of arms sales. The Saudis have recently become a major market for French technology and arms. By early 1984 the Saudis had signed $4 billion in contracts with firms owned or supported by the French government to build a sophisticated air defence system closely linked to the AWACS purchased from the United States.[9] These trade relationships have developed as part of France's efforts to build good relations with nations from which it imports large amounts of petroleum.

More than any other NATO state, France has thrown its support to

Iraq in the war against Iran. The delivery of Super Etendard fighter-bombers to Iraq in July 1983 has had important effects on the conflict, for the planes sharply improved Iraq's capability to expand the war and threaten Iran's oil lifeline. The Super Etendards, as well as the approximately 60 Mirage F1 fighters that France has sold to Iraq in past years, can carry the air-to-surface Exocet missile, which has been used to threaten shipping in the vicinity of Iran's oil lifting complex at Kharg Island. In addition, France has reportedly sold Roland anti-aircraft missiles, 150 combat helicopters, and approximately 100 tanks to Iraq since the war began.[10]

As a result of such sales, Iraq has incurred heavy financial debts in France: by the end of 1983 Iraq owed the French government approximately 13 billion francs (about $1.9 billion). Short of cash, Iraqi President Saddam Hussein reportedly offered France petroleum to offset part of the debt.[11] By December 1984, France was importing 6.7 per cent of its crude oil supplies from Iraq.[12] French companies are heavily engaged in Iraq, with an estimated 6000 French nationals constructing large-scale communications systems, public housing and buildings, and a range of infrastructure projects. These projects are insured by COFACE, the French government's investment insurance agency. The financial success of such projects is important, for several of the construction companies owned or supported by the French government are already experiencing financial difficulty.

Should Iraq fail to pay its debts and the French government be forced to absorb the losses by paying the insurance in the event of default, the economic and political repercussions for President Mitterrand's government could be serious.[13] The Iraqis have threatened that any French effort to curtail the projects would be met with a cutback in oil supplies. In May 1983 Iraqi Foreign Minister Tarik Aziz told a French reporter that once the war is over and Iraq's oil industry regains normal proficiency, 'we shall favour those who cooperated with us in our time of difficulty'.[14]

An Iraqi defeat in the war with Iran could reduce or eliminate an important, and probably growing, source of France's petroleum supplies, as well as jeopardize substantial French investments. The stated Iraqi preference for dealing with French rather than American companies has more vague implications, but is in keeping with past Iraqi efforts to oppose a substantial American presence in the Gulf. At a minimum, France has the opportunity for strengthening its ties to a nation that holds some of the largest oil reserves in the world.

The Federal Republic of Germany and Italy

The Federal Republic of Germany has taken a stated position of strict neutrality in the Iran–Iraq conflict. Should a crisis threatening NATO interests develop in the Gulf, constitutional restrictions would presumably prohibit the West Germans from engaging in any military operations in the region.

In December 1984, 22.4 per cent of the FRG's crude oil imports came from OAPEC, with Saudi Arabia and Libya providing half of that total.[15] Like France, the FRG contracted for greater supplies of natural gas from the Soviet Union in order to diversify its sources of energy supply. Currently, 20 per cent of its gas supplies come from the Soviet Union, with that share projected to rise to 30 per cent by 1990.[16]

In the last five years Italy has broken with practices of the previous three decades by taking a more visible political and military role in the Middle East. The Italian government has sent representatives to the Multinational Force and Observers in the Sinai, as well as a contingent to the MNF and minesweepers to the Red Sea in August and September of 1984.

Italy is yet another NATO country that reportedly has significant investments in the Persian Gulf, as well as a clear dependence on foreign energy supplies. In the third quarter of 1984, 52 per cent of Italy's imports of crude oil came from OAPEC countries; another 13.5 per cent came from Iran, Italy's second largest supplier of petroleum, after Libya.[17] As is true of France and the FRG, Italy complements its petroleum imports with growing purchases of natural gas from the USSR; by 1990 the Soviet Union will supply 23 per cent of Italy's natural gas needs.[18]

Italy has engaged in large construction projects in Iran, where Italian workers are said to number in the hundreds and potential investments for 1984 are in the range of $1.5 billion. Exact figures for Iran's indebtedness to Italy are unavailable. However, the significant number of Italian workers in Iran works against Italy's leverage for forcing any issue of rigorously observed payment schedules for the goods and services that it provides.

Turkey

Turkey has developed critical financial interests in the Persian Gulf. Turkey's imports of petroleum are almost evenly divided between Iran and Iraq, with those two countries supplying 70 per cent of Turkey's total needs. With borders that abut both Iran and Iraq, Turkey has attempted to remain neutral in the Persian Gulf conflict and has also made repeated offers to serve as a mediator. The Turkish–Iraqi relationship has grown to be one of mutual necessity. Iraq depends upon the sale of petroleum to fund its war effort: its pipeline through Turkey reached maximum throughput (920 000 b/d) in August 1984. Iraq pays transit fees for the Iskenderun pipeline to the Turkish government, and the line provides part of the Turks' petroleum needs. In addition, Turkey allows Iraq to send several trucks of oil across Turkish territory every day – more a gesture of friendship in Iraq's hour of need than a profitable economic arrangement. On 2 August 1984, the two nations reached an agreement for a second Iraqi pipeline to be built across Turkish territory. Total trade between the two nations was approximately $2 billion in 1984, with Turkish exports to Iraq having tripled from $310 million in 1983 to $900 million in 1984.[19]

Iran has pressured Turkey to close the Iskenderun pipeline. Turkey reportedly turned down an offer of $1 billion from Iran to shut down the line when Iraq countered with an offer to allow Turkish tankers to lift oil from Kharg Island without fear of attack.[20] Turkey is Iran's largest trading partner, with two-way trade having reached $2.4 billion in 1983.[21] In January 1985, the two nations signed a $3 billion barter arrangement. Presumably, Turkey's economic importance to Iran acts as a deterrent to any Iranian attempt to sabotage the Iskenderun pipeline. However, from interviews with individuals familiar with the views of the leadership in Iraq, it was learned that the Iraqis greatly fear an Iranian attack against one of the pumping stations along the pipeline.

Thus far Turkey has found neutrality to be a profitable, but difficult, position. It appears likely that Turkey will attempt to maintain that position should the Persian Gulf conflict grow more intense.

Japan

In December 1984, 62.2 per cent of Japan's crude oil imports came from OAPEC countries located in the Persian Gulf.[22] Among the United States' closest allies, Japan arguably finds itself in the most difficult straits. With an economy heavily dependent upon industry and exports, but with a virtual total dependence on imported energy,

Japan lacks the military capacity either to protect its transportation routes or to shield its foreign sources of energy from attack.

Both Iraq and Iran have pressed Japan to terminate its dealings with the other. In May 1984 the foreign ministers of Iraq and Kuwait asked Japan to cut its purchases of oil from Iran. In July 1984 a Kuwaiti official stated that 'the continuation of Japanese aid to Iran, notably the purchase of oil, could put in jeopardy the interests of Tokyo in the Arab world and more particularly in the Gulf'.[23] For the most part Japan has ceased signing term contracts with Iran for petroleum, and now purchases Iranian crude primarily on the spot market.

Japan has few options other than to attempt to avoid alienating any of the nations of the Gulf. Its leverage there is minimal and its potential problems great should there be a sustained interruption of the flow of oil.

THE GULF STATES AND THE NATO ALLIANCE

Iran and Iraq

The protagonists in the Persian Gulf conflict have alternately pressed their attacks against each other and allowed their confrontation to drift into a war of attrition. Despite persistent but unsuccessful efforts for a negotiated end to the conflict, the potential for escalation and severe political repercussions remains great. Iran continues to demand the elimination of Saddam Hussein and his party from power, and there is no clear evidence of a serious initiative for peace emanating from the Khomeini government. Iran continues to gather war materiel suitable for an assault across Iraq's flooded southern marshlands. Iraq seeks to regain lost territory and put an end to Khomeini's appeals to its Shi'ite population. Some observers believe that Saddam Hussein's largely Shi'ite army has demonstrated its loyalty and, despite fluctuating morale, should be able to repel an Iranian assault.[24] Others who have served with the United States or allied governments in the region note that Iraq's army has never been seriously tested in battle, and believe that in a protracted engagement with their Shi'ite brethren from Iran, the Iraqi infantry would prove unreliable.

The Gulf Cooperation Council

The trust in and reliance upon the United States by such key Gulf states as Saudi Arabia, Kuwait, and Oman have diminished in relation to the steadily growing importance of France and Great Britain in the region. There are clear indications that several important non-combatant Arab states in the Gulf, in the event of a serious escalation of the Iran–Iraq conflict, would prefer that the United States not assume a position of leadership in any involvement by Western states in a crisis. The perception that the United States acted with Israel in Lebanon to consolidate the position of a Christian minority at the expense of a Moslem majority remains a serious concern to the Gulf states, some of which have growing Islamic fundamentalist movements hostile to the United States.

In May 1981, six states (Saudi Arabia, Kuwait, Oman, Bahrain, Qatar, and the United Arab Emirates) banded together to form the Gulf Cooperation Council, an organisation intended to further their economic, political, and military cooperation in the face of the threat from Iran. The small populations and traditionally weak military structures of these states mean that their capacity to repel an attack by a more powerful outside force is minimal. The organisation lacks a unified command structure and its combined forces equal only half those of Iran. The principal role of the GCC in the Gulf conflict has been that several of its members have contributed approximately $20 billion to Iraq's war chest.[25]

The fears of the GCC states extend beyond Iran to Iraq. Kuwait has had a longstanding dispute with Iraq over the configuration of their common border, and Saddam Hussein has often in the past expressed disdain for conservative Saudi Arabia. The Iraqis view financial support from the GCC as nothing short of bribe money to assure protection from Iran and win favour with Saddam Hussein. Elements of the leadership in Iraq still harbour the view that once Iran is defeated, Iraq should move down the western littoral and settle accounts with Kuwait and Saudi Arabia.

Kuwaiti and Saudi efforts to strengthen their security relationship with the United States should be understood in this light. The perceived failure of the US efforts in the Multinational Force in Lebanon fed doubts in the GCC that the United States was committed to the integrity of the GCC states. There also remains a strong current in most Gulf states that the concern of the United States for them will always be secondary to Washington's commitment to Israel.

In these circumstances, the Gulf states' ties to Britain and France gain importance in the event of a disruption of the flow of oil. Although Great Britain withdrew its forces east of the Suez in 1971 and now has no treaties assuring assistance to any of the nations of the region, it remains on good terms with several states, particularly Oman, the UAE, Bahrain and Kuwait. In Oman, Kuwait, and, to a lesser degree, Saudi Arabia the British maintain a cadre of military personnel for purposes of training local forces. Oman has given Britain limited access to certain port facilities and airfields.

Beyond the direct French assistance to Iraq and Saudi Arabia, France does not have a highly developed security relationship with any of the other Gulf states. None the less, among the MNF participants, France most clearly improved its relations with the Arab states of the Gulf. By pressing the United States to open lines of communication with the various Arab factions of Lebanon and eschewing the use of force except for purposes of self-defence, France pursued the course of action believed by these observers to have been the most fruitful.

The instability of the Persian Gulf probably means that individual members of the GCC will continue to turn to the United States, Great Britain and France for security assistance. However, it is clear that US policy towards Israel and the perceived failure of the MNF will serve as serious obstacles to cementing relationships which, in order to endure and grow, must be based on more than temporary mutual advantage.

THE UNITED STATES, GREAT BRITAIN AND FRANCE: CONFLICTING PERCEPTIONS FOR RESOLVING A CRISIS

Friction over the MNF and differences over Israel

Though the United States, Great Britain and France all have important interests in the Persian Gulf, each is driven by different judgements over how best to protect them. Britain, France and Italy view the recent MNF experience as illustrative of differences in the US and allied approaches to the Middle East. The governments of the three nations joining the United States in the MNF also believe this experience has increased the difficulty for the four nations to act together in the future in a closely coordinated manner in the region.

The British, French and Italian governments each reportedly pressed the United States to broaden its contacts in Lebanon in order to attempt to establish a consensus for action between the Amin Gemayel government and the various factions initially willing to deal with it. In the view of the French, the British and the Italians, the United States consulted primarily with the Israelis and only secondarily with their counterparts in the MNF over which course of action to follow. The result was an emphasis on a military rather than a diplomatic solution to Lebanon's problems. The allies view Washington's approach to the Middle East as too short-term and mechanistic, and have repeatedly emphasised the need for maintaining and fostering their own long-term political and commercial relations with the region.

During the bombardments by the *USS New Jersey* and air attacks by US planes against Syrian positions in February 1984, Claude Estier, a spokesman for the then French Minister Claude Cheysson, underscored 'the historical and cultural attachment of France to Lebanon which justifies on the part of Paris positions different from those adopted by Great Britain, Italy, and the United States'. He added that French forces did not request US aerial or naval protection.[26]

It is also clear that some of the United States' NATO allies are uncomfortable with the US government's close ties with Israel. Unquestionably many of this country's European allies believe they must seek to improve relations with the Arab states of the Gulf because of their requirements for petroleum. The historical ties of Britain and France with the Middle East as a whole also contribute to this sentiment. The European Community has called for the recognition of Israel's right to exist, but the EC's Venice Declaration of 1980 also called for the inclusion of the PLO in Middle East negotiations, with a goal of establishing the right of the Palestinian people to self-determination.

Differences over Israel between the Europeans and the United States became more apparent during the MNF presence in Lebanon. Italy openly complained in December 1983 that the United States was distorting the MNF's peacekeeping mission. Italian President Sandro Pertini said that US forces were in Lebanon 'to defend Israel and not the peace'.[27] Two months later French President Mitterrand, at the height of US military action in Beirut, pointedly remarked that French forces were in Lebanon only to assure the security of French nationals there and 'to separate the Israeli army from the Palestinian army . . . We have saved about 4000 Palestinians, whom we have moved to Tunisia.'[28] There is a clear sentiment among France, Britain and Italy that the United States must show greater balance in deciding upon questions that affect both the Arab world and Israel. Such a sentiment could prove an impediment to possible future efforts at concerted action in the Middle East.

The International Energy Programme (IEP)

Yet another potential point of division in the event of a crisis in the Persian Gulf is the differing degrees of trust of NATO states in the International Energy Programme. The IEP provides for members of the International Energy Agency to share their oil stocks in the event of a significant disruption in the flow of oil.[29] The diminishing confidence of several of the United States' allies that the IEP would actually function in a crisis might be an important incentive for their willingness to play a greater political and military role in the Gulf.

The IEP details several steps for member states to take in concert in order to soften the effects of a disruption and to prevent a sharp rise in petroleum prices. The steps range from asking oil companies to offer voluntarily cargoes in transit to the IEA for countries in need of supply, to a government-directed allocation of oil stocks among the IEA membership in the event of a major disruption. Disagreement remains among the members over the circumstances under which such steps should be taken and over the effectiveness of those steps.

The Reagan Administration has repeatedly expressed its commitment to the IEP. However, there is some question whether the United States would be an effective and active participant.[30] Though the IEP does not prescribe that member states follow particular policies, it suggests several means by which a member state might lower consumption and assure that other members in need receive necessary allocations. The Reagan Administration has argued that market forces – allowing prices to rise in the event of a disruption – might be a preferred avenue for restraining consumption in the United States.

In January 1984, the Reagan Administration indicated that it would consider drawing down the Strategic Petroleum Reserve (SPR) in the event of a disruption. Reliance upon stocks and market pricing, in the Administration's view, might obviate or reduce the need for emergency sharing among nations. On 11 July 1984, the Administration joined with other IEA members in agreeing to consider a joint stock drawdown in the early stages of a significant shortage. A stock drawdown coordinated among member states would reduce the danger of one nation seeing its stocks transferred to another nation's stocks – a development that would nullify efforts to blunt price increases. If, in a brief disruption, oil prices remain relatively stable and IEA members believe that their economies will not seriously suffer from temporary and moderate shortages, the chances are thereby diminished for an intervention by NATO states in the Gulf.

Serious obstacles to assuring that the IEP would actually function as planned persist. France is the only NATO state not in the IEA. France refused to join the IEA when it was established in 1974, for the French government was apprehensive that the United States would dominate the organisation. Successive French governments have also contended that it is more productive for France, in keeping with that country's longstanding ties to many countries of the Middle East, to pursue bilateral agreements for the nation's supply of oil rather than be lined to a 'consumer's cartel' such as the IEA. In the event of a disruption of the flow of oil from the Gulf, it is entirely conceivable that France, in the wake of its past and current disagreements with the United States, would balk at the initiation or the timing of measures designed to share petroleum, and would instead seek to utilise its commercial and political links in the Arab world to assure a continued supply.

France aside, certain members of the IEA might flinch if the moment arrived to divert supplies intended for their shores to another member in need. The United States, Britain and Norway would probably have the greatest obligations among NATO states to share with other IEA members. Some observers believe that the British government, heading a nation self-sufficient in energy but experiencing economic difficulties, would face enormous domestic political pressure not to share with the 'have-nots', thereby leaving them to fend for themselves.

Particularly if the cut-off of oil were to appear to be for more than three months – thereby depleting the 90-day stocks that most IEA members have striven to build – a scramble for oil parallel to or greater than that which occurred during the Iranian revolution of 1979 could emerge.

In addition, there is no guarantee that during a major disruption private oil companies operating in member states will volunteer cargoes of crude to the IEA for allocation and sale unless given a guarantee of a replacement cost or an assurance against competitive disadvantage in the domestic markets they serve. Even so, there is no certainty that the oil companies would cooperate. After all, companies with continued access to petroleum and sizeable supplies on hand stand to reap potentially large profits should a disruption in oil result in rapid price increases. To commit their own supplies in order to contribute to the stability of the oil markets could conflict directly with their own economic interests. Given the nature of any large oil company's far-flung operations, it is likely that a government attempting to track down and verify a company's stated reserves or cargoes in transit would face a bureaucratic task of mammoth proportions.

Possible events leading to a disruption of the flow of oil

A number of possibilities exists for a disruption of the flow of oil in the Gulf. The conflict has the potential for affecting petroleum production in regions of the Gulf not directly involved in the war. Attacks on tanker traffic in the Gulf in the spring and summer of 1984 and the mining of portions of the Red Sea in August 1984 demonstrate some of the potential for threats to the transport of petroleum. A major Iraqi attack on Iran's oil export terminal at Kharg Island could lead to possible Iranian retaliation through the mining of the Strait of Hormuz or through an attack on Iraq's principal Gulf supporters, Saudi Arabia chief among them.

The Saudi oil fields and refining industry are of critical importance. Should Saudi production capacity be significantly reduced (maximum Saudi capacity is approximately 10.0 m b/d; production as of the summer of 1985 was approximately 3.7 m b/d), then a disruption of more than three months – sufficient time to absorb the stocks of most IEA members – could occur.

Within the petroleum industry, concern is greatest over three possibilities: terrorist attacks on Saudi pumping stations at several locations; destruction of several Saudi gas–oil separator plants; and serious damage to the refining and export terminal of Ras Tanura – possibly by the crashing of an explosives-laden ship into port or storage facilities.[31] Though the pipe line is itself relatively easy to repair, the sophisticated equipment necessary to replace a pumping station is in short supply, requiring six months to a year to obtain in the best of conditions. And severe damage to the Saudis' ability to refine, store, or transfer petroleum at Ras Tanura would have important effects upon the world petroleum market.

Such catastrophic war occurrences could have unpredictable effects

upon the intentions and efforts of IEA member states to work together
to remedy shortages in petroleum. If it became quickly evident that a
supply disruption would be greater than three months, would well-
stocked IEA members still agree to transfer their oil while also under
domestic political pressure not to do so? Would wealthier nations
choose to cast aside the IEP and enter the spot market to purchase
large supplies? Would Japan, a member of the IEA but perhaps the
most vulnerable of all industrialised nations to a disruption in supply,
follow the same course it did in 1979 when it ignored US pressure to
avoid panic buying and again purchase large lots of petroleum at
spot-market prices?[32] And even if member states set in motion the
IEP, would oil companies agree to sell their petroleum as required? In
1979, the Turkish government requested petroleum under the IEP,
but US companies originally refused to agree to contracts with Turkey.
Certain petroleum executives argued that the Turks were cash-poor
and unreliable customers, a situation made worse when Turkey, after
having finally arranged to purchase oil from an American company,
abruptly cancelled the shipment unilaterally when a cheaper source of
supply unexpectedly became available.

It is clear that the efficient working of the IEP, whether a disruption
in supply be for less than three months or for as long as six months or a
year, depends upon more than having large stocks of petroleum
available and a sharing mechanism agreed to and in place. The IEA is a
stronger body than it was in 1979. None the less, the unknown form of
any sudden disruption in supply would have unpredictable
consequences upon the psychology of those who have reserves on hand
and upon those who would wish to acquire them.

DIFFICULTIES OF ACHIEVING CONCERTED MILITARY ACTION TO RESTORE THE FLOW OF OIL

There are few doubts that the United States and several of its allies
would resort to military action to prevent or limit the disruption of the
flow of oil from the Persian Gulf. The limited action begun in the late
summer of 1984 by the United States and several allies to sweep the
Red Sea of mines provided indications of the difficulty of achieving
unity should a more extensive, and overtly military, effort potentially
involving combat eventually be required. In August 1984 the United
States, Great Britain, France, and Italy sent mine-clearing equipment
and personnel to the Red Sea at the request of the Egyptian

government. The Saudis also invited the United States to send mine-clearing helicopters and naval personnel and France to send minesweepers to protect the important Red Sea ports of Jidda and Yanbu. Yanbu is the terminus of a large Saudi petroleum pipeline capable of carry 1 m b/d, a critical link in the kingdom's capacity for supplying the global market since the pipeline's oil need not be carried through the Persian Gulf. Libya, an ally of Iran, is believed by the Egyptians to have mined the Red Sea in August 1984, and may well have done so in part to underscore to the Saudis that their effort to bypass the potentially hazardous Persian Gulf may not in fact limit vulnerability.

The British view of possible military action

Two important questions for the NATO allies are the degree of unity they can muster in any potential military operation, and the scale that any operation must assume in order to protect the petroleum traffic. On 1 June 1984, Prime Minister Margaret Thatcher of Great Britain was asked under what circumstances, if any, her government would contemplate military action in the Persian Gulf. She replied:

> First we try . . . diplomatic action and secondly if there were to be anything else specific it would only be at the invitation of the Gulf countries. Thirdly you only use military means, which I suppose means keeping shipping going, as a last resort.[33]

The British have been careful to describe any projected military action as limited. Foreign Minister Geoffrey Howe, on a trip to Moscow in July 1984, informed Soviet Foreign Minister Andrei Gromyko that the British would move into the Persian Gulf only as a last resort to keep shipping moving, and that no action beyond that was contemplated.[34] Presumably, Howe was attempting to reassure the Soviet Union that a British military action would not expand into an effort to land forces that might put Gulf oil fields under the direct control of the West, as well as signalling the Soviet leadership to exercise whatever leverage for restraint it possessed with Iraq.

The French view of possible military action

The French government has directed its public warnings only at Iran. In July 1984 President Mitterrand spoke of the

> solidarity of France with the Gulf states which have asked nothing of anyone and which must not be victims of this war . . . The position of France must be clear in this matter.[35]

This was the first time that France indicated it was firmly opposed to any Iranian gains in the Gulf. A day later, speaking before journalists, Mitterand told King Hussein that 'France does not wish to be the enemy of Iran or of anyone else'. But 'she does not want . . . the ages-old equilibrium between Persians and Arabs to be broken'.[36]

There are reports that France has refused to discuss military contingency plans in any depth with the United States because of the fear that such discussions would clear away an important step inhibiting the United States from undertaking possibly precipitous military measures.[37] This concern stems in part from French economic interests in the region. France has become Iraq's largest creditor outside the Gulf, and it is probable that Saddam Hussein prefers to purchase arms primarily from France rather than develop an extensive security relationship with either the Soviet Union or the United States.

The growing depth of France's financial relationship with and potentially great dependence for oil upon Iraq raises the question of French willingness to act should it be Iraq and not Iran that brings tanker traffic to a halt in the Gulf, or should Iraq later turn upon its weaker neighbours Kuwait and Saudi Arabia, either to settle longstanding disputes or to secure a route for its petroleum across the Arabian peninsula to the Red Sea.

The United States and its allies: difficulties in achieving a united effort

President Reagan, on 22 May 1984, indicated that the United States would not intervene in the region unless invited to do so.[38] Residual concern over an uninvited US presence has persisted since the mid-1970s, when then Secretary of State Henry Kissinger and Secretary of Defence James Schlesinger remarked that the United States might unilaterally enter the region to assure its access to petroleum. The Carter Doctrine, which declared US intentions to act in the Gulf in order to prevent a disruption in petroleum supplies, and its endorsement by President Reagan have not allayed such fears.

These and other reasons complicate the efforts of the United States to assure that the allies work together in the Gulf in the event of a disruption in petroleum supplies. During the effort to clear the Red Sea of mines, both France and Italy indicated that their experiences in the MNF would lead them to follow a course of action independent of the United States, or at best parallel to it. In mid-August 1984 Italian Defence Minister Spadolini said that his government was considering sending minesweepers to the Red Sea at the request of the Egyptian government. When asked if Italy were contemplating joining a new MNF in the Gulf region, he responded: 'I would not hear of any multinational force'. Once Rome did decide to send minesweepers, it underscored that its effort was the result of a bilateral agreement with Egypt and not part of a joint undertaking with US ships in the region. The French position was similar. France joined Italy in refusing to send representatives to a naval coordinating committee established by the United States and Great Britain to oversee the efforts of allied naval forces in the Red Sea. The same was true of the current efforts of the French and US minesweeping forces in Saudi Arabia.

Turkey occupies an unusual and potentially critical position should a threat develop to Western interests in the Gulf. Turkish officials have stated that the United States Central Command (CENTCOM) could utilise Turkish bases only in the event of a Soviet incursion in the Middle East, or as part of a NATO operation.[39] The same restrictions no doubt apply to other NATO members as well. But the extensive contacts that Turkey enjoys in both Iran and Iraq could prove important in the event other NATO allies intervened in the Gulf and needed to establish lines of communication with one or both of the warring nations.

Britain and France have stated repeatedly that they must be invited into the region by an Arab government before they will take military action. Given the Saudi and Egyptian requests during the late summer and fall of 1984 to take action in the Red Sea, it seems probable that at least several Arab states affected by the Gulf war would ask for assistance if greater threats to their security become imminent.

POSSIBLE FORMS OF MILITARY ACTION

The nature of the assistance to be offered in the Gulf by the United States and its allies would depend upon circumstances. Given the GCC's strong aversion to treaties with or the large-scale presence of either the United States or the USSR in the region, the Arab states clearly prefer that any military action on their behalf be limited to achieving specifically approved ends.

Minesweeping and protection of tanker traffic

The minesweeping operation undertaken in the Red Sea has provided a possible model for a similar action in the Gulf, should mines be laid in or near the Straits of Hormuz, or in waters approaching the oil-loading ports of Kuwait, Saudi Arabia, or other western littoral states. As in the Red Sea, the United States, Britain, France and Italy have the capacity to undertake minesweeping operations. Presumably, France and Italy would once again resist close coordination with the United States and Britain. Boarding of ships in order to search for mines carried on or below decks might also be a part of such an effort. In keeping with the practice of the Egyptians during the period of the mining of the Red Sea, officials of the Gulf States, rather than from the Allied states, might be called upon for this task in order to demonstrate a measure of Arab control over the operation.

Naval escorts and aerial reconnaissance and protection

Should Iranian air attacks on tanker traffic escalate or be launched against the oil ports and refineries of the Gulf littoral states of the Arabian peninsula, the United States, Britain and France could designate elements of their navies to escort ships into the Gulf and out once again into safe waters. Aerial reconnaissance to assist in the protection from attack of refineries, port facilities, and allied and civilian ships would be intensified, though again with Arab involvement. Aerial attacks against Iranian airfields might prove necessary, in order to reduce the danger of Iranian aircraft attacking allied ships.[40] The Saudis' utilisation of AWACS under US supervision could play an important and visible role, for the information gathered by the planes is already being shared among

GCC states. According to press reports of a document authored by the former Director of the State Department's Bureau for Politico-Military Affairs, the United States has drawn up contingency plans resembling such an operation.[41]

Because of the distances involved, participating air forces would have to utilise air fields in the GCC states. Most observers agree that the leaders of the GCC – Oman, Saudi Arabia, and Kuwait – are adamant that land forces not be placed on their soil, so the presence of allied military personnel on shore would be minimal. The Italians have emphasised that they would not enter combat in the Gulf, and are therefore unlikely to join such an operation.[42]

Use of ground forces to secure pipelines, refineries, and port facilities

Should pumping stations and key elements of Saudi Arabia's refining and port facilities be attacked by terrorists or by aircraft, ground forces with naval and aerial protection from allied states could be sent to secure the damaged installations and protect efforts to rebuild them. Refining and port facilities in other GCC states, as well as the desalination plant critical to Kuwait's livelihood, could also be targets of attack.

Saudi Arabia and Kuwait would probably resist a large-scale presence of European or United States troops, even in such dire circumstances. Saudi confidence and trust in the United States remains low after the outcome of the MNF operation in Lebanon. Britain has said that it would not lend assistance unless asked, and then would limit assistance to assuring the freedom of navigation of tanker traffic. As already noted, France is strongly opposed to another operation resembling the MNF. The United States might well find itself in a position of having to act alone and without an invitation to intervene. Given the hostility of much of the Arab world to the United States and latent fears of a US take-over of Middle East oilfields, this would be a difficult step to take. It would further isolate the United States from Arab nations, and would complicate future efforts to work with the allies outside NATO territory.

CONCLUSION

The war in the Persian Gulf could pose important threats to the interests of the NATO states and Japan. The United States, Great Britain and France are the only NATO states that have shown a clear inclination to use military force should there be a disruption of the flow of oil from that area. The conflicting history of each of these nations in the region has led each to evaluate differently its interests and its methods for protecting them. It is clear that France above all would resist close coordination with the United States in the event military action were necessary to secure or restore the supply of petroleum.

In Western Europe there is general opposition to extending NATO's institutional military responsibilities beyond the European continent, particularly when a crisis does not appear to be related to fundamental East–West differences. Should events develop that require military action by several individual NATO states in the Persian Gulf, a sentiment could well be triggered in the United States that member nations not participating in the action should in the future do more to share the organisation's costs in Europe. Since many NATO states are heavily dependent upon petroleum imports but rely on others to assure the security of their supply, it is reasonable to assume that those who bear the burden of a military operation in the Gulf would ask – especially if lives are lost – that other members bear a greater responsibility for maintaining NATO's strength within the organisation's traditional boundaries. In addition, allied pressure on the Japanese to assume a stronger military role in the Pacific, such as protection of the Straits of Molàcca, could increase if Western public opinion continues to resist the bite of Tokyo's trade practices while perceiving that the West protects Japan's economic lifeline.

In the Persian Gulf, the Arab states will continue to ward off ties with the United States that are too close or direct, especially in the absence of the resolution of their differences with Israel. In part for this reason, the French and the British are also reluctant to engage in military action in the Gulf with the United States unless it is at the expressed invitation of Arab nations. Even then, with the experience of the MNF in mind, the allies will be wary of a closely coordinated joint effort perceived as being under US leadership.

The MNF demonstrated an emerging tendency on the part of several NATO states to undertake greater responsibilities for their own security outside Europe. However, those same states believe that the US policy governing its MNF contingent demonstrated poor judgement and an absence of a sense of measure in the utilisation of military force. In part for these reasons, several important European allies believe that they can best protect certain critical interests by acting outside the umbrella of US leadership of NATO.

Britain and France clearly see the Arabs' displeasure with the United States on a range of questions, as the frequent emphasis by British and French leaders on 'historic ties' and appreciation for Arab culture in the region attest. They will continue to take advantage of US difficulties in the area to build closer economic and military relationships with Arab capitals.

The question of maintaining a long-term supply of energy resources goes beyond the current problems for the Alliance in the Persian Gulf. Undoubtedly, if the IEA does not hold together in a crisis, allied unity will have failed a severe test. In the event of a disruption of the flow of oil that appears to be of more than several months' duration, the domestic political pressure upon the governments of member states to refuse to share stocks could be great, particularly if those nations designated to receive supplies have not borne a military sacrifice in the Gulf. Each day that passes without a resumption of the oil flow will bring added pressure. In August 1984 the delay of ten days between the US decision to send minesweeping equipment to Suez and the Red Sea and its actual date of arrival has again raised questions about the rapidity of a US military response to a crisis in the region.

The NATO allies have already begun to look beyond the Gulf and the West in the effort to obtain a diversified supply of energy. Many of them have already turned to the Soviet Union for purchases of natural gas to help remedy this problem. By the 1990s several of the NATO states will have a significant dependence upon Soviet natural gas. It remains to be seen if in the future, at the moment of a shortage in global oil supplies, the Soviet Union will use its sales of natural gas as a lever to pry apart allied unity.

The ultimate needs of the Soviets themselves for petroleum are a factor to consider in the event of any crisis in the Gulf. Though estimates vary as to the USSR's reserves of petroleum,[43] the Soviet Union has a clear strategic interest in a region so close to its borders. Arab leaders in the Gulf wish to restrict any possible allied military mission in the region not only because they do not desire a direct and long-term Western presence there, but because they fear the Gulf could become the locus of a conflict between the United States and the Soviet Union. Arab sensitivities aside, fear of such a conflict is a primary incentive behind efforts by France and Britain to underscore the limited aims of any possible military engagement in the Gulf.

Finally, the war between Iran and Iraq may well be fought to no clear and decisive conclusion. The outcome of the conflict, in a tightly packed geographic space consisting mostly of nations with small populations but approximately 60 per cent of the globe's known petroleum reserves, could have important repercussions for the West that fall short of a dramatic disruption of oil supplies. The conflict is as much a struggle over ideologies and values as it is for strictly military hegemony. Britain and France, and to a lesser extent other West European nations, are making a strong effort to extend their commercial and political contacts in the Arab states of the Gulf. They are doing so in the hope that whatever the coming shifts in the region's political and religious tides, they will be in a position to continue their presence. Though their interests and those of the United States in the Gulf may be similar, the different methods undertaken to protect them could continue to impede unity of action in the Middle East on a range of issues important to Western security.

4 NATO and the South Atlantic: A Case-Study in the Complexities of Out-of-area Operations

ANDREW HURRELL

For much of the post-war period the South Atlantic figured only marginally on the list of western security interests outside the NATO area. Yet since the early 1970s interest in the region has been growing for a variety of reasons: anxiety within NATO over the increased Soviet naval presence; the possible threat that that presence poses to western sea communication and, in particular, the Cape Route; continuing political instability and uncertainty in southern Africa and the countries that border the South Atlantic; increased awareness of the importance of deep-sea mineral resources; concern over the future of Antarctica.

This chapter has two main aims. Firstly, to examine the nature of western interests in the South Atlantic area and to consider the extent of the Soviet threat to those interests.[1] Secondly, to review possible ways in which NATO has responded, or might respond, to the problem of security in the South Atlantic. These responses can be divided into two groups. First, responses involving NATO countries alone, either within a formal NATO framework or on a more informal, bilateral basis. Second, responses involving one or more of the regional powers, either within some formal institutional grouping – such as a South Atlantic Treaty Organisation – or based on lower levels of military cooperation with NATO countries.

An examination of western responses to the problem of security in the South Atlantic provides a fascinating case study of the complexities of out-of-area operations. In particular, it highlights three sets of difficulties that constantly recur whenever such operations are discussed. First, there is the lack of consensus about the scope of western interests and the seriousness of the threat to them. Second, there are the divisions within NATO as to whether and how the alliance should respond to that threat. Third, there is the clear divergence of interests and perceptions that exists between NATO and those major regional states that are often proposed as potential western allies.

WESTERN INTERESTS IN THE SOUTH ATLANTIC

Both United States and NATO defence planning has traditionally paid only slight attention to the South Atlantic region. As regards Latin America, US security doctrine assumed that the level of external threat would remain low and that hemispheric solidarity behind Washington's leadership would be maintained. As regards the Cape Route and southern Africa, it was believed that the low level of Soviet challenge could be easily met by a combination of overall US naval superiority, a firm British commitment embodied in the 1955 Simonstown Agreement with South Africa and access to a range of excellent facilities along the African coast. During the 1970s, however, this situation changed significantly and the South Atlantic began to figure more prominently on the list of western security interests.[2] This change was due to the interplay of three factors: the weakening of western defence capabilities; the increased salience of western interests and the growth of the Soviet presence in the region.

The weakening of western defence

On the Latin American side of the South Atlantic, the low level of external threat meant that the inter-American security system that emerged during and immediately after the Second World War was a relatively loose one.[3] This system had three essential components: the formalisation of security relations in the inter-American Treaty of Reciprocal Assistance (The Rio Pact) of 1947 and the Charter of the OAS signed in 1948; military assistance agreements signed with individual countries; and US arms sales.[4] Yet there was never any kind of permanent multi-lateral military organisation and, as Gordon Connell-Smith points out, even the 'Inter-American Defense Board was established for political rather than military reasons'.[5]

Cooperation over the South Atlantic was even more limited. In 1959 the Inter-American Defense Board approved a Plan for the Defense of Inter-American Maritime Traffic, from which the South Atlantic Maritime Area Command (CAMAS) was created. CAMAS is made up of representatives of Argentina, Brazil and Uruguay with the overall command alternating between Brazilian and Argentinian naval officers. The aim of CAMAS is to provide an integrated command in wartime and its activities have included the Atlantic convoy and communications exercises. In addition, from the early 1960s, the United States navy based in Puerto Rico participated with the navies of Brazil, Chile, Argentina, Venezuela, Colombia and Uruguay in the regular UNITAS exercises.[6]

Yet since the late 1960s the Inter-American military system has come under increasing strain. The United States is no longer the major supplier of arms to the region. By 1979 UK military assistance to Latin America had declined to US$30 million, barely 1 per cent of the world-wide total and the number of MAP personnel in the region had dropped from 800 in the mid-1960s to less than 100 in 1979. Most significant of all, in 1977 Brazil, Argentina and Uruguay broke off Military Assistance Agreements with the United States as a result of disputes over US human rights policy. As John Child concludes, 'the Inter-American Military System as a whole may now be in danger of complete fragmentation as the strongest element (the bilateral Security Assistance Program) declines drastically'.[7]

A similar picture emerges on the other side of the Atlantic. Reflecting the overall decline in the size of the US navy from 976 ships at the height of the Vietnam War to 479 in 1976, the presence of the US navy in the South Atlantic fell steadily during the 1970s. Its presence is limited to periodic South Atlantic and West African Training Cruises and, whilst maintaining a military attaché in its Pretoria Embassy, US naval ships have not been allowed to dock in South Africa since 1967. Similarly, Britain gradually phased out its involvement in the region. In 1967 the British post of Commander-in-Chief South Atlantic and South America was abolished and was replaced by a liaison officer appointed to Cape Town. In 1974 Britain decided not to renew the Simonstown Agreement, thereby ending access both to port facilities and to the Silvermine intelligence gathering station. Finally, the Portuguese Revolution of 1974 meant the loss of western access to bases in Portugal's African colonies, especially the ports of Angola (Luanda, Lobito and Moçamedes).

Increased salience of western interests

As the western military presence declined, perceptions of the importance of western interests in the region increased. Three sets of interests can be identified. First, there is the increasing importance of the South Atlantic shipping lanes.[8] The argument here has become familiar and is based on the fact that since the mid-1960s an ever higher percentage of imports to the United States and Western Europe has been transported around the southern trip of Africa. Around 2300 ships use the Cape Route each month, of which 600 are oil tankers – in 1982 47 per cent of West European oil involved the use of the Cape Route. Some 295 million tons of cargo pass through the South Atlantic Narrows each year of which 75 per cent is bound for Western Europe.[9] In particular some 70 per cent of the strategic raw materials used by NATO are transported via the Cape Route.[10] Most reports suggest that the level of usage is likely to grow through the 1980s.

Second, the increased range of US Ohio class and Soviet Typhoon class submarines, together with the 6000 nautical mile range of Trident II and SSNX20 missiles make it likely that the South Atlantic will become an increasingly important area of operations for nuclear missile submarines. This may well lead to increased conventional naval deployments in the region as the West in particular seeks to extend its ASW capabilities to meet this development.[11] Third, western nations have a long-term interest in the development of sea-bed minerals, in the South Atlantic fishing industry and in maintaining open access to Antarctica.[12]

GROWTH OF SOVIET NAVAL PRESENCE

By far the most important factor explaining increased western concern has been the striking growth of Soviet naval capabilities in general and the increased Soviet naval presence in the South Atlantic in particular.[13] The Soviet Union, which in Stalin's time possessed only a coastal navy, now has more surface ships and more submarines than the United States. The Soviet navy first appeared off West African waters in 1969 after Ghana seized two Russian trawlers. In 1970, following an amphibious attack by the Portuguese on Conakry, the Soviet Union sent a small naval contingent to the region, thus creating the West African Patrol.[14] Soviet presence in the area increased significantly following the collapse of the Portuguese African empire and especially with the rise to power of the MPLA in Angola. In June 1976 a Soviet naval force was deployed off the coast of Angola and since 1977 the Soviet Union has stationed a permanent force of around 12 ships in Luanda. Overall Soviet presence is now around 5000 ship days a year compared to 7000–8000 in the Indian Ocean,[15] and the Soviet Union has also been making qualitative changes in the types of naval vessels, particularly submarines, operating from Cuban ports.[16] In addition to its naval presence, the Soviet Union has developed a sophisticated surveillance system over the South Atlantic, using Bear-D reconnaissance flights operating from Cuba, Luanda and, between 1971 and 1977, Conakry. Finally, the Soviet Union and Eastern Europe take the largest fishing catch from the South Atlantic. By 1980 it caught about 1½ million tons annually, about 18 per cent of its world-wide catch, followed by Poland, taking 185 000 tons annually as 34 per cent of its total catch.[17]

Before considering NATO responses to the problem of South Atlantic security, it is important to set the above discussion against a series of factors that suggest the need for a more balanced assessment of the extent of the Soviet threat. Indeed the first major problem facing the alliance is precisely the lack of consensus over the strategic importance of the region. Firstly, the Soviet naval threat is mitigated by the logistical difficulties of operating at such vast distances from their home bases. More specifically, as has been frequently pointed out, if the Soviet Union wanted to cut off western oil supplies, it could do so far more effectively by intervening in the Middle East or by blockading the Straits of Hormuz.[18] Secondly, the constraints of the nuclear balance make less likely the kind of protracted conflict in which the blockading of distant sea lanes would be a major strategic priority. In the modern period all Superpower naval rivalry is necessarily disciplined by the fear of escalation to nuclear war. Indeed one study has suggested that the disruption of western sea lanes would rank only fifth in the list of Soviet naval priorities after the defence of its strategic forces, the destruction of western offensive naval capabilities, the support of its land forces and the interdiction of resupply from the US to Western Europe.[19] Thirdly, it is dangerous as well as hypocritical to concentrate on the Soviet threat and to overlook the Soviet navy's role in protecting its legitimate interests in the region: its extensive fishing fleet, its interests in Antarctica and the need to maintain the invulnerability of its SLBM force.

Fourthly, it is misleading to merely list Soviet gains and omit any discussion of Soviet weaknesses. The Soviet Union has on several occasions failed to obtain access to port facilities from apparently friendly governments: the Congo has refused access to Pointe Noire and the Cape Verde Islands to Saint Vincent. Moreover the loss of access to Conakry in 1977 is a clear example for the volatility of Soviet gains and the difficulty of obtaining guaranteed access, preferably by treaty. Most importantly, the Soviet Union's relations with Africa is far more complex than those who draw up lists of 'Marxist-Leninist' states imply. Thus even such a 'client state' as Angola maintains very close economic ties with the West – an area in which the Soviet Union is conspicuously limited in its ability to assist its allies.

These arguments do not totally demolish the importance of the South Atlantic for western security but they do underline the need for a more balanced assessment than the many 'Cape Route lobbyists' are likely to provide. Interestingly, attention has been so focused on the military threat posed by the Soviet Union that there has been a tendency to downplay the political functions of naval power: the need for NATO to develop a role in the South Atlantic in order to establish the right to be there, to indicate that the West has interests in the region and that action will be taken if necessary to defend those interests.

NATO RESPONSES

In the light of the trends discussed in the previous section, official NATO concern over the security of the South Atlantic has increased steadily since the early 1970s. As early as November 1972 the North Atlantic Assembly adopted a resolution 'to give SACLANT authority to plan for the protection of NATO–Europe's vital shipping lines in the Indian Ocean and the South Atlantic including surveillance and communication'.[20] A further resolution in 1976 called on NATO 'to reinforce the authority given to SACLANT with regard to the protection of vital shipping lanes'.[21] In 1981 the Diligent Report to the European Parliament concluded that it was 'perturbed by the vulnerability of its sea links with Africa, the Persian Gulf and other parts of the world, since the North Atlantic Treaty does not cover areas south of the Tropic of Cancer in which the increasing seapower of the Soviet Union . . . presents a growing and calculated threat'.[22]

Yet how should NATO respond to the problem of South Atlantic security? Actual and potential responses can be divided into two groups. Firstly, actions taken exclusively by NATO member states, and secondly, responses involving one or more of the regional powers in the South Atlantic.

NATO alone

In many ways the most obvious response would be to formally extend the scope of NATO operations to include the South Atlantic and the Cape Route, but without involving any regional power. Two things would flow from this. Firstly, the need for an increased peacetime presence, involving joint NATO planning and exercises. Secondly, the development of contingency planning for war.

Some very limited steps have been taken in this direction. In August 1981 the NATO exercise Operation VENTURE did extend into the South Atlantic for the first time.[23] In February 1983 NATO set up a series of regular meetings of national experts from member states and its own services to monitor and review events in five areas outside the NATO area, including both Africa and Latin America.[24] In addition, NATO has undoubtedly drawn up contingency plans covering the region. These plans involve two distinct aspects. First, the highly developed plans for resupply to Europe would in all probability extend some way south of the Tropic of Cancer in order to minimise the threat from Soviet Backfire bombers operating from bases in the Kola peninsula. Second, there can be little doubt that contingency planning does exist for the protection of the South Atlantic sea lanes although their current status is less certain. The need for such protection was recognised as early as 1972 by the NATO Defence Planning Committee and the resulting contingency plans were endorsed in June 1981.[25] The existence of such planning receives confirmation from statements by senior NATO officials. In both December 1980 and September 1984 Dr Joseph Luns told reporters in South Africa that contingency plans did exist for the defence of the Cape Route.[26] Similarly, in 1981 Admiral Harry Train wrote: 'there is no NATO border. There never was the slightest doubt in the minds of the drafters [of the NATO treaty] that it [Article 6] should prevent collective planning, manoeuvres, or operations south of the Tropic of Cancer.'[27]

Yet, however compelling the case for the strategic importance of the South Atlantic, there is almost no likelihood of any agreement within the alliance on the extension of its geographical boundaries. The Nordic countries and the Netherlands are the least likely members to endorse such an extension but, even amongst the larger members, problems persist. West Germany has constitutional constraints [Article 87(e) of the Federal Constitution] that would preclude participation in out-of-area operations.[28] And whilst France has shown a clear interest in military operations beyond Europe both by its past interventionist history and by the creation of the '*force d'action rapide*', it remains outside the Integrated Military Structure and strongly opposes all out-of-area operations or planning under NATO auspices.

There are three basic factors that lie behind this reluctance. First, there is a strong feeling in both Europe and the United States that such an extension would be divisive and would jeopardise the cohesion of the alliance. According to this view, the alliance was never intended to be a global policeman and has survived precisely because it has had limited aims and limited scope. Certainly the long history of disagreements between NATO members over events outside Europe from Suez to El Salvador lends credence to this argument.[29]

Second, this reluctance relates to basic differences in perceptions of the character and extent of the threat posed by the Soviet Union. Whilst for the United States *détente* was very largely destroyed by Moscow's adventurist policies in the Third World, Europe has in general shown markedly less support for a hard-line interpretation of Soviet behaviour.[30] This tendency has been strengthened by the wish to avoid any policies that may threaten the perceived continued benefits of *détente* in Europe. Above all, Europeans have laid greater stress on the domestic and regional causes of instability in the Third World and have often expressed the fear that NATO efforts to meet challenges outside its area or to curtail regional instability risks transforming local issues into East–West problems.

Third, there is a common fear of being associated with an overly interventionist US policy in the Third World and of being drawn into an escalating series of commitments. Hence the widespread European concern that developing contingency plans for the South Atlantic would inevitably involve commitments to South Africa or to unsavoury military regimes in Latin America.[31] In view of these problems it is not surprising that a recent report on out-of-area operations concluded that 'a collective Alliance military response is recognised as beyond the realm of political possibility and political desirability'.[32]

A second possible response would be for western navies to increase operations in the South Atlantic but outside any formal NATO framework. Thus those with the greatest interests in the region and with the necessary capabilities would consult and, if necessary, act together, meeting challenges on a case by case basis. Several steps have been taken in this direction. Institutions such as the NATO out-of-area Working Groups provide a forum for discussion and a means of following trends in the Third World. NATO ministers have also repeatedly called on members to consult together on out-of-area operations and to meet requests for assistance from other members in so far as they are able. It has also been suggested that, even if formal transfer to NATO command of national forces involved out-of-area proved impossible, such action could still be conducted by an appropriate NATO commander.[33] Above all, it is clear that extensive bilateral consultation already takes place between western navies.

In the case of the South Atlantic any western involvement would necessarily focus on the United States and Britain, between whose navies cooperation and consultation is already particularly close. Indeed US assistance to Britain during the Falklands War, involving around US$100 million of military resupply and close cooperation over the use of Ascension Island both as a base for Vulcan raids and for ship and aircraft refuelling, provides a good example of the potential relevance of such ties.

> The South Atlantic conflict demonstrated that bilateral alliances are still extremely important . . . it highlighted the fact that America's bilateral relations with her allies, in addition to the multilateral relationship that defines the NATO alliance, are crucial to any coordinated western effort to cope with threats outside the NATO area.[34]

There can be little doubt that this kind of cooperation outside a formal NATO framework reduces the political difficulties of increased western involvement in the South Atlantic.[35] Indeed the literature on out-of-area operations has generated something of a consensus that such operations are only politically feasible on a *de facto* principal nation basis.[36] Yet there must be some doubt as to how far NATO navies are actually able to implement the contingency plans that have been drawn up for the South Atlantic, let alone to increase their peacetime presence in the area. NATO navies are already stretched thin and any additional contingencies could only be met at the expense of commitments to other areas. While serving as Commander-in-Chief of Atlantic Fleet US Admiral Isaac Kidd stated that conflict in the North Atlantic and Mediterranean would make it impossible for

NATO to send a single task element into the South Atlantic.[37] Similarly, increasing doubts have been expressed about the viability of the so-called 'swing strategy', under which, in case of conflict, units of the Pacific fleet would be transferred to the Atlantic.[38] The extent to which the British navy is overcommitted is even more striking. During the Falklands War some 50 per cent of the entire fleet was deployed in the South Atlantic and there must be real doubt as to Britain's long-term ability to maintain the present level of forces in the region.[39]

The present situation could be improved in two ways. First, by a continued build-up of NATO navies, and particularly the US navy. However Congressional resistance and economic realities make it unlikely that even the United States will be able to afford the level of increase in defence spending that would permit increased operation in the South Atlantic. A second possibility would be to reshape the present division of labour within the Alliance. This might involve Britain assuming a larger role in naval matters or perhaps Western Europe as a whole assuming a greater responsibility for conventional defence in Europe. Yet the vast literature on improving conventional defence in Europe and on burden sharing has merely served to underline the political, economic, social and demographic constraints facing all such radical restructuring of NATO's forces. It is because of the inherent limits on western capacity to operate in the South Atlantic that the potential involvement of regional allies becomes so important.

Responses involving regional powers

Given the problems outlined in the previous section, the involvement of friendly regional states has appeared to many people as the best way of safeguarding western interests in the South Atlantic. Such proposed involvement has taken two distinct forms. On the one hand, proposals have frequently been made for the creation of a formal multilateral security pact along NATO lines covering the South Atlantic area.[40] Potential members of such a 'South Atlantic Treaty Organisation' have included the United States, Britain, Brazil, Argentina, Chile, South Africa and Uruguay. To quote one example of this line of thinking:

Hopefully this [the policy of *détente* in southern Africa] might lead, in due course, to some form of Southern Hemisphere Defence Pact embracing not only South Africa but Australia and New Zealand,

Brazil and Argentina, assisted by other maritime powers such as the United States, Great Britain and France.[41]

On the other hand, other writers and officials have stressed the importance of more modest, lower-level informal cooperation between NATO member states and the regional powers. As Admiral Harry Train, NATO's former Supreme Allied Commander, Atlantic, said in Montevideo in July 1981, the need to safeguard the security of the South Atlantic 'must lead the nations concerned to develop a natural defence, even without a pact, treaty or formal agreement'.[42] In practice this option would focus on increased bilateral cooperation between the United States and Brazil, Argentina, Chile and South Africa. It would involve increased joint patrols, technical liaison, exchange programmes, lecture series and briefing teams and flag officer visits.

Signs of such increased cooperation and speculation about the formation of 'SATO' have a long history.[43] As early as 1956 Argentina responded to a recommendation by the Inter-American Defense Board that naval cooperation in the South Atlantic should be improved, and in July of that year sent invitations to Brazil, Uruguay and Paraguay for 'preparatory talks to study the bases for an organization for the defence of the South Atlantic'.[44] After lengthy stalling by Brazil, a conference did take place in Buenos Aires in May 1957, although little progress was made towards the formation of any formal pact or alliance.[45]

The next wave of speculation occurred in the late 1960s following increased contacts between South Africa and both Brazil and Argentina. When Vorster became premier in 1966, South Africa launched its foreign policy of 'outward movement' or 'dialogue' and in the same year the Argentinian and South African navies began an exchange programme for naval staff. In November 1967 a South African naval unit visited Buenos Aires and joint exercises were held.[46] During his visits to Brazil (to inaugurate the Rio–Cape Town air service) and to Buenos Aires, the South African foreign minister, Hilgard Müller, constantly stressed the need for a common approach to South Atlantic defence in the face of the growing Soviet threat.[47] In an interview in Buenos Aires he stated that a South Atlantic pact between Brazil, Argentina, Uruguay, the United States and South Africa was a likely development, although this was later denied.[48] Despite this denial, together with others from Brazil and Argentina, speculation continued and was further fuelled by the nine-day visit to

South Africa in May 1969 of the Argentinian naval chiefs of staff.[49] This speculation was strengthened by the Brazilian government's support for Salazarist Portugal and became linked with the idea of a Luso-Brazilian Community, a rather vague and romantic attempt to join Brazil, Portugal and the Portuguese territories in Africa in a kind of commonwealth.[50] In 1969 it was reported that Brazil nearly took part in naval exercises with Portugal and South Africa.[51] Yet despite the rumours, nothing concrete emerged and in July 1969 Brazil issued a formal note in the United Nations, denying any involvement in a South Atlantic pact. Nor did Brazil take up Caetano's proposals for greater Brazilian involvement in West Africa and the South Atlantic under the aegis of a Luso-Brazilian Community.[52]

In 1976 there was a renewal on speculation about South Africa's alleged involvement in 'SATO' following the visit of the head of the South African navy, Vice Admiral James Johnson, to Brazil and Argentina during the annual UNITAS naval exercises between the United States and several Latin American countries. In an interview in Rio de Janeiro, Admiral Johnson declared: 'The Communists are turning the area into a Soviet lake . . . On any day you can see 30–35 Soviet ships pass by here and there's nothing we can do. We are all alone.'[53] In 1976 the Argentinian foreign minister, Rear Admiral César Guzzetti, expressed his country's grave concern 'that the South Atlantic might be the object of a modification . . . that could endanger our sea communications'.[54] Commenting on the visit of the head of the Brazilian navy, Azevedo Henning, to Buenos Aires in April 1976, the Argentinian paper *La Nación* emphasised the concern in the armed forces over the growing Soviet threat in the South Atlantic and the belief that this threat could only be effectively countered by joint action and military cooperation between Argentina, Brazil and South Africa.[55]

With the advent of the Reagan administration it appeared that the concern of US defence planners over the South Atlantic would be far more closely reflected in actual policy. An improvement in relations with Buenos Aires, Pretoria and Brasilia became a major priority. The dominant concern of American foreign policy became the country's strategic capability *vis-à-vis* the Soviet Union and the need to build up strong regimes in the Third World to counter Soviet adventurism. This triumph of the globalist viewpoint and the obvious enthusiasm of certain members of the new administration for closer relations with various Latin American military regimes fuelled speculation that a South Atlantic pact might soon emerge. Closer military cooperation with Latin America was viewed as essential because, to quote Jeane Kirkpatrick, the United States is 'being surrounded by a ring of Soviet bases on and around our southern and eastern borders'.[56] In 1980 a top Reagan aide, General Daniel Graham, was reported to have said in Buenos Aires 'that Mr. Reagan would favour a NATO-like treaty linking the militaristic nations of South America with South Africa'.[57] The successive visits to Buenos Aires in 1981 of General Vernon Walters, General Edward Meyer, General Richard Ingram and Admiral Harry Train clearly pointed to the American desire to establish closer military ties.[58] Similarly, in his speech in Brasilia in August 1981, Assistant Secretary Thomas Enders stressed his concern for the security of the South Atlantic.[59]

Such speculation also resulted from the improvement in relations between Brazil and Argentina following President Figueiredos's visit in May 1980. At the time of this visit the Argentinian foreign minister, Carlos Washington Pastor, spoke of this rapprochement as laying the basis for 'an alliance against world communism' and specifically mentioned the possibility of a South Atlantic defence pact.[60] It is thus no coincidence that a conference on 'SATO' in May 1981 was held in Buenos Aires.[61]

Yet despite the consistency with which proposals for a SATO have been made, there have always been formidable political obstacles both to the creation of such an organisation as well as to the expansion of lower level military cooperation. These obstacles can be illustrated by examining the attitudes, interests and policies of three major regional powers, South Africa, Argentina and Brazil.

SOUTH AFRICA

South Africa is the country which has most consistently favoured the formation of 'SATO' and promoted attempts to develop a more tightly-knit system of South Atlantic security. Clearly, South African membership of such a grouping would have obvious military advantages, given the country's strategic location and its own military capabilities, particularly in the field of intelligence and reconnaissance.[62] Moreover, from Pretoria's point of view membership of such a pact would have important political advantages. A central theme of South African foreign policy has been the emphasis on the country's strategic importance to the West and on the extent of the Soviet threat to western interests in both southern Africa and the

South Atlantic.[63] South Africa is thus a country which has a definite
stake in poor relations between the Superpowers. A military grouping
in the South Atlantic, however informal, has been viewed as an
important means of gaining allies and respectability, of overcoming
the country's political isolation and of defusing the antipathy
generated by apartheid. This policy has led South Africa to seek to
develop both political and economic relations with the countries of
Latin America.[64] Thus South Africa's own concern for South Atlantic
security and its desire to use the concern felt by others as a means of
overcoming its own diplomatic isolation has been a constant theme of
the debate on South Atlantic security.

Against this, however, it is precisely the political problems created
by South Africa that have done most to ensure that SATO has never
emerged. The political costs of close ties with South Africa have been a
constant factor in the policies of both Argentina and Brazil, as well as
the United States and Western Europe. The example of the United
States is particularly telling. According to the logic of the Nixon
Doctrine, South Africa appeared an obvious candidate for regional
delegation and for playing an increased role in western defence. Yet in
terms of South Atlantic defence, the administration did very little to
promote such a role and even upheld President Johnson's ban on the
sale of naval reconnaissance aircraft.[65] In the face of this policy, the
ending of the Simonstown Agreement and the country's ever-growing
diplomatic isolation, South Africa substantially altered its naval
policy, converting its Buccaneer aircraft from a maritime patrol role to
conventional bombers and placing major emphasis for its navy on
Israeli coastal patrol vessels.[66]

Under President Carter the chances of any military cooperation with
South Africa were negligible with the United States supporting the
1977 UN arms embargo. However, the incoming Reagan
administration did appear to favour building up South Africa as a Cold
War ally through its policy of 'constructive engagement'. There were
increased contacts between military officials, coastguards were trained
in the United States and the restrictions on 'dual use' equipment such
as planes and computers were eased.[67] Yet the all-too-obvious limits of
'constructive engagement' have made it far harder to draw closer to
Pretoria than many in the Reagan administration had hoped. The lack
of political progress inside South Africa, continued domestic
instability and waning optimism over the prospects for a settlement in
Namibia have forced the administration to rethink its policy.[68] Above
all, the growing campaign within Congress – among both Republicans

and Democrats – for some form of economic sanctions against South Africa make it increasingly unlikely that South Africa's role in South Atlantic defence will increase in the near future.[69]

ARGENTINA

As is evident from the earlier outline of proposals for a SATO, there has been a considerable body of opinion within Argentina, both official and unofficial, that has favoured the creation of a South Atlantic pact. The basis of this opinion can be found in the fervent anti-communism of the Argentinian military and perhaps also in the common interests and perspectives of military-ruled Argentina and South Africa generated by their pariah status. It can also be related to the strongly held geo-political views of many military officers. As John Child has pointed out, if there is one part of the world where geo-politics is a flourishing subject, it is in southern Latin America.[70] Apart from, and in some ways in response to, the obsession with Brazil and the potential Brazilian threat, this geo-political tradition has a strong maritime emphasis, highlighting the significance of the South Atlantic and the need to safeguard Argentina's claims in Antarctica.[71] It sees Argentina as having special responsibility for the control of several key exit and entry points to both the South Atlantic and Antarctica. According to this view, Argentina's future lies in the integration of all its national territories and in the exploitation of its ocean resources. Only by doing so can it recover its lost status and overcome the acute sense of internal and external vulnerability that has characterised the country's recent foreign policy.[72]

Yet although this kind of thinking is significant and reflects serious national concerns, Argentina's attitude to the South Atlantic must be viewed within the context of the country's overall foreign policy.[73]

Edward Milenky has suggested that Argentina's foreign policy can be seen as a series of alternations between what he calls a 'statist–nationalist' foreign policy and a 'classic liberal' foreign policy.[74] The first views Argentina as a non-aligned, strictly Latin American, developing country and can be seen in the long tradition of independence and universalism: in Perón's proclamation of the 'Third Position', equidistant between the United States and the Soviet Union; in the 'developmentalism' of the Frondizi period (1958–62); in the ideological pluralism of the Lanusse government (1970–3); in the revived Perónist foreign policy of 1973–6; and the certain elements of current Argentinian foreign policy under the Alfonsin government.[75] The second views Argentina as a nearly developed, western, Christian nation and can be seen in the strongly pro-western and violently anti-communist tendencies of Onganía (1966–70) and the regimes that ruled from 1976 to 1983. It is no surprise to find that speculation about Argentinian involvement in a South Atlantic pact and the promotion of closer ties with South Africa and the West should have been prominent during these two latter periods.

Certainly the overall orientation of current Argentinian foreign policy makes an overlap with western interests in the South Atlantic extremely unlikely. President Alfonsin has repeatedly stressed the importance of overcoming the country's militaristic image, created by the previous government's appalling human rights record and its foreign aggression. Moreover he has emphasised that economic issues and the debt crisis will be the country's overwhelming priority in foreign policy.[76]

Four specific features of current Argentinian foreign policy should be stressed here. First, there has been a substantial reorientation of the country's foreign policy towards both the Third World in general and Latin America in particular. Strenuous efforts have been made to overcome the dispute with Chile over the Beagle Channel, to continue the improvement of relations with Brazil and to promote common positions on economic issues, particularly on the debt. More generally, Argentina has been seeking to build up a leading role within the Non-Aligned Movement, as illustrated by Alfonsin's visits to Algeria in October 1984 and India in February 1985.[77] The foreign minister, Dante Caputo, underlined this new policy in March 1984. 'We are non-aligned because we see with grave concern the negative effects of the East–West conflict on our countries.'[78] In terms of the South Atlantic the most significant aspects of this shift have been the decision in May 1986 to break-off diplomatic relations with South Africa and Alfonsin's support of Brazilian proposals to create a nuclear-free zone in the South Atlantic.

Second, whilst Argentina would like to improve its relations with Washington, the outlook is not encouraging. In addition to the legacy of bitterness and mistrust created by Washington's support for Britain during the Falklands War, there are likely to be serious differences over debt management, over trade issues, over US Central American policy, over Argentina's close relations with Cuba and over its nuclear programme. In this respect the present government is maintaining a historic norm. Superficial ideological common interests have often obscured the extent to which Argentina and the United States must be seen as historic rivals. Argentina's globalist pretensions, its affinities with Europe, its pioneering advocacy of the principles of non-intervention and the juridical equality of states all made Argentina a traditional opponent of Pan-Americanism and hemispheric solidarity under United States leadership. Thus Argentina remained neutral in both world wars. It delayed ratification of the Rio Pact for four years and the Charter of the Organisation of American States for eight. In 1954 it abstained from supporting the US-sponsored Declaration of Solidarity for the Preservation of the Political Integrity of American States against International Communism and again in 1962 over the resolution expelling Cuba from the OAS. The postwar period has seen frequent disputes over trade issues, foreign investment, policy towards Cuba, nuclear energy and human rights.

Third, there is the question of relations with the Soviet Union – a crucial point if we are talking about Argentinian involvement in a pact aimed at countering Soviet expansionism. Argentina was the first Latin American country to send a representative to Soviet Russia and ever since has tried to maintain an independent position towards both Superpowers. Perón established formal diplomatic relations in 1946 and in 1953 the first trade treaty was signed. Economic ties were significantly strengthened with the signing of a three-year trade agreement in 1971 and, politically, the two countries were moving closer together in the two years preceding the coup of 1976.[79] Despite the virulent anti-communism of the military regimes that governed from 1976 to 1983, these relations continued to develop. In 1980 Argentina sold 80 per cent of its grain to the USSR and a long-term supply agreement was signed in July of that year.[80] Soviet turbines are installed in the Salto Grande hydroelectric project and the Soviet Union has assisted Argentina in fishing, oceanography and offshore oil exploration.[81] Although the economic basis of the relationship has undergone some strain, the determination of the Argentinian government to maintain its links with the Soviet Union was well illustrated by the signature in March 1986 of a new fisheries agreement and by Alfonsin's visit to Moscow in October 1986.

Finally there is the crucial question of the Falklands. Clearly the war itself dealt a very serious blow to any cooperation between Argentina and any NATO country over South Atlantic security. It both engendered virulent antipathy towards a leading member of NATO, Britain, and had indirect effects on Argentina's relations with both the US and the EEC. Argentina remains adamantly opposed to any multilateral solution of the dispute dressed up in security terms, seeing this as a way of merely legitimising Britain's militarisation of the islands and cementing British control.[82] The islands remain a powerful nationalist symbol and there appears to be little sign of agreement, with Britain entrenched in its 'fortress Falklands' policy. Given such a stalemate, this issue more than any other will continue to complicate western efforts to develop closer military cooperation in the South Atlantic.

BRAZIL

Brazil is the other Latin American country which has a major stake in developments in the South Atlantic. Brazil's externally oriented development model, together with the constraints of the debt crisis, have meant that foreign trade and the expansion of exports have been of critical importance to the country's economy. In 1980 98 per cent of Brazil's foreign trade was transported by sea. This importance is increased still further by Brazil's dependence on imported oil and in 1980 83 per cent of its oil imports were transported via the Cape Route.

Since the late 1960s Brazil has made increasing efforts to use its ocean space and resources more effectively. The country's merchant marine and shipbuilding capability has increased dramatically: the merchant marine increased from below 1 million tons in 1967 with an average age of 10 years to over 5 million tons in 1977 with an average age of 4 years.[83] In 1970 Brazil extended its territorial sea to 200 miles and conducted an extremely active diplomacy at the United Nations Conference on the Law of the Sea. It has developed offshore oil; its annual fish catch ranks about eighteenth in the world and in 1968 it established an Interministerial Commission on the Exploration and Utilisation of the Sea Bed and Ocean (CIEFMAR).[84] In addition, Brazil has maintained a consistent, although discreet, interest in Antarctica and in 1975 received adherent status to the Antarctic Treaty, emphasising both its security requirements and its wish to participate in the exploration of Antarctic natural resources.[85]

In the light of these factors and given Brazil's geographical position it is hardly surprising that the Brazilian military should have long viewed the South Atlantic and the west coast of Africa as an area vital to the country's national security. As General Golbery do Couto y Silva, Brazil's leading geo-politician, wrote in 1957:

We must take it upon ourselves vigilantly to observe what takes place along the whole west coast of Africa, for it is incumbent upon us by self-interest and even tradition to preserve it from domination by aggressive imperialist forces.[86]

More recently, military writers have sought to go beyond this stress on the defensive importance of the South Atlantic and to propose that Brazil should develop a more dynamic role in the area. Thus Vice Admiral Hilton Berutti Augusto Moreira wrote in 1972:

To provide Brazil with adequate maritime power and to take maximum advantage of the country's geo-strategic position are essential decisions for the attainment of the national objective of rapid development and for support for a high degree of effective national security.[87]

Another leading strategist, General Meira Mattos, proposed in 1977 that Brazil should develop a new, far more ambitious 'South Atlantic Strategy' based on a large increase in the country's air and naval capabilities.[88]

Again not surprisingly, the victory of the MPLA in Angola, the continued presence of Cuban troops in Africa and the growth of Soviet naval influence in the South Atlantic all served to increase the concern of the Brazilian military for the region's security. In December 1975 the navy minister, Azevedo Henning, emphasised the dangers of Soviet military expansionism in the South Atlantic in a widely reported speech to the Escola Superior de Guerra (the Brazilian Higher War College).[89] In 1976 an article in the college's journal *Segurança e Desenvolvimento* pointed to two types of threat:

In times of peace: a higher level of ideological penetration and greater infiltration of agitators mainly via diplomatic and commercial missions . . . In a war situation: the transformation of Angola into a communist country represents a very considerable increase in the aggressive power that can be levelled against South America in general and Brazil, because of its geographical position, in particular.[90]

This line of thinking was vigorously taken up by the conservative press and together with a number of official visits of Brazilian and

Argentinian naval chiefs, fuelled speculation through 1976 that a South Atlantic pact was in the making.[91]

Yet despite this clear interest in the security of the South Atlantic, Brazil has consistently ruled out participation in any form of South Atlantic pact. In September 1976 the foreign minister, Antonio Azeredo Silveira, stated: 'There is not the slightest possibility of establishing a collective security system in the South Atlantic, especially with the awkward and unwanted presence of South Africa.'[92] When such a pact was proposed in October 1977 by the Uruguayan admiral Hugo Marquez, Brasilia issued an immediate denial.[93] In an interview in 1979, the navy minister Maximiano dismissed the necessity of a South Atlantic pact.[94] For Brazil talk of a 'SATO' is, to quote an official statement, 'inopportune, superfluous and dangerous'.[95] Inopportune, because the Brazilian government does not believe that the level of threat can warrant the formation of a new defence pact; superfluous, because the security of the region is already covered by the Rio Treaty;[96] and dangerous, because such a pact would needlessly militarise the South Atlantic and escalate Superpower rivalry in the region.[97]

Yet as with Argentina, Brazil's interests in the South Atlantic need to be set within the overall context of the country's foreign policy. The very close pro-American and narrowly anti-communist line that followed the 1964 military coup had already weakened by the end of the 1960s as Brazil increasingly sought to diversify and widen the range of its international and regional ties. As economic growth continued apace, Brazil's international needs and interests widened and became more complex. Flexibility, pragmatism, independence and diversification became the dominant themes of the country's foreign policy. Economic ties with Western Europe and Japan developed rapidly and, as the 1970s progressed, Brazil expanded its relations with other developing countries and began to adopt a more 'Third-Worldist' foreign policy stance. Three features of this policy should be stressed here.

First, there is the switch in Brazil's Africa policy and the decision to concentrate on developing relations with black Africa and to minimise all formal contacts with South Africa. In November 1975, despite misgivings from within certain parts of the military, Brazil became the first non-communist country to recognise the MPLA government in Angola. Since then Brazil has worked hard (and successfully) to expand economic ties in Africa, particularly with Nigeria, Angola and Algeria.[98] Second, as with Argentina, Brazil's economic relations with the Soviet Union have expanded steadily through the 1970s and in July 1981 a US$5 billion, five-year trade agreement was signed in Moscow.[99] Third, as the overall economic importance of the United States for Brazil decreased, and as Brazilian leaders more confidently asserted their independence, the relationship with Washington became more troubled. Brazil was upset by US protectionism, by President Carter's policies on human rights and nuclear proliferation, and by the high level of US interest rates. The United States was irritated by Brazil's recognition of the MPLA government of Angola in 1975 and its policies in Africa and the Middle East, by its hardening attitude on North–South issues and by its refusal to abide by the 1980 grain embargo. The growing tension was best exemplified by Brazil's unilateral renunciation in 1977 of the 1952 and 1956 Military Assistance Agreements.

These factors explain Brazilian reluctance to become involved in any formal security pact in the South Atlantic. Do they also rule out lower levels of military cooperation with western countries? A number of recent developments work in favour of increased informal cooperation between the United States and Brazil. First, the debt crisis has resulted in a significant reorientation of policy towards Washington and the Reagan administration has made great efforts to overcome the damage to the relationship that occurred in the 1970s.[100] Second, there has been some progress in improving military ties between the two countries. A limited agreement covering the exchange of personnel was signed between the US and Brazilian navies in March 1978, and in February 1984 a Memorandum of Understanding on renewed military cooperation was signed in Brasilia. In December 1984 a further agreement was signed on the exchange of air force scientists.[101] In addition, the annual UNITAS exercises have in recent years evolved away from a formal political exercise into a more demanding and serious training programme.[102] Above all there can be no doubt about the continued willingness of substantial sections of the Brazilian military to cooperate informally with the United States.

Third, Brazilian concern for developments in the South Atlantic has, if anything, increased.[103] The Falklands War profoundly upset the implicit assumptions of much Brazilian military thinking, namely that actual conflict in the region would remain a remote contingency.[104] In the aftermath of the war, there were frequent statements by military spokesmen expressing concern that the country's military weakness and proposing improvements.[105] In terms of the South Atlantic, proposals have included the installation of an improved acoustic facility on the island of Fernando de Noronha, the construction of a base on the island of Trinidad and general updating of the Brazilian navy.[106] However the country's financial difficulties pose very severe constraints on the likelihood of any such improvements being realised in the short term. As a recent study made clear, Brazil's ability to influence events in the South Atlantic remains limited:

> The bitter reality is that at present the navy cannot control even small selected South Atlantic areas and has painful difficulties patrolling, even for a short time, the entire Brazilian coast.[107]

In the final analysis, however, both longer-term trends in Brazilian diplomacy and the recent foreign policy of the Sarney administration suggest that security cooperation between Brazil and the NATO countries will be increasingly unlikely over the coming years. Under President Sarney the main lines of Brazil's Africa policy have continued. Brazil has made a formal proposal in the United Nations for the creation of a nuclear free zone in the South Atlantic. Cooperation with Argentina has become a high priority and Brazil has repeatedly reaffirmed its support of the Argentinian position over the Falklands. Above all, security for Brazil has continued to mean economic security and Brazilian attention has been focussed overwhelmingly on the debt crisis and economic issues – areas where friction with the developed countries has increased significantly since 1985. Against this background Brazil will continue to be extremely reluctant to enter into any kind of formal military agreement with either the United States or NATO and is likely to maintain its increasingly distant and uncommitted policy towards East–West issues.

CONCLUSION

Out-of-area issues can be divided into two broad types. On the one hand there are those problems or threats outside the NATO area that relate directly to western security or to NATO's ability to fulfil its basic purposes. The vulnerability of Middle East oil is the clearest example of this kind of issue. On the other there are those crises in the Third World that can have an indirect spill-over effect on to core Alliance concerns. The divisions between Europe and the United States over Central America are a good example of this category of problem.

Many commentators have seen the security of the South Atlantic as belonging to the first type – an area where NATO has vital security interests, particularly the defence of the sea lanes and oil supplies around the Cape, and where a vigorous NATO response to the Soviet threat is called for. Yet once one moves beyond the rhetoric the inherent complexity of out-of-area operations emerges all too clearly.

First, what are western interests in the region? As we have seen, there has been a substantial debate over the strategic importance of the South Atlantic and the seriousness of the Soviet threat. This lack of consensus has carried over into the political realm with European members of NATO in general prepared to adopt a more relaxed interpretation of recent developments in the region than the United States. On a deeper level the Falklands War should serve as a reminder of the difficulties of defining 'western' interests. Which 'western' interests were more important, Washington's concern over maintaining its regional ties with pro-western Argentina or London's determination to recover the islands and uphold its prestige?

Second, even if a compelling case for the existence of vital western interests is accepted, how should NATO respond? On the one hand there is a firm consensus that the present boundaries of NATO should not be extended. On the other, beyond continual calls for greater consultation, there has been very little agreement as to what practical steps should be taken.

Third, even assuming the willingness, has NATO the ability to protect its interests in the region? As we have seen, current evidence suggests that at present NATO navies would be hard pressed to do so. Yet to demand changes, either in the form of overall increases in defence spending or in terms of redefining contributions, would inevitably reopen the divisive question of burden sharing that has dogged the Alliance for so long.

Finally, in view of these difficulties, many writers have stressed the importance of strengthening ties with friendly regional states. Yet the problems here are, if anything, even greater. On the one hand some potential allies such as South Africa (and perhaps also Chile) create more political problems than they solve strategic ones. On the other the difficulty of increasing military ties with countries such as Brazil or Argentina point to the danger of assuming an identity of interests between regional Third World states and the industrialised nations of the Atlantic community. The reality is one of divergent attitudes, interests and policies and the possibility of such leading Third World states accepting a narrow western-orientated definition of security is likely to decline. First, security against the Soviet Union has to be set against other security concerns, both internal and regional. Thus to most Latin Americans conflicts between Argentina and Chile over the Beagle Channel or between Britain and Argentina over the Falklands have a far greater salience than an undefined Soviet threat about which they are in any case able to do very little. Second, security concerns can rarely dominate the list of priorities of even the most anti-communist Latin American government. The problems of economic development remain paramount and it is arguably the lack of western initiatives in this area that has most impeded attempts to develop closer relations. Finally, it is possible to argue that the interests of even generally 'pro-western' Third World states such as Brazil or Argentina can actually be best served by the decline of western influence, and particularly US power, and the creation of a situation of balance or equilibrium with the Soviet Union.

The South Atlantic is not likely to become a major issue of intra-alliance politics or even to rank particularly high on the list of out-of-area priorities. Yet the example of the South Atlantic underlines the difficulties facing all attempts to extend NATO's interests and activities beyond their traditional limits.

5   Africa as an Out-of-Area Problem for NATO

DOUGLAS T. STUART

INTRODUCTION

From time to time during the last 36 years events in Africa have intruded upon the debates within the North Atlantic Treaty Organisation. In a few cases the result has been a coordinated allied position on an issue of recognised common interest. More often the result has been acrimonious dispute within the alliance. In only one case, Suez, did the dispute reach the stage of intra-alliance crisis, but in a few instances – most notably, Algeria – resentments that were harboured by one or more of the alliance members as a result of disagreements over African policies contributed to subsequent crises within the alliance.

In an earlier article this author identified four types of out-of-area situations that have been confronted by NATO planners since 1949:

1. Burden-sharing situations, in which a NATO member involved in an out-of-area action has solicited the direct or indirect support of other NATO members;
2. situations in which NATO members have been concerned about the possibility of 'guilt by association' with the out-of-area actions of another ally;
3. situations in which one NATO member has seen another member's out-of-area action as an infringement upon its *domaine reserve* in the Third Word and;
4. out-of-area events which have highlighted fundamental differences between NATO allies regarding the nature and degree of threat posed by the Soviet Union.[1]

This study will survey four cases in intra-alliance debate regarding Africa during the last three decades; the Algerian War (1954–62),

Angola (1961), the Congo (1960–62) and Zaire (1977–8). Each case will be discussed as an instance of the four types of out-of-area situations cited above.

ALGERIA: BURDEN SHARING

During the preliminary discussions relating to the formation of the North Atlantic Treaty Organisation the US delegation took the position that the alliance should have a very limited membership, and that its geographic scope should be restricted to the North Atlantic region. Initially the US delegation favoured an expansion of the 1948 Brussels treaty (US, France, the Benelux states) to include the US and Canada.

The participants at the Washington Talks were extremely reluctant, therefore, to accommodate France's request for two additions to the membership list of NATO: Italy and the French department of Algiers. France's interest in including Italy in the alliance was due in large part to Paris' desire to shift the base of gravity of the evolving defence arrangement. France could not accept membership in an alliance that did not extend security guarantees into the Mediterranean, as well as the North Atlantic. Paris sought the participation of Rome as a means of enhancing NATO's Mediterranean identity and of establishng a Mediterranean voting bloc within the alliance.

The desire to increase the Mediterranean identity of NATO also served to partly explain the French demand for the inclusion of Algiers. But a more fundamental issue was at stake on the Algerian question. France had been attempting since the end of the Second World War to re-establish French *de jure* and *de facto* influence in North Africa. De Gaulle had come out of the war convinced that the Anglo-Saxons were intent on subverting the French presence in the region, and he undertook several initiatives during the two years of the provisional government which were designed to reconstruct the politico-military system which had tied the North African colonies to the French metropole in the pre-war period. In 1945 this strategy was reflected in De Gaulle's (unsuccessful) efforts to reinforce the French garrisons in Syria and Lebanon as a means of blocking the growth of a British military presence in the Levant and in the General's rejection of Franklin Roosevelt's proposal that the two leaders meet in Algeria on FDR's return from the Yalta conference. De Gaulle explained that he could not accept a 'summons from a head of a foreign state to go to a place that is part of our national territory'.[2]

The French delegation to the Washington Talks exhibited this same prickly sensitivity on the Algerian question during discussions relating to the geographic scope of the alliance. In the face of concerted US opposition Paris quickly abandoned its initial request for the inclusion of all of France's North African territories in the treaty area. But on the issue of Algerian participation in the alliance, the French delegation was inflexible. Henri Bonnet, the Chief of the French delegation to the Talks argued that 'Algeria was part of France and in the same relation to France as Alaska or Florida to the United States'.[3] In effect, the French government threatened the participants in the Washington Talks with its own domestic weakness, arguing that the inclusion of Algeria was essential to insure mass and élite public approval of France's participation in NATO. The US, British and Canadian representatives at the Talks could not discount the possibility that the existing Fourth Republic government might fall over the Treaty question, and the Western allies would then be faced with the problem of negotiating with an even weaker and less accommodating successor government in Paris.

Still, the US delegation was extremely reluctant to extend the alliance to the southern littoral of the Mediterranean. Robert Lovett reflected the concern of many American policymakers at the time: 'to get into Africa would open up a limitless field' and unnecessarily jeopardise the ratification process in the US Senate.[4] Washington pressed Paris to accept verbal guarantees of support for the French position in Algeria rather than a specific commitment in the treaty. The French delegates continued to hold firm on the issue of formal Algerian inclusion in the treaty, however, and in the end they succeeded through sheer persistence. In retrospect, the ability of the French delegation to increase the southern orientation of the Atlantic alliance by its sponsorship of Italian and Algerian membership represents one of the most impressive foreign policy successes in the generally abysmal record of the Fourth Republic.

The US delegation to the Washington Talks was certainly not insensitive to French arguments regarding the geo-strategic importance of North Africa. The US position was summarised in a memorandum by the Policy Planning Staff dated 22 March 1948:

> With the rapid development of air power, the geographical position of North Africa assumes added importance. In hostile

hands, the air and naval bases of this area, especially those in French Morocco, could exercise control over the Atlantic approaches to the Mediterranean and the sea lanes down the West African coast. Such hostile bases could neutralize potential U.S. Atlantic bases in the Azores or other neighbouring islands and cut the most direct line of access to the petroleum of the Middle East. . . . Conversely, a North Africa in friendly hands could afford corresponding advantages to the U.S. It would be a valuable base for the launching of air attacks, naval operations or amphibious landings against an enemy-occupied Europe. Its utilization by the U.S. or a friendly power would complement and strengthen any U.S. bases in the Atlantic islands.[5]

This analysis illustrates the enduring influence of the lessons of 'Operation Torch' – the allied landing in North Africa as the first stage in the Southern European counter-offensive of 1943 – on US defence planners during the late 1940s. In the event that the much discussed Soviet offensive against Western Europe became reality, Washington recognised that North Africa would once again serve as a source of geo-strategic depth, resources and manpower until such time as the region could be utilised as a 'logical springboard' for a Western counter-attack.[6] US policymakers were therefore anxious to insure that North Africa remained firmly within the Western security ambit although outside NATO.

The French government played upon this US security concern in order to obtain material and political support for its neo-colonial campaigns in North Africa during the period of the Fourth Republic. French defence experts developed an extensive geo-political literature to justify their requests for NATO backing. The central element of this literature was the *guerre revolutionnaire* thesis, which stressed the global nature of the Moscow-dominated communist threat, bent on the eventual encirclement of Western Europe and the isolation of the United States. Moscow found its greatest opportunities in the Third World, where it was involved in the subversion of nationalist movements and the encouragement of revolution. In the face of this challenge the best strategy for the West was to rely upon those allies (read France) which maintained the most extensive colonial and post-colonial networks in the Third World. According to this argument, France was doing more than its fair share as a NATO ally by its military campaigns first in Indochina and then in Algeria – and was therefore entirely justified in its frequent demands that it be treated as an equal by the Anglo-Saxons in their formulation of Western security plans.[7] Rather than representing a diversion of NATO arms and *materiel*, the Algerian War was treated by Paris as the front line of NATO's defence system. The French were willing to do the fighting for NATO in Algeria. All that they asked in return was economic and political support, and non-interference.

But US defence planners harboured serious reservations about France's reliability in Francophone Africa. First, there was the problem of French overall military weakness in the post-war era. By 1950 France's limited military resources were seriously over-extended in pursuit of the 'war without war aims' in Indochina. According to one internal US memorandum dated 20 November 1950 the French war effort in Indochina represented a serious drain on France's contribution to NATO (in fact, by the end of 1951, only three fully equipped metropolitan divisions were available to the alliance). The report warned of a 'six month delay in the date when North Atlantic Treaty forces will be adequate to resist Soviet aggression' if the US complied with French requests for arms and material for Indochina.[8]

The second, and more fundamental, problem with the French, from the point of view of many US policy makers at the time was policy incoherence. In North Africa, according to Dean Acheson, 'the real difficulty . . . was that France had no policy . . . except repression and hanging on'.[9] Washington none the less maintained its policy of providing financial and arms aid to France under the NATO military assistance programme in spite of the fact that France allocated much of this aid to the Algerian campaign. Washington also helped the Fourth Republic to carry the burden of the Algerian War by maintaining large numbers of US troops in Western Europe and by integrating the Bundeswehr into the alliance. As Edgar Furniss has noted, however, this last initiative was viewed with concern by France, particularly when 'a Bonn–Washington axis thus filled the void left by the Fourth Republic's departure for Algiers'.[10]

The Eisenhower administration initially committed itself to a continuation of Truman's policy of non interference in France's North Africa sphere of influence although in 1953 it rejected 'as a matter of principle' a French request for a specific declaration of American non-interference in North Africa.[11] Non-interference became more difficult and less important for Washington as the Algerian War dragged on, however. An important turning point was the 1956 Suez intervention by French, British and Israeli forces, which was interpreted by Eisenhower as a personal betrayal as well as a betrayal of Western solidarity. Eisenhower considered that he had been presented with a choice between 'following in the footsteps of Anglo-French colonialism in Africa and Asia, or splitting our course from their course'.[12] After 1956 the President was much more willing to consider the second option.

Starting in 1957 the Eisenhower administration also had to deal with domestic political criticism of its 'hands off' approach in North Africa. The most influential US critic of France's policies in North Africa during this period was John Kennedy. Kennedy explicitly called for Algerian independence in a Senate Speech in July 1957, arguing that France had proven itself to be incapable of understanding the independence movement which was 'spreading like wildfire' throughout Africa.[13] The Eisenhower administration made it clear at the time that it rejected Kennedy's arguments and regretted the Senator's interference in an issue of French domestic politics, but it became increasingly more difficult for Eisenhower and Dulles to align themselves, even implicitly, with French policies in North Africa after this period.

Washington and London felt that the French were particularly misguided in their policies toward Tunisia which France identified as one of the major sources of assistance and arms for the Algerian rebels (FLN). The US and Britain were anxious to maintain the loyalty of Tunisian President Habib Bourguiba and it was felt that the most expeditious means of enduring Bourguiba's commitment to the West was by the provision of arms. In view of French sensitivities the Anglo-Saxons initially attempted to include France as a third supplier to Tunis. But when Paris rejected the offer, the US and Great Britain went ahead with the arms transfers to Bourguiba. For the French, who were at this time in the process of constructing more than 200 miles of electrified fence and mines along the Tunisian border (the famous Morice Line) in order to cut off Tunisian support for the FLN, the Anglo-Saxon initiative represented an indirect subvention of the Algerian revolution. French Prime Minister Felix Gaillard warned that 'If the Atlantic Pact should fall to dust one day, we will know the authors of its failure.'[14]

Jacques Soustelle had been even more foreboding in an article written for *Foreign Affairs* shortly after he was removed from the office of Governor General of Algeria in 1956. Soustelle bemoaned what he considered to be the 'apparently inexhaustible complacency' of France's NATO allies with regard to Arab arms transfers to the FLN.

It is not surprising, in these circumstances, that the Atlantic Alliance has lost much of its credit in France. People cannot see how they can be allied on the European Continent and not allied elsewhere, especially in regions which are of strategic concern to the Continent itself.

Soustelle concluded his analysis with a warning to the NATO allies.

Should France as the result of an unprecedented disaster actually have to quit Algeria, and consequently North Africa in general, the chances are that she will be thrown back into neutralism and soon after that into communism . . . somewhat as the defeat of 1940 broke her ties with England and, under the leadership of Vichy, linked her to Germany. Not just for the sake of France, then, but for the whole Western world must her position in North Africa be maintained. If the tricolor is lowered in Algeria the red flag will soon fly in Paris.[15]

When De Gaulle returned to office in 1958 he embarked upon a foreign policy of *triage* in Africa. Extricating France from Algeria took over three years, during which time he laid the groundwork for a new pattern of relations with Francophone Africa and with the NATO alliance.[16] In order to insure an uninterrupted link between the metropole and Africa in the event of future crises De Gaulle removed the French fleet from the Mediterranean command of NATO in March 1959 – seven years prior to the French departure from the NATO military command. De Gaulle explained that the decision was taken because of the 'absence of a common policy' on African security among the major NATO allies. De Gaulle's Prime Minister Michel Debré was more specific during a conversation with Secretary of State John Foster Dulles. France felt compelled to remove its naval forces from NATO control 'because the Allies have not been supportive of us in Algeria'.[17]

As had been the case in Indochina, US financial and arms aid for the Algerian war effort did not encourage French gratitude. Indeed, anti-Americanism seemed to increase in France even during those periods when US sponsorship of the war effort was increasing. When De Gaulle finally succeeded in ending the war in Algeria he quickly decommissioned the bulk of the Algerian forces in spite of a long-standing commitment by France to reassign most of these troops to the European NATO command upon their return. The money that

De Gaulle saved by his troop cuts went to France's *Force de Frappe* – which De Gaulle in later years was to treat as both the symbol and the guarantor of France's independence from NATO's integrated military command.

PORTUGAL IN AFRICA: GUILT BY ASSOCIATION

During the Second World War the US accorded priority to gaining access to bases on the Azores, although many in Washington were reluctant to deal with the Portuguese government on the grounds that it was dominated by 'Germanophiles'. George Kennan recounts in his memoirs that influential groups within the US policy-making community viewed Salazar as 'a dangerous fascist and in league with the enemy'. Rather than negotiate with Salazar, 'various eager beavers in General Donavon's OSS' recommended US sponsorship of a revolt in the Azores to acquire independence from Lisbon.[18] This strategy was ultimately abandoned, in favour of negotiated base access in conjunction with the British, an arrangement which extended into the postwar era. In February 1948 the United States succeeded in renewing its bilateral basing agreements with Lisbon for an additional five years. The Director of the State Department's Office of European Affairs, J. D. Hickerson described the 1948 agreements as 'highly satisfactory' in a memo to Secretary of State George Marshall. But Hickerson noted that the Joint Chiefs still preferred some arrangement that would assure longer term access to the Azores facilities.[19] Thus the US instructed its ambassador to Lisbon to let Salazar know that the participants in the 1948 Washington negotiations were moving in the direction of considering Portugal's membership of NATO. Both the US and Britain could be expected to support such a proposal.[20]

As the cold war intensified, support for Salazar increased among the Washington policy élite. In 1952 Acheson contributed a new distinction to the lexicon of US foreign policy when he described Salazar as 'not a dictator in his own right as Stalin was, but a dictator-manager employed and maintained by the power of the Army.'[21] NATO relied heavily upon the Lajes base in the Azores during the 1950s. By 1957 transient flights were averaging about 1200 per month. The Lajes facility also served as an important refuelling point during the 1958 Anglo-American intervention in Lebanon.[22] As Portugal's economic situation worsened in the late 1950s the

Eisenhower administration increased its financial and arms aid to the Salazar government.[23] But it was explicitly agreed between Washington and Lisbon that US arms aid would not be used in the Portuguese colonies.

Along with the specific US interest in the Lajes facility, US policy toward the Portuguese colonies in Africa was influenced during the Truman and Eisenhower years by the general tendency among the US policy élites to defer whenever possible to the NATO allies on colonial issues. As late as 1959 the US government was still clearly dominated by this 'Eurocentric' approach to Africa,[24] as illustrated by the following excerpt from a Department of State Bulletin entitled 'The Role of the United States in Africa: Our Interests and Operations'.

In terms of trade, administration, political and economic development, and education the European colonial or former colonial powers have contributed far more than have we. Moreover, these powers are continuing their interest and contributions, adapting them in an enlightened and sympathetic way to the rapidly changing situation . . . We have no desire to interfere with the fruitful development of these new relationships, and in fact we are taking particular care to avoid slipping into such a position, which could only result in friction and rivalry contrary to the best interests of the new African states, of our European allies and of ourselves.[25]

George Ball described the foreign policy approaches of Truman and Eisenhower as based upon 'the assumption that the United States . . . was a status quo power. . . . If stability could be assured for a reasonable period through colonial structures, such as Portugal's, there was no reason for America to rock the boat.' The Kennedy administration, according to Ball, 'frontally challenged this approach'.[26] Kennedy campaigned on a platform of 'new beginnings' in foreign policy. If elected, he promised to 'get things moving again' and, in particular, to adjust US foreign policy to the realities of change in Africa and Asia.

In the winter of 1960/61 Portugal was singled out for special attention by the incoming Kennedy administration. The country was considered to be politically as well as geographically on the margin of the NATO alliance and of limited value for US or Western security aside from the Azores facility that it provided. Salazar himself was a subject of some ridicule by the Kennedy group. Ball described him as 'a sixteenth century man' and telegrammed Kennedy after a meeting with Salazar that Portugal was 'ruled by a triumvirate consisting of Vasco deGama, Prince Henry the Navigator and Salazar'.[27] Portugal's claims that it was instituting reforms in the colonies were likewise disdained by the New Frontiersman within the Kennedy administration. Roger Hillsman notes in his book *To Move a Nation* that the popular joke in Washington at the start of the Kennedy term was that the Portuguese had granted university degrees to three Angolan students and were now ready 'to embark on their second five-hundred-year plan'.[28]

Portuguese colonial repression had been subjected to special criticism by Chester Bowles in his study of *Africa's Challenge to America* in 1956. Bowles noted that 'now that Portugal is a member of the United Nations it will be possible to focus more international attention on a system that appears second only to the Union of South Africa in its harsh treatment of the Africans'.[29] When Bowles was appointed to the position of Under Secretary of State in the Kennedy administration he pressed the case for just such a policy of pressure within the United Nations. The opportunity came two months after Kennedy's inauguration, in the form of a United Nations resolution calling for an enquiry into Portugal's management of its overseas 'non self-governing territories'. Lisbon had consistently rebuffed UN efforts to monitor its colonial policies, on the grounds that the African territories had been made 'overseas provinces' of Portugal in 1951 and were therefore an integral part of Portuguese sovereign territory. From time to time during the 1950s the Salazar government also used this argument in NATO forums to press the case for extension of the NATO treaty guarantee to the colonies, citing the France/Algeria precedent. The argument carried very little weight in NATO circles, however, and the 'overseas provinces' claim was rejected out of hand by the Afro-Asian bloc within the UN.

Arthur Schlesinger has discussed the US vote against Portugal in the UN in his book *A Thousand Days*. According to Schlesinger, the US vote in the United Nations represented a turning point in US policy toward the Third World; it 'had liberated the United States from its position of systematic deference to the old colonial powers'.[30] Schlesinger and others scored it as a major victory for the 'Africanists' at the expense of the 'Europeanists' within the administration. One month after the Oslo Ministerial Conference the United States again criticised Portuguese policies in Angola. US military assistance for 1961 to Portugal was cut from a proposed figure of $24.75 million to

$2.75 million and Washington blocked US commercial sales to Portugal.[31]

Among the 'old colonial powers' in Europe the new American policy was greeted with concern. The European allies had little love for and only limited economic or political interest in their Portuguese NATO ally, but they saw Kennedy's initiatives as the first step in a dangerous trend. British cabinet members were reportedly concerned about the President's 'penchant for making sweeping statements encouraging nationalist aspirations in Africa', while France and Belgium saw the attack on Portugal as one element in a broader campaign of US meddling in the colonial affairs of all European NATO allies with responsibilities abroad. Even some states which did not have residual colonial responsibilities saw in Kennedy's policies an unfortunate degradation (or, what Pierre Hassner in a different context has called a 'relativization') of NATO in US global policy.[32] James Reston summarised the mood in the *New York Times* on 4 June 1961, when he noted that during Kennedy's first three months in office 'he has seemed to give equal weight to a whole grab-bag of policies. Thus, Laos and Angola have seemed for the moment as important as the unity of the Western alliance'.[33]

Portugal responded immediately to what it saw as America's meddling in an issue of Portuguese sovereignty. Salazar interpreted Kennedy's actions as a betrayal of understandings implicit in the North Atlantic Treaty. In 1949 he had advised the Portuguese National Assembly that although the colonies were not formally covered by the NATO treaty 'it is likely that the procedure for consultations which is provided for by Article 4 of the Pact . . . might be extended to all other regions where difficulties are of a nature to create troubles'.[34] Salazar saw the events of early 1961 to be just such a case of extra regional trouble. Major riots had broken out in Luanda in February of that year, forcing Portugal to deploy most of its continental European troops in Angola. But rather than offering to increase its military assistance, Washington chose to join the Afro-Asian bloc in the UN in its attacks against Portugal.

During the NATO ministerial meeting in Oslo in May Portuguese Foreign Minister Alberto Nogueira pressed the allies for support for its colonial war in Angola while at the same time making it clear that NATO membership did not give any allies the right to interfere in Portugal's internal problems. Citing the example of Algeria, Nogueira requested allied permission to send troops armed with NATO weapons to fight in Africa. Finally, the Portuguese foreign minister solicited the backing of Portugal's allies to oppose any further diplomatic attacks against Lisbon in the UN. In Oslo all of these initiatives were rejected or sidestepped by Portugal's allies.[35] The European allies felt justified in expressing concern about the foreign policy direction of the Kennedy Administration, but these governments were not about to be driven by Washington into closer affiliation with the unsavoury policies of Salazar. The NATO allies were particularly unreceptive to Portugal's arguments for a common position against the Afro-Asian bloc in the UN. According to the Royal Institute of International Affairs: 'It was felt that to be asked automatically to underwrite one another's policy in the colonial field as an obligation concomitant of NATO membership was more than could be expected of any member.'[36]

Washington's initiative at the UN forced some NATO allies to clarify their own positions on the issue of Portuguese colonial policy. Denmark came out strongly in favour of the UN anti-colonial campaign and explicitly rejected the Portuguese request for a unified NATO position in opposition to the Afro-Asian bloc. The Norwegian government announced in June that it had stopped the sale of ammunition to Portugal owing to Lisbon's policies in Africa. One week after the Norwegian announcement the British government clarified its own position; weapons for use in Portuguese overseas territories would no longer be sold to Lisbon, although arms sales for use within NATO would continue. Other NATO allies followed suit. Ultimately only France among NATO governments was to continue to sell arms to Portugal with no geographic restriction on their use. But none of the NATO allies established procedures to assure that arms supplied to Portugal for use within the alliance treaty area were not subsequently shipped to Africa.[37]

If the Kennedy administration had gone much further in its campaign to 'get on the right side of change' in Africa it could have made it extremely difficult for Lisbon to persist in its colonial policies. By the end of the year, however, the 'Europeanists' in Washington had regrouped their forces and Kennedy had become much more sensitive to their arguments in support of Salazar. Three developments during the second half of 1961 contributed to the change in Kennedy's perspective.

1. During the summer of 1961 the Joint Chiefs of Staff pressed the argument that the Lajes base in the Azores would become

indispensable if Washington was faced with a crisis in Berlin. As East–West tensions subsequently increased over Berlin, it became much harder for JFK to disregard the advice of the JCS.

2. Kennedy became increasingly more frustrated with Bowles during the summer and fall of 1961. The breakpoint in their relationship occurred in September, following the Belgrade international conference of neutral governments. Kennedy was infuriated by the neutral leaders' 'stupefying forebearance' in response to Khrushchev's resumption of nuclear testing just prior to the conference. Schlesinger notes that Adlai Stevenson and Bowles, 'the chief local champions of the Third World policy' were singled out by Kennedy for special criticism for their failure to solicit stronger criticism of Moscow among the Belgrade neutrals. Bowles and Stevenson were described by Kennedy as 'the real losers . . . at Belgrade'.[38] Two months later the 'Thanksgiving Day Massacre' took place. Bowles was replaced as Under Secretary of State by George Ball and persuaded to accept a vague status as 'Special Representative and Adviser to the President for African, Asian and Latin American Affairs'.

3. Salazar and Noguiera continued their counter-offensive against Kennedy during the second half of 1961 – in Washington and in the capitals of Western Europe. The Portuguese government pursued two strategies during this period; first, it explicitly linked the colonial issue with the renewal of US base rights in the Azores and second, it sought to convince the 'old colonial powers' that if America's pressure campaign against Portugal succeeded it would be only a matter of time until Washington turned its attention to their separate colonial situations.

In the end, it was the prospect of losing the Azores base which was the most important determinant of change in Washington's policy. The five-year basing agreement was due to expire at the beginning of 1962, and Kennedy was still extremely sensitive to the risk of a new crisis over Berlin. Furthermore, the new US strategy of Flexible Response and forward defence was expected to place an even greater premium on air transport of troops and *materiel* from the United States, and the JCS was not forthcoming with alternatives to Lajes that would be available, affordable and politically reliable. Finally, the administration had to consider that the US had already invested about $100 million in the Azores facility.[39]

By 1962, therefore, the US had backed away from its campaign of pressure on Salazar. In January the US obtained a renewal of its base rights in the Azores, but Portugal agreed only to a system of one-year access agreements which could be abrogated with six months' notice rather than a new five-year treaty. Washington reversed its policy of economic pressure on Salazar. The US approved an EX-IM bank loan of $69 million to Lisbon and agreed to bear half the costs of three new ships for the Portuguese Navy.[40] By the end of 1962 the United States was once again voting against UN resolutions critical of Portugal in Africa, leading S. J. Bosgra and C. Van Krimpen to conclude that 'the Kennedy administration had re-joined the club of NATO'.[41]

For the next 12 years US policy makers avoided a conflict with Lisbon over its African policies. The Nixon administration, in particular, was anxious to maintain good relations with Lisbon up until the time of the Portuguese military revolt which led to the collapse of the African empire. In 1968 Eduardo Mondlane, head of the Front for the Liberation of Mozambique (FRELIMO) advised the Tanzanian newspaper *The Nationalist* that 'we are fighting Portugal and all her NATO allies' because of the financial and arms support which Lisbon obtained from its NATO allies and subsequently siphoned off to its African campaign.[42]

THE BELGIAN CONGO: DOMAINE RESERVE

Belgium was the country within the alliance that was most sensitive to the precedents being set by the Kennedy administration in its initial forays against Portugal.

By the time that Kennedy and the 'Africanists' came to office in 1961 the Belgian government had already stored up a list of grievances against Washington for the latter's policies toward the Congo. As previously mentioned, the Eisenhower administration was inclined to defer to its European colonial allies whenever possible on issues relating to Africa. In the case of the Belgian Congo, deference to Brussels was the totality of US policy. Thus, when Brussels announced plans in January 1960 for granting independence to the Congo in six months' time the US government discovered that it had virtually no intelligence data to refer to as a basis for articulating an independent policy during the transition period.[43] An active policy was deemed to be essential by the US government, in order to pre-empt the Soviet Union in what was considered to be an inevitable race for the hearts and minds of the leadership of the new African republic. Washington therefore set to work to acquaint itself with the key players in the Congo and shortly thereafter came to the conclusion that Patrice Lumumba, an ardent nationalist who had organised the first party (the *Mouvement National Congalais* – MNC) with national as opposed to regional or tribal support, was the individual most likely to maintain effective control of the Congo during the initial period of independence. Control was associated with stability and inversely associated with outside communist influence in the US foreign policy equation for the Third World at this time. Washington consequently communicated to its Belgian ally that Lumumba appeared to be the best choice for leading the transitional government.

Brussels resented even this degree of US 'interference' in the difficult transition process. The Belgian Resident Minister in charge of the transfer of authority in the Congo complained subsequently about 'The consular agents of foreign states in Leopoldville, and particularly those of signatory states of the Atlantic Pact' who 'not without a certain naiveté' had attempted to press their support for Lumumba.[44]

The leader of the MNC was indeed the closest thing to a strong national figure in the Congo at this time, but he had proven to be particularly intransigent in transition talks with the Belgian government, and had, in fact, been placed in prison in Brussels at the start of the year. The Belgians were inclined to favour the more moderate, if politically weaker Joseph Kasavubu. Ultimately, a government was established in the Congo comprised of both Lumumba (Prime Minister) and Kasavubu (President).

During the first six months of independence Lumumba proved to be worse than the Belgians had warned – more obstreperous and, in particular, more pro-Soviet. Washington suddenly found itself confronted with the very real possibility that the Soviet Union would be invited into the Congo to bolster Lumumba's internal position.

The Congo situation achieved the status of an out-of-area problem for NATO within days of its admission to the UN (7 July 1961). Riots in several areas of the Congo led to a rapid redeployment of Belgian forces between 9 and 19 July, with the approval of the key NATO allies. The situation became even more complex when Moise Tshombe, took advantage of the internal disorder to announce plans for the secession of the Katangan region from the Congo. The Belgian government leaned in favour of supporting Tshombe, who encouraged Brussels to believe that he would be pro-Western in his politics and that he would work closely with the Belgian government to protect its extensive financial interests in the region. Once in place, therefore, the

Belgians appeared to be quite reluctant to leave the Congo and Katanga in particular.

The new Congolese government complained of a Belgian attempt to 'occupy the country' and called for a 'foreign neutral army' to help restore order and get the Belgians out. Moscow did not miss the diplomatic and propaganda opportunity provided by the crisis. The USSR argued that NATO was behind the Belgian intervention: 'The fact that the Belgian government sends troops to the Congo which are subordinated to NATO command and based in the German Federal Republic demonstrates once again the role that the aggressive NATO bloc, by assuming the role of international policeman, plays in the colonial enslavement of the peoples of Africa.'[45] Lumumba was particularly supportive of such Soviet arguments, and Washington was anxious to pre-empt any more active solicitation of Soviet assistance by the Congo leadership or by other Afro-Asian states.

It was in this context that Washington agreed to support a UN peacekeeping presence in the Congo. Belgium had committed itself to a policy of 'deliberate speed' in the removal of its troops. Once in place, however, UN forces began to press Brussels for the immediate withdrawal of all of its troops. On 18 July Belgian Prime Minister Gaston Eyskens stated that there was no need for UN forces to 'meddle in the internal affairs of a country' and Brussels undertook to delay the arrival of UN troops in the Katanga region.[46] Washington's subsequent efforts to work with Hammarskjöld and the ONUC forces was viewed in Brussels as a breach of the tradition of transatlantic solidarity and a reversal of Washington's long-standing policy of deference to the separate NATO allies in their respective spheres of influence in Africa. Even the Belgian Secretary General of NATO, P. H. Spaak expressed considerable disappointment at the lack of support provided to Belgium by Washington during mid-1960. In his memoirs, however, Spaak admits that 'one of the errors of the Belgian government was not having assured itself of the backing of its allies at the moment that it decided on its policy [of intervention]'.[47]

The accusations of US betrayal of Belgian interests were, in fact, unreasonable. Weissman concludes that US Congo policy during the latter half of 1960 was 'qualified and even shaped by her deference to Belgian policy'.[48] The Eisenhower administration attempted to work within the UN framework to protect Belgian interests while at the same time blocking the efforts of Moscow to insert itself into the Congo situation.

Whether it was justified or not, the Belgian government harboured a good deal of resentment and suspicion toward Washington by the time that the Kennedy administration came to office. The new administration naturally distinguished between the Portuguese and the Belgian cases in Africa, but many of the same arguments that had been employed by the Africanists against Lisbon's policies in Angola were presented in support of a more active involvement in the Congo situation as well. On the day of JFK's inauguration (20 January 1961) the Africanists completed a 73-page single-spaced report on the Congo situation in which it was noted that the Eisenhower administration's concern for 'NATO solidarity' had prevented it from pursuing a coherent policy 'in favour of the speedy implementation of the UN resolutions', particularly on the issue of the removal of Belgian troops. The report recommended that the US support a policy in the UN aimed at the neutralisation of all armed forces in the Congo as expeditiously as possible.[49] In his quest to 'get things moving' the new president gave Stevenson the authorisation to pursue such a policy at the UN.

The 'Stevenson Plan' was introduced in the UN in the first half of February. It called for the removal of all 'foreign military or para-military personnel' in the Congo and explicitly condemned 'those Belgians . . . providing military advice and assistance to the Congo'.[50]

Madeleine Kalb describes the Belgian response as 'furious', in particular because Brussels had not been consulted about the US plan before it was introduced at the UN. 'They [Belgians] argued that the American failure to consult with a NATO ally, especially one with an overriding responsibility in the area, placed Belgium on the same plane as the neutralists and the Soviet opponents of NATO'.[51] The intensity of the Belgian criticisms was partly due to the fact that the Belgians were already on the defensive and extremely sensitive to any initiatives by the UN in the Congo which would disrupt their 'deliberate speed' strategy. It was also a matter of the Kennedy administration's style. By the time (1960) that disputes arose between the US and Belgium over Congo policy, Eisenhower had long since established his *bona fides* as a faithful Atlanticist. The new administration was barely in office when it began to make controversial statements which led key allies to question whether the alliance still mattered in Washington.

The US policy in the UN contributed to Spaak's decision to resign from the Secretary Generalship of NATO. On 13 February he sent a recriminatory letter to Kennedy in which he advised the president of his decision to quit and complained of Washington's lack of attention to the interests of its allies:

> Regarding problems which occur outside of the geographic limits of the Alliance, the practice of consultation is generally accepted, but the results are not always very satisfactory. What occurs is that states act without consulting their partners. It occurs, above all, that consultation does not result in the harmonization of policies. The last unfortunate example of this occurred quite recently in the case of the politics relating to the Congo. The American ideas, as made public, could be approved neither by France, nor by Belgium, nor by the Portuguese nor, I believe, by the English; that is to say by none of those states most directly interested in African problems. What has come to be called the American plan was never made the object of discussion within NATO. The allies of the United States were apprised of it at the same time as their enemies. . . . I remain convinced that a basic choice has to be made. For the moment, the choice can be summarized as follows: Does the United States accord more importance to the UN than to NATO? In other words, in order to assure itself of the support or friendship of the non-aligned states is it willing to sacrifice the interests or bruise the feelings of its allies in NATO? This is what occurred in the past in Suez and Algeria. It has occurred more recently in the case of the Congo and the case of the Portuguese territories of Africa. The repetition of such situations will seriously weaken the cohesion of the Atlantic Alliance.[52]

One month after his departure from NATO Spaak became Vice Premier and Minister for Foreign and African Affairs. He none the less continued to involve himself personally in NATO politics throughout the year, and continued to press the case for allied solidarity in the UN and the Congo.

The Belgian government could count on much more sympathy and support from the key European allies than Lisbon could in its parallel campaign. Great Britain was impressed by the fact that the rich Katanga region was the most stable area of the Congo, in large part because of the Belgian military presence. London was concerned about a too-rapid departure of Belgian forces which might create instabilities in Katanga that would quickly spill over into the neighbouring Federation of Rhodesia and Nyasaland. The UK also recognised a common interest with Belgium in the protection of investments in Katanga, where the British firm Tayanyika Concessions owned 14 per cent of the *Union Minière* company and controlled the Benguela railway which shipped ore through Angola to the coast.[53] The British were also convinced that the case of Brussels was quite different from the case of Portugal, and London felt more directly threatened by its implications of the Congo precedent. Shortly after Stevenson's UN proposals were introduced in the UN, the *New York Times* reported that London was very concerned about the direction of US policy, and that the UN was 'determined not to be "hurried" in Central and East Africa' and quoted an official 'close to Macmillan' who had asserted that 'we are not going to be jockeyed into the sort of solution the Belgians reached in the Congo'.[54]

Brussels also found an ardent supporter in De Gaulle, who harboured his own grudges against the US for its policies in North Africa. In the Congo case, De Gaulle also had the opportunity to vent his anger against one of his favourite *bêtes noires*, the *nations dites-unies* for its attempts to transfer its 'global incoherence to the local scene' in the Congo. De Gaulle refused to contribute funds for the UN Congo operation and even refused overflight privileges to Congo-bound UN aircraft. He also convinced the Francophone African states to refuse overflight rights. As John Newhouse has noted, 'a glance at the map shows quickly the extraordinary inconvenience this hostile gesture produced'.[55] It is worth mentioning, however, that France and Belgium tended to have fundamentally different ideas about allied policy coordination beyond the NATO treaty area. This is perhaps best illustrated by De Gaulle's choice of the Congo as a test for his three-nation directorate scheme.[56] The General was quite willing to leave Belgium out of the Congo picture altogether in 1960 and to solve the problems of the Congo within an exclusive club comprised of London, Washington and Paris if given the opportunity.[57]

The Kennedy administration was caught off guard by the allied opposition generated by the Stevenson proposals. By April of 1961 Kennedy was backing away from any positions in the UN that could be interpreted by Brussels as anti-Belgian, and Washington was attempting to reassure its major colonial allies of its commitment to Atlanticism. In mid-April the US abstained from a vote in the UN which was critical of Belgian policy in the Congo, and Washington subsequently muted its position in favour of the expeditious removal of all foreign troops. Spaak expressed 'satisfaction' with the 'encouraging words' of US Secretary of State Dean Rusk in their discussions relating to the Congo at the NATO ministerial meetings in May.

By the end of 1961, however, Hammarskjöld was pressing Washington to take action. The US policy of accommodating Brussels was seen by the UN Secretary General as contributing to the stalemate in the Congo which could not be maintained indefinitely. Washington at least partly agreed. The US was convinced that Tshombe was encouraged in his intransigence by the support he received from foreign troops and mercenaries in Katanga. Kennedy also concluded that Hammarskjöld was correct in his desire to increase the pressure on Tshombe by forcing the foreigners out. He therefore offered limited and conditional US support for new military initiatives by ONUC during December. The decision triggered even more allied criticism than had been the case ten months earlier.

Dean Rusk was dispatched to the NATO ministerial meeting in Paris in mid-December, to plead the US case. He reported to Kennedy that the Congo was 'the most pressing item of business' on the NATO agenda.[58] Indeed, the intensity of the disagreement in Paris led one newspaper to conclude that the alliance was 'already in danger of joining the Council of Europe and Western European Union on the scrapheap of obsolete western political institutions'.[59] Rusk cautioned the president to reduce US involvement – already marginal – in the ongoing UN operation in order to avoid further disruption of the alliance. Harold Macmillan also pressed the case for 'reconciliation rather than conquest' in the Congo in phone conversations with Kennedy and Rusk.[60] Kennedy complied.

The European reaction to the US/UN Congo initiatives of December 1961 appears to have had a particularly chastening effect on Kennedy. The US again retreated into a policy of relative quiescence in the UN and reassurance in NATO. But again, for the US the situation of stalemate in the Congo became a source of increasing frustration. Kennedy seems to have learned during 1961 that Washington had to coordinate its policies with its key European allies prior to any new initiatives in the UN. During the autumn of 1962, therefore, the US cautiously developed a case for increased economic and, if necessary, military, pressure on Tshombe to break the deadlock in the Congo. By November, the US administration was happily surprised to discover that Britain and (more importantly), Belgium, appeared willing and even anxious to join the US in achieving a solution. According to Stephen Weissman, three things had occurred over the year to soften the Belgian attitude regarding US interference in the Congo.

1. Some Africanists maintained that long hours of rational persuasion finally paid off.
2. Some Europeanists said the courteous diplomacy of 1962 soothed many sore spots.
3. Tshombe's position had deteriorated in the past year.[61]

Spaak met with Kennedy in Washington in late November to discuss the basis for a common policy. By mid-December Spaak had publicly broken with Tshombe (referring to him as 'a rebel') and expressed support for UN recourse to military force if necessary to end the Katangan secession. This was enough of a *carte blanche* for Washington, which assured UN Secretary General U Thant of American support for 'Operation Grand Slam' against Tshombe's forces in Katanga. The ONUC operation began on 28 December and proved to be easier than expected. Very little direct US support was in fact required. On 14 January the ministers of Katanga announced that they were 'ready to proclaim to the world that the Katangan secession is ended'.[62]

ZAIRE: DIFFERING PERCEPTIONS AND MOTIVATIONS IN AFRICA

Shortly after coming to office in 1974 Valery Giscard d'Estaing made it clear that his administration would accord a much higher priority to Africa than had been the case under either De Gaulle or Pompidou. Giscard also departed from Fifth Republic tradition by discussing African issues in the context of the politics of blocs and justifying some French initiatives in Africa as contributions to the preservation of the East–West geo-strategic balance.

The new attention that France paid to Africa, and the new willingness of the Giscard government to coordinate French policy with other NATO members was based upon the French President's conviction that the West's circumstances in Africa had changed in fundamental ways during the 1970s. Giscard's Presidency (1974–81) did in fact coincide with the beginning of a new era in African politics, the most notable characteristics of which were the intensification of intra-African jockeying for sub-regional hegemonies, the collapse of the Portuguese empire and the new willingness of Cuba, East

Germany and the Soviet Union to become directly involved in African conflicts. In an interview for *US News & World Report* in 1976 Giscard explained that French activism was also conditioned by US post-Watergate and post-Vietnam paralysis:

> It is true – say, recently in Africa, the US appeared to be experiencing certain difficulties in implementing its foreign policy, compared to nations enjoying full freedom of decision and action. These difficulties undoubtedly created a sense of anxiety in the world.[63]

Giscard argued that France had a special responsibility to resist the 'local disequilibrium of forces' in Africa not only in the name of narrowly defined French national interests but in the interests of Western security as a whole.

The French President's willingness to coordinate French policies in Africa with other members of NATO was demonstrated during the Ogaden crisis of 1977 and during the 1977 and 1978 Shaba crises.[64]

At the time of the first Shaba crisis the recently elected Carter administration's policies in Africa were dominated by Cyrus Vance and Andrew Young, who favoured 'African solutions to African problems'. The US government rebuffed some of Giscard's early efforts to solicit allied support for Zairian president Mobutu's resistance to an attack of approximately 2000 Katanganese rebels (FLNC) primarily on the grounds that there was no clear evidence of Soviet or Cuban participation. When pressed by a reporter to speculate on US policy if a significant Soviet/Cuban military presence in Zaire could be proven, however, US ambassador to the UN, Andrew Young, admitted that 'after Vietnam, there is almost no way you could get the United States militarily involved in Africa'.[65] Giscard had treated Zaire as France's most important African ally since 1974, and felt compelled to assure the stability of the Mobutu regime in 1977. He therefore acted on his own when it became apparent that the Carter administration had no interest in being drawn into a central African conflict. Paris provided the air transport for 1500 Moroccan troops, as well as arms supplies and 65 French military advisers. The ease with which Moroccan and Zairian forces crushed the Shaba revolt relieved the Western allies of the need to consider a more active and perhaps, a more coordinated response to the crisis.

When a much larger FLNC force (est. 4000) attacked the Shaba region one year later, it was harder for key Western governments to maintain a sense of remove. Giscard encouraged Western concerns in 1978 by arguing much more forcefully than he had a year earlier that the USSR, Cuba and Angola were actively supporting the FLNC action and that East bloc victories in Africa would doom East–West *détente*.

Giscard's arguments reached a somewhat more receptive audience in Washington than had been the case one year earlier. By the time of the 1978 crisis the influence of the Vance/Young faction in Washington had declined significantly and the 'globalists' within the administration – most notably, Zbigniew Brzezinski – were much more powerful. This group accepted French and CIA arguments of Soviet, Cuban and Angolan complicity in the 1978 FLNC attack and felt that a strong US response was long overdue.[66] Carter continued to waffle, however. He was pleased by Giscard's demonstrated willingness to share the Western defence burden in the Third World, and he was willing to assist the French President in his efforts to solicit support from other NATO allies. The President was none the less opposed to any use of US military personnel in the Shaba crisis because it would represent the first test of the administration's war powers authority since coming to office, and it would be in support of a regime which was generally considered to be repressive and corrupt and viewed by many experts as close to collapse.[67]

Carter therefore limited Washington's contribution to a 'carefully limited, one-time deployment of US transport aircraft' to lift arms, *materiel* and 'logistical personnel' into Zaire.[68] Every effort was made to avoid a confrontation with Congress in the context of the 1973 War Powers Act. According to White House testimony following the crisis, 'no military personnel of any kind were carried on U.S. planes, and the U.S. pilots were not even equipped with sidearms. In addition, the U.S. planes and personnel were never within 100 miles of actual combat.'[69]

Several other NATO allies shared Washington's concern about becoming too involved in Africa in support of Mobutu. Great Britain was sensitive to the negative reactions that a NATO-approved intervention would trigger among the Anglophone states of Africa.[70] Denmark and Norway had been consistently critical of Giscard's military activism in Africa, and both governments opposed efforts to introduce African security issues in the NATO forum.

Even Belgium, which had by far the greatest economic stake in Zaire, was reluctant to risk being once more tied down militarily and politically in Central Africa. The Belgians were particularly cynical about Giscard's efforts to elevate the Zaire crisis to the status of a common Western security interest. As Belgian Foreign Minister Renart Van Elslande observed at the time of the 1977 crisis, France's concern for stability in Africa tended to be focused on 'African countries that possess important resources'.[71] Brussels consequently resisted French and Zairian solicitations to intervene until the crisis threatened the lives of the European residents in Southern Zaire. Even then, Brussels hesitated and Paris was forced to send in its contingent one day ahead of the larger Belgian force.

Brussels continued to reject French efforts to place the intervention in an East–West political context. It continued to treat the operation exclusively as a humanitarian action and attempted (unsuccessfully) to terminate the operation 72 hours after it began. Belgian Foreign Minister Henri Simonet distinguished between the French and Belgian philosophies in a televised interview at the time of the crisis: 'The French government has an African policy which is not the same as ours. France seeks to maintain *points d'appui* in the dark continent, while Belgium seeks cooperation with a country rather than a regime.'[72]

The discomfort which various NATO allies experienced over Giscard's campaign to elevate the Zaire operation to the status of a common Western security interest was brief. The rescue operation was a success that virtually all NATO members were able to applaud on humanitarian grounds. Carter went further in a statement to the NATO Council of Ministers in Washington shortly after the rescue operation. He publicly applauded the 'efforts of individual NATO allies for the help they gave to nations and peoples who need it – recently in Zaire' and concluded that 'our alliance is centered in Europe but our vigilance cannot be limited to that continent'.[73] But, Carter, and virtually all the other NATO allies baulked when Giscard subsequently solicited allied political and economic support for an 'inter-African force' to replace Belgian and French troops in Zaire and to be available for other interventions in Africa in the future.

France's NATO allies confronted the issue directly at the aforementioned NATO Ministerial Meeting on 30 May 1978. When pressed for a statement the NATO allies came down strongly on the side of ambivalence. President Carter noted after the meeting that the allies had ruled out any coordinated NATO action in Zaire as 'outside the bounds of its [NATO's] charter' but he concluded that there was a 'general feeling that the Cubans have exceeded any bounds of propriety in having massive placement [sic] of troops in Africa'.[74]

Giscard subsequently convened a meeting of Belgian, French, US, British and West German representatives in Paris to press his case for allied sponsorship of an inter-African force. Specifically, he sought a Western commitment to equip, train and provide logistical support for a 4000–5000 man force constructed mainly from the Francophone African states. The proposal was quietly smothered by the other allies at the meeting, although a commitment was made to provide Zaire with some financial aid for purposes of economic resuscitation.

One month after the second Zaire crisis, an article was published by the French Armed Forces Chief of Staff, General Guy Méry, in which he called for greater allied cooperation to extend security guarantees to Africa, noting that France was 'at the moment, on the western side, rather alone in our action'.[75] Giscard's efforts to stimulate debate within NATO on African security in general and the issue of Zaire in particular, met with some expressions of sympathy and gratitude, but very little in the way of active support.[76] The French President's contentions that the allies were insufficiently attentive to Soviet and Cuban activism in Africa foundered on three factors.

First, Giscard had considerable difficulty both at home and abroad in articulating a coherent theory of foreign policy in which France was presented as the main defender of Western security in Africa and at the same time as the principal spokesman of East–West *détente*.

Second, France, in particular among NATO allies, has traditionally had difficulty in convincing other Western governments of its altruistic motives in foreign affairs. French arguments about common security interests in Africa were inevitably viewed with suspicion by European governments which had historically competed with France for influence in Africa and, to some extent, by the United States, which had become more accustomed to being the victim than the beneficiary of French foreign policy *gestes* since the late 1950s.

Third, and most importantly, despite the fact that most NATO allies were more alert to the dangers of regional and subregional instability in Africa by the mid-1970s there was no agreement within NATO regarding the role of the Soviet Union or Soviet proxies as a source of this instability, and no agreement on the need for a NATO multilateral peacekeeping approach to the region.

SOME CONCLUSIONS

In the introduction of this chapter the reader was presented with a typology of four kinds of NATO out-of-area situations. It will have become obvious that these categories are not mutually exclusive. Each of the four cases discussed exhibited characteristics of more than one type of out-of-area situation. An attempt was none the less made to consider each of the cases as illustrative of one particular type of out-of-area problem.

Algeria was selected as an example of the problems of burden sharing because the French government could not have carried on its 'savage war of peace' in North Africa without the financial and arms support provided under NATO auspices. This situation of dependency was a source of special frustration for France. The Algerian War was fought under the banner of sovereign right and sovereign duty, yet Paris' reliance on allied sponsorship of the war effort was recognised by all parties as proof of the limited nature of that sovereignty.

During the period of the provisional government (1945–6) De Gaulle had argued for the preservation of the remnants of the French Empire to aid France in reasserting itself as a great power in the post-war era. But by the time that he returned to power in 1958, the General had concluded that the interminable colonial wars had in fact kept France weak and reduced its freedom of movement and its influence in world politics and, in particular, within the Atlantic Community. The solution – cut French losses in North Africa – was evident for De Gaulle by 1961, but highly unattractive. The process of retrenchment from Algeria was made somewhat easier for France, however, by the projection of much of the blame on to France's principal financial backer, the United States. According to French public opinion America had always provided just enough support (material and moral) to keep French forces fighting in North Africa but never enough for victory. The historical record supports Alfred Grosser's conclusion that 'Algeria dominated everything and explained everything, from Suez to the wave of bitter and xenophobic nationalism which swept across France or carried in its train a deep though veiled crisis which hit deeply into the very heart of the Atlantic alliance.'[77]

The case of Portuguese colonial rule in Africa fits fairly comfortably into the 'guilt by association' category. Portugal's membership in the alliance had been something of an embarrassment since 1949. It became even harder for the allies to look the other way after Lisbon embarked upon a brutal war in Angola in 1961. It is none the less apparent from our brief survey of the Portuguese case that the Alliance would have adjusted itself to the events in Angola without much difficulty if the issue had not been picked up by the newly-installed Kennedy administration. To the extent that Kennedy's criticisms of Lisbon looked like criticisms of European colonialism in general they elicited negative reactions from the 'old colonial powers' within NATO. But in general, France, Britain and Belgium saw themselves in an 'alliance of convenience' with Portugal in its campaign within NATO to resist US pressure and criticism. Had Washington chosen to press its case against Portugal, and resisted the tendency to relate the Portuguese question to the more general issue of colonialism in Africa, Kennedy could have obtained much greater support within NATO for a policy of coordinated pressure on Lisbon.

But Kennedy mismanaged the Portugal question from the start. He came to office looking for situations in which he could demonstrate his commitment to change in the Third World at minimal cost. Portugal's management of its overseas territories seemed to be ideally suited. But the president gave insufficient attention to the risk that his policies toward Portugal would trigger a negative response from the major European colonial allies and from the still-influential Europeanist policy élite in Washington. Above all, Kennedy does not seem to have been prepared for the well-orchestrated campaign of opposition that Lisbon undertook on its own behalf. As George Ball noted, Portugal saw itself with 'its back to the wall' on the question of preserving its colonies too poor and too financially dependent upon metropole/ colon trade to even consider decolonisation.[78] Salazar therefore took full advantage of the leverage provided by the US dependence on the Azores facility to press Washington to abandon its campaign of criticism. In the face of Portugal's political counter-offensive, the Kennedy administration retreated.

The Congo was chosen as illustrative of a *domaine reserve* situation within the alliance. General histories of African colonialism refer to Belgian policy in the Congo before 1959 as uniquely 'paternalistic'. According to Henri Grimal 'in the eyes of the Belgian authorities . . . as the blacks were 2000 years behind, the Belgian presence and domination would be essential to the Congo for a long time to come. The civilizing mission was therefore conceived without any regard for the time factor.'[79] The civilising mission was in itself sufficient justification for Belgian colonial rule and sufficient justification for refusing any efforts by outsiders to meddle in Belgium's Congo policies. Allies were expected to be especially sympathetic to Belgian sensitivities in this regard. Brussels was quick to complain during 1960–62 whenever it appeared that the United States was straying from this tacit agreement.

But Belgian opposition to US interference in the Congo never took on the characteristics of psychodrama that were so common in French responses to American 'betrayals' in Indochina and North Africa. Two factors account for the difference between the Belgian and French cases. First, by the time that Washington became entangled in the Congo the fundamental break between the metropole and the colony had already taken place. After January 1960 Brussels no longer viewed events in the Congo as issues of domestic sovereignty – the most extreme form of the *domaine reserve* perspective. Paris, on the other hand, continued to treat the struggle in Algeria as a *guerre civile* until the final break in 1962. Second, Belgium's concern for allied deference in the Congo was always balanced by the priority that Brussels accorded to consultation and policy coordination within NATO. More than any other figure, Spaak personified this dualism between the exclusively national and the Atlantic commitment. The result was that Belgian challenges to Eisenhower's and Kennedy's policies in Africa stayed at the level of intra-alliance political dispute and were not permitted to run out of control.

Indeed, the Congo case appears in retrospect as an example of US/European disagreement in which both sides of the Atlantic placed a premium on intra-NATO cooperation. In all three instances in which the US was considered by Belgium to have meddled in the Congo without proper consultation Belgian criticisms were followed by US Policy adjustments – in favour of the Belgian position. This occurred in the autumn of 1960 (following US support for the initial UN intervention) in the spring of 1961 (in the wake of the Stevenson proposal) and in 1962 (after the UN attempt to force all foreign military personnel out of the Congo). For its part, Belgium gradually adjusted its position on the Katanga secession issue so that by the end of 1962 Washington, Brussels and London had achieved the semblance of a common policy. The Congo case is therefore best understood as an instance of consciously moderated dispute within NATO. No one, however, would describe it as a model for allied policy coordination.

Zaire (1977 and 1978) represents one of several cases in which a NATO ally tried to 'educate' other members of the alliance to what it considered to be a common security interest in Africa. It is distinct from the Algerian, Angolan and Congo cases in that it occurred in the post-colonial era in Africa. Significantly, it was also the latter part of the post-Vietnam period in the United States and the beginning of the period of Soviet interventionism in the Third World. This combination of circumstances was a source of concern for most of Washington's European allies in the latter half of the 1970s, but it was viewed with special concern by the government of Giscard d'Estaing in France. To the extent possible, Paris sought to convince the other NATO allies that situations of instability in Africa had a direct bearing on East–West relations and, especially, on the politics of *détente*. He also attempted to convince the French mass and élite public with this argument: 'I should like to tell the French that Africa is quite close'.[80]

Virtually all NATO allies disregarded Giscard in 1977. The US was particularly uncomfortable with the French President's efforts to elevate the first Shaba crisis to the status of a common Western security problem. Giscard was none the less accorded high points by most allies for his coordination of the first Shaba intervention, in which Morocco provided most of the troops, and Paris provided the air transport. Giscard was somewhat more successful in obtaining US and Belgian participation in the second Shaba crisis a year later. But attempts by NATO SACEUR Alexander Haig and others to interpret the 1978 action as a first step toward a coordinated NATO peacekeeping role in Africa were rejected. At the close of the NATO Council meeting in Washington shortly after the second Shaba crisis NATO Secretary General Joseph Luns announced that 'it was the consensus of all the leaders that the situation in Africa was not something for NATO to be concerned with as an alliance'.[81] Pierre Lellouche and Dominique Moisi reflected the Giscardian interpretation of these developments in their assertion that 'French military interventions are objectively serving overall Western interests. However, the cost of such interventions is borne by the intervening state alone.'[82]

Since the mid-1970s the geo-strategic value of Africa has been reassessed within the Western security community in light of changing circumstances. On the basis of the historical record, however, it is hard to imagine that this reassessment will result in consensual support in favour of a renegotiation of the NATO treaty so that the alliance *per se* can play a more active role in Africa. We are more likely to see a continuation of the tradition of ad hoc policy coordination among concerned NATO governments in response to events in Africa. NATO can perform a useful role, by providing a loose and adaptive institutional framework for such policy coordination. To ask more of the alliance would risk the situation that Robert Lovett warned against during the Washington Treaty negotiations: 'spreading the butter so thin that nobody gets fed'. More fundamentally, any attempt to renegotiate the 'transatlantic bargain' to include Africa would run foul of the first law of good management – when something is running reasonably well, leave it alone.

6 France, NATO, and Regional Conflict in Africa

JOHN CHIPMAN

From the end of the Second World War, France's commitments in the African continent have had a major impact on the formulation of her declaratory policies as well as on the substance of her defence plans. Immediately after the war, the defence of North Africa and of the 'French Union' virtually received a higher priority than the defence of Europe, where a fresh outbreak of hostilities seemed unlikely.[1] Once negotiations on the Atlantic Treaty began, France made substantial efforts to use the Atlantic framework to retain her colonial possessions, by insisting that the United States consider giving greater commitments to Allied interests outside the treaty area.[2] The reluctance of the United States to do so (despite the initial inclusion of France's North African territories within the Treaty area), must be seen as one of the root causes of France's later desire for independence within the Atlantic Alliance. Since many of France's major military responsibilities were in areas not covered by the Alliance, it would eventually appear proper and logical that France take a more aloof stand in respect of direct collaboration for European defence. France would 'independently' prepare for her defence within Europe, just as she was 'forced' to stand alone in defence of her outside obligations in Africa.

Out of these practical needs to ensure the security of extra-European areas a theory of the French place in the world has developed over time that in turn has been used to justify persistent commitments outside of Europe and especially in Africa. More precisely, French relations with the African continent have held a specific place in French foreign policy since decolonisation. While the French position in the world is symbolised by the possession of nuclear weapons and membership of the UN Security Council, the ability of France to act with considerable freedom in her ex-colonies serves to justify a foreign policy which is written in large terms. In general, the French have believed that for France to maintain her position as a medium power the state must undertake a degree of activity which has implications for those living outside its borders. In the French conception, to maintain, or to aspire to a great foreign policy, a medium power must be able to exert control or influence in places where no other power can do quite the same. To compensate for an incapacity to exert influence in all parts of the globe, as would a Superpower, a medium power, such as France, must try to preserve for itself a certain exclusive influence in a region.

The maintenance of influence in the francophone African states has been directly linked to the French need for *rayonnement* (or 'glory'). The early French reports on economic aid to Third World countries stressed that the diplomatic power of France, either regionally, or in global conferences, depended in part on the relations which France was able to keep with developing countries.[3] Close relations with the newly decolonised areas of Africa gave proof of a continuing French ability to adapt to different circumstances, and a policy which was 'active' would ensure that France could preserve for herself the place that de Gaulle had created for her on coming to power. The French colonialist, Jules Ferry, asserted that at the end of the nineteenth century France would become a power of the third or fourth rank if she adopted a policy of '*rayonner sans agir*' ('shining without acting'). Presidents of the Fifth Republic have taken similar if less consistently dramatic attitudes towards the French role on the continent. The annual Franco-African summit meetings, which were begun on African initiative in 1973, have come to indicate the extraordinary diplomatic power France possesses in large sections of Africa, and which has been used to imply a type of great power status.

If Africa is important to France for these elemental reasons relating to the French place in the world, it also helps her to give meaning to her manoeuvres on the world stage. One of the enduring aspects of Gaullist foreign policy, which has resurfaced in different forms during the presidency of each of de Gaulle's successors, is the desire to play a moderating and independent role between the two Superpowers. While the French membership in NATO and France's basic interests put her clearly in the Western 'Bloc' it has always been a French desire not to be defined in relation to either of the two Superpowers but rather as a unique force in world politics. It was de Gaulle's nascent insistence on French independence from the two blocs which made him more receptive than might have otherwise been the case to the calls of independence from France issuing from the French colonies in Africa.

Since 1960, France has claimed that it is her independent position in world politics which should make her a more attractive option for states of the Third World. Ostensibly untainted by the stigmas associated with Superpower rivalry, the French offer of economic and military aid to less developed countries has been represented as part of a formal desire, within these states, for the politics of non-alignment. This tendency was, if anything, heightened by the French Socialists in the early 1980s who viewed France's particular aims as a third force to be co-extensive with the general aims of the Third World.[4]

From the point of view of French diplomacy, the Franco-African relationship is a symbiotic one. French leaders have claimed that France belongs to the councils of the great powers because she has retained influence in such a large section of the African continent, and have claimed, equally, to the peoples of the ex-colonies, that it is their share of French power, grandeur and independence, which gives them a special status. On the other hand, a good deal of French activity in Africa has been taken not only with the compliance, but at the request of the Africans. French influence in the region has therefore come to be related not only to the nature of power as deployed by French leaders, but also to the definition given that power by the Africans. Indeed the Africans have to some degree been the determinants of French power in Africa in that they have given juridical sanction (through the signing of cooperation agreements, and in maintaining their membership of the Franc Zone) to the importance of France on the continent. Because the French themselves have put so much stake on their influence in Africa, any move by the Africans radically to divest themselves of the French presence would have to be carefully managed by France. This is especially true in respect of its military policy on the continent which has important political consequences for the European dimension of its foreign policy. More than one French leader has pointed to the fact that French steadfastness on the African stage demonstrates willpower which is useful in strengthening France's general policy of deterrence. French ability to manage and deploy power on the African continent in defence both of African allies and of international principles confirms a special place for France both in the international system generally and within the Western Alliance in particular. In 1945 the French statesman Gaston Monnerville argued that: 'Without her Empire, France would today be nothing more than a liberated country. Thanks to her Empire France is a victorious country!'[5]

This idea persists, and the fact that Africa provides a 'field of action' for French power is fundamental to French military and therefore political confidence.

While the French insist at Franco-African summit meetings that the closeness of Franco-African relations derives entirely from a sense of mutual self-respect, within the French domestic debate reference is always made to how Africa helps France to maintain her political stature, and furthers her economic well-being.[6] Though the numbers involved are not high, it is noteworthy that the francophone states still import 40–60 per cent of their goods and services from the ex-metropole, and that Africa as a whole is the only major geographical region where France is consistently able to show a surplus on its foreign trade. Africa also provides France with a substantial amount of her raw materials. Nearly all France's uranium comes from Africa (Southern Africa, Niger and Gabon); a third of her copper comes from Zambia and Zaire, a third of her phosphates come from Tunisia, Morocco, Senegal, Togo and Algeria; and a fifth of her iron ore is supplied by Mauritania and Liberia.[7] France also imports almost 18 million tons of crude oil annually from various parts of Africa, which represents almost one-third of France's total oil imports.[8] Clearly a great deal of French aid to Africa is sent with a view to ensuring continued supply of these important materials. On the other hand, the very high price that France sometimes pays for these resources (such as uranium from Niger) is itself a disguised form of aid. In any case, much of the aid sent to African countries comes back to France in the form of purchase orders for French goods and services.

It remains the case that all of the francophone black African states are dependent on France. For the African states directly concerned, relations with France are a vital element in the formation of their domestic and external policies. Aid received from France is crucial to their economies, and has an equally important effect on the training and formation of national armies, as well as on the choices that countries in a given region make in respect of the types of alliance or military pacts they might wish to construct. While the foreign policies of francophone African states are by no means dictated by France, the French presence in certain African countries makes shifts in foreign policy – in terms of the diversification of trading partners in Europe, or

the establishment of special links with non-francophone African states
– particularly awkward (though not impossible).

The right wing government of Jacques Chirac, which came into
power following the legislative elections of March 1986 altered the
direction of some of Mitterand's southern Africa policy, but the
general interest in francophone Africa persisted. But all French
governments have made their own interpretations of African problems
(particularly in the dispute over Namibia) and this raises the question
of the degree to which French policy in Africa is in the service of
'Western' interests, at least as defined by the United States.

Three general points can be made. First, French success in
maintaining influence in the francophone African area guarantees a
continuity of political experience in Africa which is generally valuable
to the West. Moreover, French declaratory support for policies of
non-alignment in Africa show a sensitivity to the local ideologies of
independence which can reflect well on the Europeans as a whole. In
the early days of the European Community, France implicated the
other Europeans in her Africa policy by helping to create a European
development policy for Africa. This policy has helped to heighten
Western influence and prestige in the area. Second, the particular
influence which France is able to maintain does much to prevent the
deep penetration of Soviet influence. If French decolonisation had
proceeded suddenly, if the French had not shown a strong interest in
their ex-colonies, it might well have been possible for the Soviet Union
to exploit local vulnerabilities to her advantage. Because of the close
relations between France and her ex-colonies the African states had
little incentive radically to shift allegiances, and this continues to be the
case. Third, the maintenance of a rapid action force (*Force d'Action
Rapide* or FAR) with an ability to intervene effectively on the African
continent and the existence of French bases in various African
countries allows France to contain the expansion of Soviet influence
once it has begun to make itself felt either directly or through African
states who receive Soviet aid. In this connection the French garrison at
Djibouti clearly plays an important role. It is the only Western outpost
at the southern entrance to the Red Sea. Yet it must be kept in mind
that the French presence there serves as much to keep a precarious
balance between opposing states in the area (each having a
Superpower patron) as it may serve to support a purely Western
interest.[9]

To balance these last two considerations, then, is the very special way in which French policy in Africa is presented. French policy has rarely been aimed overtly at keeping the Soviet menace at bay or at propagating a particular 'Western' or 'NATO' policy. The French have traditionally been reasonably relaxed about the degree of Soviet influence on the continent. The decision of Guinea to turn to the Soviet Union in 1958 was one which de Gaulle did little to prevent. The adoption by countries (like Benin) of Marxist governments and the signing, by countries like Madagascar, of military cooperation agreements with the USSR were things to which the French governments of the day were relatively indifferent. The first French military intervention in Zaire (Shaba I, 1977) may well have taken place for 'cold war' reasons, but the 'East–West' dimension of the problem formed only part of the justification for French action. Furthermore, while the Americans supported the French, the West Europeans were less enthusiastic. The claim of President Giscard d'Estaing that he had intervened on behalf of Europe[10] annoyed several EC member states who did not see how European interests were engaged in central Africa at the time, and who therefore felt that the French President had used Europe's name in vain.

If the French have confronted difficulties on those occasions when they have tried to present their activities as being in the general Western interest, they have also been challenged by those African states who know that national interest makes the Western interest divisible. African leaders who may formerly have thought only in terms of playing West against East are now successfully (from their point of view) able to play West against West. Francophone states are beginning to test ways in which they might break out of the French mould, and reintroduce into Africa a degree of competition between the Western powers. Soon after the Mitterrand election in 1981, for example, the President of Gabon pointed out to the new French President that, if his requirements in terms of military or economic aid were not met by the French, he would turn to the United States. This strategem, employed on occasion by other African leaders, works primarily to pit Western states against each other, even if only in small matters. As a new generation of African leaders is appearing, who have a less sentimental feeling towards France than their predecessors, resistance to the French presence may emerge more forcibly than before, and will have its effects on the military arrangements existing between France and certain African states.

There is, therefore, no necessary identity of *interests* between France and the West as a whole. Paradoxically (given the French fear of being associated too closely with the Atlantic Alliance as a body) there is one sense in which there is an identity of *aims* between France and NATO in Africa. Recent NATO statements on the effect that developments outside the NATO Treaty area might have on Western security, have stressed that 'respect for genuine non-alignment is important for international stability'.[11] The first French Minister for Cooperation in the Mitterand Government, Jean-Pierre Cot, expressed a view that can be taken to represent an unchanging French attitude when he declared that 'we think that the best way of maintaining our interests (outside the NATO area) is to support non-alignment, and particularly in Africa'.[12]

Naturally, the 'support of non-alignment' has not always been the dominating motive for French military intervention in Africa. The need to retain influence in the states closest to France has required military activity of different kinds, in varying degrees, and for a number of complex and related reasons. The maintenance of defence agreements with eight African states (Cameroon, Ivory Coast, Comoros, Central African Republic, Djibouti, Gabon, Senegal and Togo), and of Technical Military Assistance agreements with these eight and 17 others, has created in some cases an explicit, in others an implicit, obligation to intervene in Africa in periods of political turmoil. Yet only when the need to protect French civilians embroiled in a conflict is evident, could a French military intervention be considered automatic. Even the call of a political leader having a defence agreement with France would not necessarily result in immediate French action. The pressure of various African states, and clear evidence of foreign intervention, might force a French reaction (as happened in Chad 1983–7), but France's longstanding desire for 'independence' would certainly rule out promises of an open-ended character. The preservation of French economic interests, important as these may be, would equally never be the sole motive for military action. Finally, given the currently highly complicated political environment in Africa, France would prefer to remain neutral in the event of conflict between francophone African states; as happened during the Christmas 1985 border war between Mali and Burkina Fasso. However when France's prestige on the continent might be at stake an intervention in support of a friendly state is difficult to refuse. Thus when Togo in September 1986 asked France to re-establish order in Lomé after a series of riots, 200 French paratroops were sent from nearby Gabon and the Central African Republic without much hesitation.

Since 1960, there have been at least 19 instances of overt intervention by France in Africa to suppress riots, support a political leader, or defend a country against external aggression. There have equally been numerous 'warnings' and military activity of subtle kinds that have influenced events in Africa. Ever since the French established an intervention force in 1962, in fact, French power located in the metropole has served as a deterrent to politically inspired unrest in many francophone African states. The continued presence of French troops in Senegal, Ivory Coast, Gabon, CAR, and Djibouti, has also had a restraining effect. The key to understanding the military role of France in Africa lies, therefore, in an understanding of how France's military capacities in Africa serve to deter adventurous activity.

THE PRESENT STRUCTURE OF FRENCH–AFRICAN MILITARY RELATIONS

The Mitterand Government put its own stamp on French security policy in the 1984–8 Military Programme Law.[13] Its principal innovation lay in the reorganisation of the Armed Forces and in particular, the creation of a new intervention force, the *Force d'Action Rapide* (FAR) which became effective in August 1983.

The establishment of this new intervention structure was an attempt to reconcile France's African (and Middle East) military vocation with the need to be able to come to the aid of France's allies in Europe. A rapid action force which could contribute both to the maintenance of peace in the Third World and to the conventional defence of Western Europe reflected France's position as a 'Eurafrican power'. As the FAR has developed, analysts and policy-makers have asked whether it primarily serves France's European needs (and therefore brings France closer to her NATO allies), or whether the new force, in strengthening France's intervention capability, merely emphasises France's existing guarantee of support to her African allies. In principle, French leaders have insisted that the FAR can do both at the same time. It gives meaning to France's defence policy which is contained in the phrase 'independence and solidarity' often used by officials of the Mitterand government. French power allows France to act (by her own volition) in defence of countries politically close to her. Like other elements of the French Armed Forces, the FAR also serves a symbolic purpose. At the end of 1983 a group of civil servants of the

Ministry of Defence noted that the existence of the FAR and the doctrines governing its use allowed France to maintain her place in the world:

> The FAR is an expression of our will, of our capacity to be a nation with worldwide interests and universal vocation: neither hegemonic Super-power nor mediocre province, France and her civilisation must continue to bring to the world her message of liberty and independence in the service of peace.[14]

In practice, given the relative unlikelihood of an outbreak of hostilities in Europe, the restructuring of France's intervention forces is of greater relevance to overseas commitments, even if some of the units assigned to the FAR are more appropriate for action in Europe than in the African bush. Its *Force d'Hélicoptères Anti-Char*, or FHAC, is especially designed to fight alongside NATO forces attempting to contain Soviet Operational Manoeuvre Groups (OMG). Action by the FAR in Central Europe, beyond the reach of French supply lines, would depend on substantial NATO logistical and air support.[15] The implication of the FAR's creation is that the Mitterand Government, more than any of its predecessors, chose to give substance to the axiom that the conventional defence of France is inseparable from that of its West European neighbours.

Still, while the FAR has a politico-military *significance* for the European theatre, the continued instability of Third World states who desire outside support means that the FAR is likely to be of greater immediate *utility* for overseas tasks. The modernisation of France's intervention capability would allow France to conduct more effectively the type of operations overseas that she has traditionally seen necessary. The creation of the FAR has not, however, changed the dimension of France's extra-European power, or the substance of her day-to-day military relations with African states. There are still potential outside challenges for which the FAR by itself would be an inadequate instrument, while the nature of Franco-African military cooperation has been untouched by the recent structural reforms.

The FAR and Africa

The FAR comprises five divisions and a logistic formation totalling approximately 47 000 men: the 9th Marine Infantry, the 11th

Parachute, the 6th Light Tank, the 27th Alpine, and the 4th Aeromobile Divisions. The 9th and 11th are untouched Divisions of the former *Force d'Intervention* (mostly *Troupes de Marine*); the 6th Division is an outgrowth of the 31st Brigade (much of the Foreign Legion is attached to this Division); the 27th Division is assigned to the FAR more or less intact; and the 4th Division is a totally new formation (see Table 6.1).

The reorganisation therefore does not materially affect the *Troupes de Marine* who have traditionally acted overseas.[16] Though the FAR has been joined under a single commander it is not intended to fight as a unit and the separate divisions do not often exercise together. Its first large manoeuvre took place in June 1985, code-named *Farfadet*, including 12 000 men from all three services, and as the FAR is improved it is likely that many larger joint exercises will take place. The FAR is, nevertheless, not an independent army corps able in the European theatre to take on an enemy without other logistic or communication support. The FAR rather provides a command structure and a reservoir of forces from which the commander may draw for deployment in areas of crisis. All that its five divisions have in common is their relatively high mobility. Of the five, the 4th Aeromobile was isolated as the most important for combat in Europe. Composed in part of three regiments of combat helicopters (Gazelles and Super Pumas) the 4th Division has been presented as a valuable potential complement to NATO forces trying to contain Soviet attacks into Western Europe. The 27th Alpine Division also has a more obvious mission in Europe than in Africa. In the event of war in Europe, however, the other three divisions, although more accustomed to overseas action, could be deployed in the European theatre.

While the precise conditions under which the FAR would act in Europe remain necessarily somewhat ambiguous, given France's general attitude to NATO, the FAR's overseas missions have been given clearer definition. First, it is to guarantee the security of French citizens abroad. Second, it is to protect the territorial integrity of the *Départements Outres Mer* (DOM) and the *Territoires Outre Mer* (TOM). Third it should be able to defend energy and raw material supplies as well as France's commercial routes. Fourth, it must fulfill the defence and cooperation agreements which France has signed with other states. And, fifth, it must be able to participate in international peacekeeping missions.[17] The President's capacity to act quickly in the event of some overseas crisis has been increased by the fact that nearly

TABLE 6.1   Composition of the Force d'Action Rapide (FAR)

Fourth Air-mobile Division	Three regiments of combat helicopters each to receive: 30 *Gazelle* helicopters (*HOT* missiles) 22 *Puma* helicopters Support and protection helicopters One infantry regiment equipped with 48 *Milan* missiles One command, manoeuvre, and service regiment equipped with 30 *Super Puma* helicopters
Sixth Light Tank Division	Two regiments equipped with 36 AMX-10 RC Two infantry regiments in VAB One artillery regiment with 24 155mm guns (tractor drawn) One engineer regiment One command and service regiment
Eleventh Parachute Division	Six infantry regiments One light armoured cavalry regiment One artillery regiment Two command and service regiments
Ninth Marine Infantry Division	Three motorised infantry regiments One tank regiment (*Sagaie* tanks), with anti-tank squadrons One command and support regiment Two engineer companies
27th Alpine Division	One regiment equipped with AML and anti-tank squadron One artillery regiment equipped with 24 105mm guns (tractor drawn) and a ground to air component Six motorised infantry regiments (mortars and *Milan* missiles) One engineer battalion One command and support regiment

SOURCE   SIRPA: Service d'Information et de Relations Publiques des Armées France.

all members of the FAR are professional servicemen. Under French law, short-term conscripts may not be sent overseas without parliamentary approval. The professionalisation of France's intervention capability means that a large force may now be sent overseas without parliamentary debate.

This has not gone uncriticised. In February 1984 the *Mouvement d'Information pour les Droits du Soldat* (IDS) issued a communiqué stating that 'with the professionalization of a quarter of our armed forces . . . the government has given itself an intervention capability of a colonial type – without the parliamentary debate considered a democratic minimum'.[18] The professionalisation of France's intervention capability has nevertheless been seen by the government as an essential reform and, on the basis of recent experience, has been extended to include certain types of technicians. In the summer of 1983, when the Mitterand Government was mounting *Operation Manta* for its intervention in Chad, it was unable in the first instance to send a fuel detachment as the technicians were all conscripts. It has since ensured that essential logistic units of this kind are made up entirely of professionals.[19]

While the size of the FAR (47 000) is double that of the old *Force d'Intervention*, there are still considerable limits to its ability to act overseas. The 1984–8 Military Programme Law guarantees the air force 450 combat aircraft, but its transport capacity remains low. Any rapid overseas action obviously requires a large transport capacity for which the French have been forced to rely almost exclusively on their *Transall* aircraft. At the end of 1984, all the planned 25 of the second generation *Transalls* (C-160S) (which can be refuelled in the air) were in service to complement the 48 first generation aircraft (in service since 1967 and due to be phased out between 1995 and 1998). Neither the first not the second generation *Transalls* are truly adequate for France's overseas needs. Aircraft of the second generation can deliver a payload of only 8 metric tons over 5000 kilometres; the maximum payload of 16 tons is deliverable over a distance of only 1800 kilometres.[20] Even with its refuelling capability, the *Transall* would require the use of staging bases for a distant overseas intervention. The French government has dismissed the idea of trying to buy American C-141 *Starlifter* aircraft on the grounds that some basic problems would not be solved by its acquisition. In any case the US Air Force felt that it needed all its C-141s (now out of production) for use by the Military Airlift Command. The government has chosen instead to augment its military transport capabilities by relying on national civil air lines to provide aircraft (such as the *Airbus*) at short notice for specific missions. From time to time, as is the case in Chad 1986–1987, France was able to borrow from United States *Galaxy* aircraft stationed in Europe.

In the light of these deficiencies, the *Commandment du Transport Aerian Militaire* (COMTAM), which is in charge of all logistic and tactical missions associated with military transport, clearly needs to improve its carrying capacity and certain criteria for a new transport have been established.[21] In mid-1984, Charles Hernu the French defence minister, held discussions with various European and American officials in order to prepare a programme for the development of an American–European transport aircraft, but the realisation of such plans are still well in the future.

While airlift is therefore likely to be a problem affecting France's intervention capability until well into the next century, sea transport presents fewer problems. Any intervention action by sea will, of course, be considerably slower than transport by air but the sea does offer some advantages: transport can usually be effected without violating areas of national sovereignty; the cost is lower; the range of material which can be transported more varied. Distance is less critical and the establishment of a 'sea presence ' can often help to complement the deployment of ground forces.[22] The 1984–8 Military Programme Law has made provisions from the improvement of France's sea transport capabilities. Three new landing ships (*Transports de chalands de debarquement* or TCD) have been ordered, to be delivered in the early 1990s. These ships, of about 10 000 tons displacement, are intended to maintain the navy's capacity to transport tanks overseas and any other material not easily transported by air.[23] Plans to develop a nuclear-powered aircraft carrier to replace *Clemenceau* have also been put into effect since the 1984–8 Military Programme Law was presented which will give France a greater capacity to establish an overseas presence. In February 1986 the defence ministry signed authorisations for the *Richelieu* carrier.

Nevertheless, given that France's links are often to landlocked African states, it will be difficult for the French to exploit the advantages of sea transport. For the intervention in Chad in 1983, some equipment was transported by sea to Cameroon and then taken overland to Chad, a process which took some time to organise and put into effect. Without relying on US transport aircraft, or on the goodwill of a number of African states, it will be difficult for France in the foreseeable future to deploy an interventionary force much larger than that sent to Chad in 1983 – which was the largest overseas expedition launched by France since the Algerian War. At the height of the peacekeeping mission about 3300 troops from all three branches of the armed services were present in Chad and between August 1983 and September 1987 almost 10 000 men completed a period of service.[24]

Even if certain types of African contingencies could be dealt with by sea, the French will still have to rely extensively on air transport for the initial stages of any intervention in Africa. They must also rely on the cooperation of African states politically close to France for the prolongation of any intervention. The present capacities of the French interventionary forces are such that, though they can be very effective for long-term peacekeeping operations (as in Chad or the Lebanon), their capacity to fight long and intense wars on the African continent is very limited. The FAR is primarily a 'first aid' instrument, able to put down uprisings or invasions not involving sophisticated opposing forces.

The far and parachute assault capability

French military action in Africa may be of two types: long-term peacekeeping activity; and short-term firefighting action. The rapid instigation of a major expedition is subject primarily to the availability of sufficient transport and the ability of the target states to receive French forces at the same rate as they can be despatched. If there are airstrips large enough to accommodate civil aircraft, then troop deployment can be expected to take place rapidly and efficiently. One of the advantages of French action in Chad in 1983–7 was that French engineers were able to rebuild the Ndjamena airstrip so that large civil and military aircraft could land there. While such work has also civil implications, it naturally increases France's capacity to bring in an intervention force rapidly when required. Although it would be wrong to suppose that the French have an interventionist *idée fixe*, action is taken where possible to improve the quality of African military infrastructures (for a variety of motives). In the specific case of Chad, the experience gained through *Operation Manta* during 1983–4 could be expected to improve France's ability to react quickly to any future crises. When France reinforced its presence in Chad in 1986–7 it also brought in sophisticated equipment such as radar, which help the host country to defend itself.

But not all French interventions in Africa can be expected to take place in good conditions and the French are continuing to make efforts to improve their capacity to land troops in all environments. In principle, all members of the 11th Division are parachute-trained. Having seized and cleared an airfield, these assault troops could then be followed by air-landed elements from the 9th Division or other units of the FAR. Moreover, in each regiment of the 11th Division there are units who have been trained to conduct intelligence-gathering or minor combat roles deep behind enemy lines. These 'pathfinder' troops might well be sent into a crisis area before other troops of the 11th Division were deployed. These units, which are known as *Commandos Recherches et Actions dans la Profondeur*, are specially trained to drop onto hostile territory in order to secure military installations (including airstrips) which could then be made available for French reinforcements. In peacetime there are only some 200–400 such specialist troops operational at any one time, far too few to engage in a long-drawn-out war without immediate support. The French also rely on the paratroops of the Secret Service (Discretion Generale de Service Exterieur) who in Chad in 1987, for example, helped Hissene Habré's government troops to prepare battle against the Libyans.

Among the most specialised of French units to have operated in Africa is the 1st RPIMA (*Regiment Parachutistes d'Infanterie de Marine*). This unit (which like that from the DASE does not belong to the FAR) is at the direct disposal of the French President. It can be used for rescue missions or sensitive intelligence operations. In practice, however, for a mission such as the Shaba rescue, these commandos are likely, possibly with *Jaguar* aircraft support, to be reinforced as soon as possible by additional troops from the 11th or 9th Divisions. As long as African armies or insurgent bands remain small and dispersed, the French can remain reasonably confident of their 'firefighting' capacity even though, in the first instance, they may rely on the unique abilities of only a few hundred troops.

The creation of the FAR has in no essential way changed the means by which France deploys force in Africa, even if recent reforms have improved France's ability to manage its overseas power. New communications systems now allow French commanders to work more effectively with marine or air forces supporting African land operations. In late 1984 a new satellite was launched by the *Ariane* rocket with two military communication channels. The *Syracuse* network, operational from the beginning of 1985, allows for secure, jam-free communication between fixed and mobile stations.[25] As a result, the French President can communicate directly with French forces deployed in Africa, something which is often essential given the political sensitivity of much of French military policy.

Some constraints on intervention

There remain, however, certain natural restrictions to the deployment of French power in Africa. The logistical problems associated with any substantial military action overseas are immense: the organisation of the initial intervention must be such that units are able in the first instance to act autonomously; and, once forces are deployed, they must be able to take advantage of stocks which have already been prepositioned overseas. The maintenance of prepositioned stocks in key areas of interest to France naturally saves a considerable amount in initial transport costs, but all French action in Africa since decolonisation has been *sui generis*, and it is impossible to calculate the amount or type of equipment which the FAR would have to take with it in the future in order to ensure success.[26] French forces intervening in countries having defence agreements with France will be able to make use either of local stocks or (in countries where French forces are stationed) equipment in the inventory of the French *Force de Presence*. In other cases all supplies would have to come direct from France which might require the case-by-case negotiation of appropriate overflight or transit rights with the countries involved.[27] The transport of heavy equipment (such as tanks) can perhaps be effected by air but this will always be extremely expensive. In the past, the cost of such transport has sometimes exceeded the book value of the cargo. The *type* of intervention naturally affects the *organisation* of its support. For a rapid intervention like Shaba in which everything is sacrificed to speed the stocks taken in with the troops are minimal. For more deliberate peacekeeping missions, such as the 1983 Chad operation, after the first stage of rapid troop deployments has passed, most of the resupply is done by sea and a substantial infrastructure has to be set up in the host country to deal with supplies.

A second problem concerns specifically those forces stationed in certain African countries (and not part of the FAR) including the 23rd BIMA in Senegal, 43rd BIMA in the Ivory Coast and the 6th BIMA in Gabon, as well as the various marine infantry troops in Djibouti.

The defence agreements signed with each of these countries explicitly prohibit France from using the territories of the signatory states for interventions elsewhere but, by special agreement, France may use her facilities in these countries as staging posts. During the 1983 intervention in Chad, for example, the garrison in Gabon (near Libreville) and in the CAR (in Bangui and Bouar) effectively served as rear bases for French action. Forces permanently prepositioned in

Senegal, the Ivory Coast or Gabon may be re-deployed elsewhere for a French intervention. In extreme circumstances the French would ask the host government if the forces stationed could temporarily be moved to another theatre. The political importance of these forces, however, which serve as a deterrent to internal unrest, is such that it is difficult to imagine that permission would be granted unless they were soon replaced by units coming from France. The French government would also only ask for permission in the most extreme circumstances. Even the transfer of certain pieces of equipment at the disposal of prepositioned troops to other parts of Africa would cause some concern locally and this would normally be done only on the understanding that replacements would be sent as soon as possible. Jaguar fighter aircraft based in Gabon, for example, would (in principle) only be transferred to another field of action with the approval of the Gabonese President who would have to balance the relevance of a specific French action to Gabonese interests against the problems associated with the temporary absence of French aircraft from the country. If the mobility of the FAR is restricted by transport problems, that of the prepositioned forces is partly constrained by the juridical terms which govern their actions in the host countries. Nevertheless, the existence of permanent French garrisons increases the reach of the FAR and allows it to have at least some capacity to intervene in almost any African area of direct interest to France.

Because of the manner in which training and exercising of these forces is organised, elements of the FAR arriving in Africa are able to act effectively with other French units stationed there and with African armies. Elements of the FAR are often sent abroad as rotating units (*unités tournantes*) to complement other French forces permanently stationed there. This rotation of personnel gives the FAR direct experience of African conditions and makes large exercises of metropole-based and overseas-based forces (in collaboration with local armies) much simpler. As the training of African troops is, in the case of those countries having defence agreements with France, coupled with participation in Franco-African joint exercises, interoperability problems are reduced, though not entirely eliminated.

Furthermore, the general policy of military cooperation pursued by France ensures that African armies remain dependent on France for the replacement of equipment. Through her policy of military cooperation, France is able to control the size and capabilities of most francophone African armies. Arms transfers remain at a modest level and the general policy is to give only those types of equipment which the Africans are able to maintain themselves. Only very rarely does the French Ministry of Cooperation give the Africans equipment which has been recently developed. The preference is to transfer armaments which are appropriate for African conditions and which are not expensive to maintain. France often refuses African requests for equipment either because the equipment demanded is too expensive, or because the French have other priorities. Each African state connected to France by a cooperation agreement makes its annual requests through the local French Head of Military Cooperation, who passes the request on to Paris. The Ministry of Cooperation then distributes aid as it sees fit to all the countries under its jurisdiction, thus subordinating particular African demands to France's general strategy for Africa. It is worth recalling that most French arms *sales* are to the Maghreb countries and to the Middle East, areas where France's diplomatic power is important but not nearly as predominant as it is in sub-saharan Africa. Francophone Africa is therefore not a *market* for France's arms industry, though certain more advanced pieces of equipment, such as *Mirage* and *Alpha Jet* fighters, are occasionally sold to the richer states. The others have largely to satisfy themselves with what the French decide to give them, a fact which allows the French to ensure that appropriate regional military balances are maintained.

There is, therefore, a conscious attempt by the French in their dealings with African countries to develop a common military policy. Careful not to over-endow African armies, the French are able to ensure that it is difficult for one country to launch an attack on another. The fact that France maintains agreements with so many countries also serves as a stabilising factor in that leaders would be uncertain who the French might support in any interstate conflict which might occur and consequently they are likely to be deterred from letting any dispute lead to war. More particularly, the relations with states in which France has prepositioned troops are intended to ensure that France is able to act alongside local forces with ease. Although interoperability is obviously generally high because the troops have been trained and equipped by France compatability of forces still varies from country to country.

The discovery and solution of the problems which might affect joint operations takes place through the system of joint manoeuvres which are essentially of two types. First there are national manoeuvres, in which the armed forces of the African country exercise with the French *Forces de Presences*. The armies of Senegal, Gabon, and the Ivory

Coast almost never go on a major exercise without including French troops. Second, there are bilateral manoeuvres, which the French organise on average once a year. These include elements from the local African army, French forces stationed in Africa and units of the FAR. These are costly and complex but deemed to be worthwhile because they are demonstrations of political solidarity as much as tests of military effectiveness. Again the most important take place in Senegal, Ivory Coast and Gabon. In the CAR, where the French forces are labelled *Elements Français d'Assistance Operationelle* (EFAO), and are rotated once every four months from the FAR, the French units hold small exercises almost on a weekly basis, and undertake major exercises once in their tour. Full bilateral exercises sometimes take place in countries with which France has defence agreements but in which there are no prepositioned forces. This, for example, was the case for *Katcha 83*, a bilateral manoeuvre held in the north of Togo in June 1983 which involved metropole-based troops of the FAR and also elements of the EFAO coming from the CAR.[28]

In the many exercises that took place in the 1970s and the first half of the 1980s, a tradition of action with a small nucleus of African armies has been established. These exercises have also allowed the French to test new weapons on African soil. They have proved as challenging for French as for African troops, primarily because troops coming from the metropole are forced to adapt themselves to several different generations of equipment. During the *N'Diambour III* manoeuvres in Senegal in November 1982, for example, French soldiers used AMX 30 tanks (introduced to African soil for the first time) and AMX 10 RC infantry vehicles together with older vehicles, such as the AML, now used only by French supplied armies overseas.[29] Though the different generations of combat equipment in the FAR and African armies does not pose serious problems, it does require a certain versatility on the part of soldiers involved in any joint action. Of more concern, as was demonstrated in the bilateral manoeuvres which took place in the Ivory Coast during 1984, is the question of communication.[30] Radio equipment in African armies is often incompatible with more modern French systems, so that liaison between elements of French and African armies is often awkward.

Over time, the bilateral exercises have helped the French and the Africans to develop complementary forces which would be useful in meeting certain African contingencies but these exercises have not necessarily improved the capacity of African armies to fight *independently*. It is doubtful whether any francophone African army could, even today, successfully mount a major expedition outside its own territory although the Senegalese, for example, have tried to gain international recognition for their armed forces and they have participated in peacekeeping operations far from national territory (in Chad and Lebanon) and in an intervention (Gambia) much closer to home. Troops from Zaire have often been sent to Chad. Yet for the most part the capacities of francophone African armies are modest and uninspiring. While their ability to put down internal disputes is adequate enough, defence against an external aggressor would in most instances require outside help, and francophone African leaders of countries closely affiliated to France openly declare that defence in such contingencies depends on French support. The French, for their part, are likely to become increasingly reluctant to deploy forces to Africa except in the most extreme of circumstances, yet the option of working with other Western states to manage conflict in Africa (thus distributing responsibility and possibly dampening criticism), has not been seriously considered.

OTHER NATO STATES AND COLLABORATION WITH FRANCE

Precisely because French *national* interests are so tied up in Africa, the idea of collaboration with other powers to manage African conflicts is antithetical to the French scheme of things: influence shared is influence lost. In most military interventions made by the French in Africa, consultation with European and NATO allies has been minimal and after the fact. When the French mounted a considerable amount of logistical support for the Moroccan airlift of troops and equipment to Zaire in 1977, for example, President Giscard d'Estaing stressed that his action had been taken without consulting the Carter administration.[31] Any claims that Giscard's policies in Africa in fact implied closer relations with the United States or NATO were always strongly resisted by the French President, and this has remained the case. The French have accepted a general duty to inform their allies as to their actions in Africa (once they have taken place), but have not thought it necessary to seek advice. Only on rare occasions, when their own policy would have failed without it, have they recognised the need for outside assistance.

Intelligence support from the United States has been essential in most interventions of the 1980s. Throughout the 1983–7 French intervention in Chad the Americans provided important information on Libyan troop movements. The efficacy of American intelligence gathering in the region was even a cause of some embarrassment to the French. After the French had signed a joint withdrawal agreement in September 1985 with Libya that called for the simultaneous and complete withdrawal of both Libyan and French forces from Chad, it was the Americans, who several weeks later, revealed that while France had loyally completed her part of the bargain, most Libyan forces had not budged. While the United States has taken an increasing interest in the affairs of sub-Saharan Africa, and has provided important logistic support for French action, the fears expressed in certain French quarters that Washington was preparing to 'replace' the French in Africa appear unfounded. These fears do, however, limit the times when France will actively seek US assistance for any action in Africa. In Chad, however, close consultation has taken place between the Americans and the French whose aid given to the Hissene Habré government was thus well coordinated. This is the principal, if minor example of French–US military cooperation in francophone Africa.

Yet if the French accept outside help reluctantly it is also true that it is sparingly offered, especially in the case of other European states. Former President Giscard d'Estaing proposed some time ago in the pages of *Foreign Affairs*[32] the creation of a European Rapid Deployment Force (ERDF) that would be able to intervene in areas where European interests were engaged (principally in the Middle East or Africa) to quell a conflict or keep the peace. None has been created. A number of European countries have developed rapid action forces. The British after the Falklands war have made considerable efforts to upgrade the capacities of their rapid action force. The Italians in the 1985 White Paper have argued for the creation of a *Forza di Intervento Rapido* (FIR). The Portuguese and the Spanish are also improving and reorganising their rapid action and special commando units. But the prospect of any of these units being pooled into a general European capacity remain extremely low. While there has been some experience of collective European action out of the NATO area (Sinai, Red Sea, the Lebanon), these have been rarely coordinated, and do not serve as relevant precedents for collective Western involvement in Africa.

If there is to be collaboration among Europeans in the future for the management of political and diplomatic problems in Africa it will only take place if a small collection of states have a direct and verifiable interest in helping to solve a problem, believe that a collaborative approach will be both more effective and serve their national interests in some way, and if (though this is perhaps of lesser importance), the target states accept the style and content of the European initiative. These conditions are stiff ones, and limit the sort of collaboration possible. To the extent that types of conflicts and problems that occur in Africa are often complex and intractable then the deterrent to collective action will be high, in that a fear of failure will affect any decision to mount a diplomatic or military enterprise in these regions. While the fact of cooperation might be an aim to pursue in and of itself, it will rarely be compelling enough a motive to risk a national embarrassment in the Third World.

CONCLUSION

The French are likely, therefore, to continue to have an individual and relatively exclusive responsibility for sub-Saharan African security. Because it is to the mutual benefit of all parties, the Franco-African security system which now exists is likely to remain in place, even if occasionally modified, at least until the end of the century. Although the French would like to reduce the sometimes annoyingly high political and economic costs of their policy in Africa, they would like to continue to derive the benefits of it. Whether a right wing or a left wing government is in power, the essential lines of French African policy will remain constant. Disputes, domestically, will be on questions of nuance and of tone rather than on principle or substance.

In the December 1985 Franco-African conference of heads of state, President Mitterrand drew the lines of French policy in Africa. These are likely to determine the parameters of French action in Africa for any likely French government of either the moderate left or moderate right. Mitterrand went to great lengths in his opening speech[33] to stress that France was not in a position to provide answers to the various African dilemmas. France would continue to provide a modest level of economic aid to those countries (mostly francophone) to which she was still close owing to historical and cultural ties, though there were limits to her capacity to subsidise African treasuries. The French government would continue to offer military assistance to those countries who asked for it, though Mitterrand insisted that France could not be expected automatically to intervene in any circumstance. Rejecting the roles of 'paymaster' and of *gendarme*, Mitterrand

nevertheless happily promised to play advocate, and gave his word
that he would do as much as possible to plead the African case in every
relevant international chamber.

The 1985 summit conference confirmed a secular trend in France's
Africa policy basically unchanged by the experience of 'cohabitation'
with the Chirac government: while France's interest in Africa remains
high, her ambitions have declined. There is no sense in which one can
now speak (if this was ever possible), of France 'managing' African
affairs. While France in the 1960s seemed anxious to play a leading role
on the continent, French leaders are now happier with a policy which
seeks only to manage relations with African countries in such a way
that France is in a position to *react* to African political and military
developments. The fact that in the last week of 1985 two small
francophone African states (Mali and Burkina Fasso) were able to
begin, fight and conclude a short war without any appreciable or at
least obvious French involvement, also shows that African states are
taking less account of possible French attitudes than was once the case.
The fact that a francophone African regional organisation (the *Accord
de Non Aggression et d'Assistance en Matière de Defense* or ANAD),
of which both the belligerent states were members, was successfully
able to bring about a ceasefire, despite the competitive attempts of two
African powers (Nigeria and Libya) to do the same, also proves that
francophone African states are now developing both the will and the
diplomatic capacity to keep the peace in West Africa.

If recent French declarations have shown that France has been
serious about giving meaning to the oft repeated maxim 'Africa for the
Africans', it remains the case that France has a vital role to play in the
final dénouement of the post colonial period. For some time, France
has pursued a carefully regulated policy of bilateral aid to a number of
African countries. The logical outcome of an effective policy of aid is
that its recipients require it less as time goes by. If the economic and
political stability of Africa depends, as the French have often argued,
on more efficient regional systems of cooperation, then French aid
should increasingly be directed towards improving the means of
multilateral cooperation among Africans. While the maintenance of
the network of defence and cooperation agreements between France
and most francophone African states is an essential factor contributing
to military stability in francophone Africa, the strengthening of
regional institutions will be a high priority for those African states who
truly wish to release themselves from a continuing dependence on
outside powers for so many of their security needs. An enlightened

French policy that would seek to encourage the development of such organisations as the ANAD would do credit to France's longstanding African vocation, as well as reinforce generally the standing of the West in Africa.

7 Southern Africa and the West in the Post-Nkomati Period: The Case of Mozambique

BERNHARD WEIMER

At the beginning of their lucid analysis of the potential and dynamics of the conflict in South Africa, John Saul and Stephen Gelb qualify the present crisis as structural or 'organic' rather than merely 'conjunctural'.[1] This implies, so the authors contend, that the state, in an attempt to manage and finally resolve the crisis cannot – as in the case of the conjunctural – resort to reactive, *defensive* measures of adjustment, but is forced to design and implement *formative* efforts:

> A new balance of forces, the emergence of new elements, the attempt to put together a 'new historical' bloc, new political configurations and philosophies, a profound restructuring of the state and ideological discourse . . . new programmes and policies . . . a new sort of 'settlement' within certain limits[2]

have to be constructed, which supersede and replace previous 'forces', 'configurations' and 'programmes'. From this perspective Botha's reforms as well as his 'Total National Strategy' are far from cosmetic and can be seen as formative efforts, which, on the one hand have considerably eroded the rationale and practise of apartheid, without, on the other, yielding to the political demands of the Black majority. Thus both the reforms and the reactions to it (from the split within Afrikanerdom to the attempt by the 'young comrades' and the ANC to make South Africa ungovernable) are a reflection of the continued 'organic/structural crisis' in South Africa as well as the inability of the

139

Botha government to cope with it in analytical and political terms. In the words of Stanley Uys

> the pattern is always the same: reforms which are meant to strengthen a regime in fact weaken it . . . To expect Botha . . . to grant blacks 'meaningful political rights' is to miss the whole point of the current process. By the time he is ready to give blacks these rights, the game will be over: this is the end of the process of change, not the beginning.[3]

For the mid-eighties, some of the most important economic aspects of the crisis can be summarised as follows:

— low respectively negative real growth of GDP with the growth of the population exceeding growth of GDP;
— unemployment and 'job scarcity' for approximately 4.5 million Blacks out of a population of some 25 million;
— change from a position of a net capital importer to a capital exporter;
— dramatic drop of the Rand's external value as well as drop of gold reserves;
— a shrinking real economic base with widening money supply; increasing secular inflation;
— an 'end of the road' for import-substitution–industrialisation without prospects for export-led growth; dependency on mineral commodity exports (gold);
— highly skewed income distribution resulting in depressed domestic demand;
— increasing rate of bankruptcies and industrial strike action; plus serious under-utilisation of installed capacity in key sectors;
— a financial crisis in food producing agriculture with dramatically increasing indebtedness of commercial farmers.

This economic crisis – the worst in more than five decades (according to government officials) – exacerbated by selective international sanctions and disinvestment moves of multinational companies, is in many ways directly and indirectly linked to the political crisis of the Botha regime, both in domestic and in external, namely regional relations as well as to the widespread and increasing Black struggle against apartheid and vice-versa. Taken together, these factors constitute the most explosive, dramatically sharpening conflict in South Africa's history, in which the government reacts – often brutally – rather than acts, thus increasingly losing the initiative and whatever little international support it might still have.

If this diagnosis is correct, what does it imply for Western policies towards Southern Africa? Can the United States policy of 'constructive engagement' with Pretoria, or whatever is left of it, succeed?[4] Or are we presently witnessing the beginning of the end of the Pretoria regime, as the ANC suggests in its Freedom Radio broadcasts from Addis Ababa, and the birth of a 'new nation', the 'post-apartheid South Africa' as suggested in titles of conferences and scholarly works? And what are the consequences for the West's policies towards South Africa's neighbours, the majority ruled Frontline states?[5]

In this context it is noteworthy that the West is not perceived as a homogeneous group of states sharing uniform perceptions of and attitudes towards the crisis in Southern Africa. In Michael Howard's assessment of the differences there is a 'widespread feeling' in *European* attitudes towards an 'objective revolutionary situation' in South Africa, 'that in the last resort the collapse of the present white regime would have to be accepted and that we would have to learn to live with the successors as we have learned to live with successor regimes elsewhere in Africa'.[6]

In contrast the *United States*, under the Reagan Administration with its preference for geo-political concepts, anti-communist ideology and neo-interventionist strategies entailed in the 'Reagan Doctrine', has a tendency to see the conflict in the globalist terms of a Superpower quest for Southern Africa's mineral wealth, the strategic sea lanes around the Cape, etc., which South Africa as the economic and military hegemonial power of the region can play an important role in safeguarding. The 'constructive engagement' policy; the 'linkage' of the Cuban withdrawal from Angola to the independence of Namibia; the ideological and – since July 1985 – overt material support for UNITA and the very late and haphazard recognition of ANC and SWAPO as most important organisations of the Black minorities in South Africa and Namibia are a reflection of this perception. Table 7.1 summarises the differences between the US and Europe (with the inclusion of the FLS and South Africa).

While both the United States and Europe deplore apartheid, their efforts and methods for its abolition differ. Washington's principal European allies have adopted a wait and see attitude, or, as a diplomat put it, one of 'constructive fence-sitting'. In contrast, the United States is more actively engaged in pursuing distinct policies or rather

TABLE 7.1   Conflict in Southern Africa: perceptions, attitudes and strategies[7]

	RSA	FLS	Europe	US
perception of causes	'total communist onslaught'	apartheid	apartheid	apartheid East–West conflict
attitudes	prevention of revolution by all means; entrenchment of apartheid	containment of damage, learn to live with successor regime; support for liberation movements	containment of damage, learn to live with successor regime	containment of damage, averting of revolution
strategies	TNS	'Lusaka Manifesto': armed struggle-cum-negotiations	'peaceful change' through cooperation with all parties	'peaceful change' by constructive engagement and dialogue

programmes. This pertains both to the US Congress with its sanctions legislation ('disinvestment campaign') and to the White House with 'constructive engagement' which, despite its failure, has still not been abandoned but has been reinterpreted as moving into an 'active' phase – a reference to the imposition of sanctions against South Africa and to the talks between Secretary of State Shultz and ANC President Tambo in early 1987. For the US, South Africa's continued apartheid policies and regional aggressiveness are apparently no major obstacles to the maintenance of a concept in which Pretoria as 'natural ally' (albeit of a pariah status) fits well into Washington's geo-political designs and globalist 'zero-sum-games'.

The attitude and perception appears to neglect the indirect *destructive* effects (both in South Africa and the region) which 'constructive' engagement with Pretoria has yielded. Only recently there has been an attempt by the US administration to increase its economic – and in special cases such as Botswana, military – support to selected Frontline states in the SADCC. It also seems to underrate both the structural weaknesses ('organic crisis') with the inherent dynamics of an 'objective revolutionary situation' of a highly militarised and economically still relatively strong South Africa and the importance of the question of the 'successor regime'.

If the foregoing analysis is correct then it is apartheid South Africa which, despite (or because of?) its military and economic muscles, is 'organically' weak, vulnerable, unstable, and as a result has a tendency for aggressive 'fits'. In the words of the Zimbabwean military historian Michael Evans,

> there is an inherent paradox in the strategic equation between South Africa and the Frontline States . . . South Africa is strong militarily and economically but she is weak ideologically, since 80 per cent of her population rejects apartheid. In contrast, the Frontline States are strong ideologically but are weak militarily and economically.[8]

In such circumstances can the republic play an important role in Western policies or should the Western powers look increasingly to South Africa's neighbours?

This chapter attempts to provide some answers to this question by looking at the People's Republic of Mozambique. As a point of departure I assume that the crisis this country has been facing in the last few years also qualifies as an 'organic' structural crisis with similar features to that of South Africa. The past years have seen the dramatic accumulation of inter-linked crises in the economic, security and political fields, which have almost overwhelmed it. The partially home-made economic crisis (drop in production, foreign and domestic trade, foreign exchange reserves, etc.) was interlinked to and aggravated by South Africa's undeclared war and the terrorist activities of the MNR, as well as the prolonged drought and other natural disasters. Interwoven in this pattern is a political crisis of legitimacy of the FRELIMO state, notably among the peasantry, which, after having actively supported the anti-colonial struggle, but deprived of the material gains which the 'new Mozambique' was able to offer, turned its back on the state and party.[9] According to government estimates, the quantifiable losses resulting from this accumulated crisis amount to at least $5.5 billion.[10] The political and economic cost of winning back the 'hearts and minds' especially of the rural population to FRELIMO and of integrating the 'nationalist faction' of the 'armed bandits' have yet to be evaluated.

With the assumption of a continuing 'organic' structural crisis both in South Africa and Mozambique I shall argue that the recent policy shifts both in South Africa and Mozambique are political responses to the respective crises. These responses, which have the Nkomati Accord of March 1984 as a common denominator are examined in some depth. In the case of Mozambique, the focus will be on the

present policy options of the FRELIMO Government, which can be
summarised as an attempt to realign internal and external relations
under conditions of war. With regard to South Africa, the Nkomati
Accord as part of the minority regime's Total National Strategy will be
examined, principally as it affects its relations with Mozambique.
Pretoria's relations with its other neighbours will be touched upon only
briefly.

One conclusion rather than a prediction drawn from the
examination of the 'organic crisis' and the respective responses is that –
under certain conditions – both countries may be witnessing the
beginning of the end: whereas in South Africa – according to some
government officials – the 'beginning of the revolutionary warfare' is
evident, in Mozambique 'things cannot get much worse' so that one
might be about to see the light at the 'end of the tunnel' of war,
hardship and hunger.

What are the ramifications of this analysis for Western policies
towards Southern Africa and towards Mozambique in particular?
With the use of two conflict scenarios it is suggested that the West
should attempt to meet the present policy option of Mozambique and,
indeed, of the Frontline States as a whole. This would include
increasing political, economic and military support and assistance. I
shall end by considering aspects of military cooperation with
Mozambique.

MOZAMBIQUE: THE OPTION OF EXTENDED REGIONALISM AND PARTIAL CAPITALIST TRANSFORMATION

I have argued elsewhere[11] that three foreign policy options can be
distinguished, which the FRELIMO government has pursued since
Mozambique's independence in 1975, without either having to
fundamentally alter its national principles and objectives or the
administrative structures and personnel involved in foreign-policy
making:[12]

— the period June 1975–January 1981 which saw an option for socialist
  transformation and integration into the Council of Mutual
  Economic Assistance (CMEA);
— the period January 1981–September 1982 which witnessed the
  'double track' option and 'opening to the West';

— the period from September 1982 onwards which saw the option of extended regionalism and partial capitalist transformation.

The switch from one option to the other can be linked analytically and empirically to the deepening 'organic crisis' which was partly a result of the colonial heritage, partly of the government's own making and partly caused by South Africa's undeclared war. This crisis had fundamental ramifications for Mozambique's social-political fabric as well as its economic performance and, with the spread of 'armed banditry', on the security situation, in some provinces more than others.

January 1981, the date of the transition from the first option to the second was marked by two key events: the 'crossing of the Matola Threshold' by South Africa,[13] i.e. the beginning of the intensification of its 'undeclared war' against Mozambique; and the decision at the CMEA meeting in Prague, not to admit the country as a new member.

September 1982, the date of the first high-level meeting between South African and Mozambican government officials during the period of 'undeclared war' at the – now historic – Inkomati River (at Komaatipoort) symbolised the beginning of a new policy which – inter alia – sought to redefine the relations with South Africa.

What are the major elements of this policy?

Although Mozambique's foreign policy has always had a very strong regional orientation, the latter nevertheless has been rather selective. While relations between Mozambique and South Africa, Swaziland and Malawi have been of a rather functional, pragmatic nature with little or no political links in common (except for SADCC with regard to Swaziland and Malawi), Zimbabwe, Tanzania and Zambia have been FRELIMO's 'natural allies' in the region with whom the party and government have a special affinity. Neither its excellent relations with these 'natural allies' however nor the existence of multilateral regional institutions such as SADCC and the FLS, in both of which Mozambique is a leading member, provided enough leverage to decisively counter if not eliminate the forces responsible for Mozambique's deepening economic and security crisis.

The first step in Mozambique's efforts at completing and realigning its regional relations was the signing of the Nkomati Accord with South Africa in March 1984.[14] The second, third and fourth steps respectively were the signing of a security pact with Swaziland in August 1984[15] and Cooperation Accord with Malawi in October of the same year,[16] and the security cooperation agreement (Lilongwe Treaty) with President Banda's Government in December 1986.

As regards the second element of Mozambique's present policy, i.e. partial capitalist transformation and membership of such international institutions as the International Monetary Fund (IMF) and the International Finance Corporation (IFC) one has to return briefly to Mozambique's participation in the regional and world economy during the two decades preceding its independence. As Babu observes by analysing what he calls the 'shameless spectacle' of the Nkomati Accord, pre-independence Mozambique was – as a colonial service economy – firmly incorporated into the economic orbit of South Africa and Portugal – both of which were structurally dependent semi-peripheries of the European and American economies.[17] This 'axis', together with the British settler colony Rhodesia sometimes referred to as 'ASPRO-alliance'[18] not only cooperated militarily in counter-insurgency operations but also used the instrument of regional economic integration in an attempt to establish economic bulwarks against the advancing liberation struggle in the Portuguese territories and later as an instrument to co-opt the nationalist movement by offering economic and social rewards for more moderate policies. In Mozambique, the Cabora–Bassa scheme exemplified such a 'dual purpose' project.[19]

Today, twenty years after the firing of the first shot in Mozambique's struggle for liberation, FRELIMO has chosen to opt for the partial revitalisation and reconstruction of those very structures and links (including those through South Africa and Portugal to the West) which, as a liberation movement, it once sought to destroy. Having analysed some of its earlier mistakes in trying to establish a centrally-planned economy and a socialist society based on the principle of democratic centralism, FRELIMO has obviously come to the conclusion, that the inherited socio-economic structures as well as the politico-economic environment (both internal and external) were not conducive for achieving these objectives. Apparently certain stages of dependent capitalist development (with its internal and external implications) cannot simply be by-passed on the path from underdevelopment to a socialist society, nor were there to be linear processes towards this end.

Hence, it has opted recently for extended regionalism and closer economic cooperation with South Africa, partial domestic capitalist transformation, participation in international capitalist institutions such as the International Monetary Fund, the World Bank and the

Lomé Convention, as well as more or less successful attempts at strengthening economic ties with South Africa, Portugal, the EEC countries and the US.

The realignment of external relations both at the regional and international level has been matched by a process of fundamental internal readjustment and change since September 1982. According to Joseph Hanlon, between 1981 and 1983 a rift occurred in the ruling alliance which was accompanied by a shift of economic and political power from the 'state group', the 'technocratic bureaucracy' and the 'workers' to the 'commercial group' or 'aspirants to the bourgeoisie'.[20] In this context it is important to note the conclusions of the IV FRELIMO Congress in April 1983, which, having analysed the failures of previous policies, opted for a strengthening of the peasant sector and a programme of decentralisation. Coupled with a new agricultural and investment policy, the late President Machel resolved to decentralise the decision-making process, as well as mobilise and arm the masses in the hope of 'winning the battle' for the hearts and minds of the peasants.[21] These steps were to be followed by IMF-inspired economic reforms, including a drastic devaluation of the local currency.[22]

Taking into account both the internal and external dimensions of the government's present policy, a preliminary evaluation of its successes would have to include the following observations:

1. The Nkomati Accord – despite the increase of MNR operations since its signing in March 1984 – has resulted in a deepened understanding of the nature of 'armed banditry' and the various external 'connections' of the MNR (South African, Portuguese, Arab Malawi etc.). This has enabled FRELIMO to conduct more appropriate counter-insurgency measures including the deployment of troops from Zimbabwe, Tanzania and Malawi.

2. With this Accord Maputo was able to prove – both before and after its signing – that South Africa had been one of the centres from where MNR destabilisation originated.[23] At the same time the Accord provided Mozambique with an instrument to exert pressure on Pretoria to honour the 'letter and spirit' of the treaty. The same is true for the cooperation accord with Malawi.

3. The present option has enhanced Mozambique's reputation as a country with firm principles (peaceful coexistence, good-neighbourliness, anti-apartheid stance, non-alignment, etc.), and pragmatic policies in the national interest. As a result the West has increasingly recognised Mozambique's potential role as a stabilising

force in the region, irrespective of its structural economic weaknesses. This in turn has resulted in an increased flow of resources and aid to the country, a case in point being the substantial assistance for the 'Beira-Corridor' Project.

4. Increased Western – and Eastern – economic assistance, the accession as a new member to the Lomé convention and the IMF (with a quota of some \$60 bn), the successful rescheduling of parts of its debt in 1985, the opening of new credit lines, etc., have widened Maputo's scope and manoeuvrability in economic and fiscal matters. This has aided the government in its austerity programme and contributed to the economic reforms which are presently underway. Despite its socialist orientation Mozambique's standing with the IMF has appreciated considerably. Officials of the IMF and of national investment corporations have guardedly expressed optimism that Mozambique's economic recovery programme is likely to work, provided the security situation can be improved. In April 1987 a deal with the IMF looked near, which was expected to result in a structural adjustment facility for Mozambique. This would release about US\$35 m on easy terms from the Fund and \$90 m from the World Bank, paving the way for more credits from bilateral donors and further rescheduling of the country's \$3.2 bn foreign debt.[24]

5. With regard to tackling the security crisis, the present policy options hold out some promise, too, despite continued MNR operations throughout the country, but especially north of the Zambezi, in Zambezia and Tete, bordering Malawi. In this context mention should be made of South Africa's somewhat haphazard affirmations that it will fully adhere to its obligations undertaken at Nkomati, namely to curb support for the MNR within the South African security forces, to undertake the strict surveillance of its borders and airspace with Mozambique, to protect the Cabora Bassa power lines and to establish a joint 'Nkomati Operational Centre'. This has to some extent led to a shift of military activity from the south (Maputo, Inhambane, Gaza provinces) to the north, where combined Mozambican, Zimbabwean and Tanzanian forces have recaptured strategic towns and areas north of the Zambezi from the MNR in an offensive in October/November 1986, successfully preventing the establishment of supply routes to the rebels from South Africa via the Indian Ocean.

The 1982 military cooperation agreement with Portugal has also been resuscitated. The proposed establishment of Portuguese-trained mobile counter-insurgency units ('*corpos de intervencao rapida*')[25] seems to have some chance of realisation, especially since the Reagan Administration has indicated its readiness to provide limited ('non-lethal') military assistance to Mozambique.

A major breakthrough for Mozambique, however, lies in the increasing military cooperation with Britain, which sponsors a military training programme for the Mozambican Army in eastern Zimbabwe as well as providing – through a private security company – logistical and other support for Mozambican units guarding the Nacala rail line to Malawi.

6. Finally, if one takes together the various components of the present policy, significant – yet unstable – progress seems to have been made in some of Mozambique's central and southern provinces, and notably in the Beira Corridor, straddling Manica and Sofala, where MNR activities have decreased markedly over the past few years.

The partial achievements of the present policy, however, are too few and fragile to allow extrapolation into the future. Especially in the economic field it remains to be seen whether an economic recovery can be instituted under conditions of war and whether the partial achievements can be consolidated, Mozambique's own resources mobilised and a – potentially food-surplus-producing – family subsistence economy successfully rehabilitated.[26] Further economic progress will require conditions of internal and external peace which is precisely why the major components of Mozambique's present policy are all inextricably linked: peace, good neighbourliness and cooperation with South Africa; increased military and diplomatic endeavours to eliminate the MNR including indirect contact with the movement (via South Africa) in the context of the 'Pretoria Declaration' of October 1984 and the co-option of its 'nationalist faction(s)' possibly through the offer of an amnesty; re-capitalisation of the economy by way of selective capitalist transformation and increased cooperation with the West. The key to success lies, for the time being, in the creation of militarily protected zones of production and distribution, where food, clothes, seeds and consumer goods can be distributed to the peasants in order to meet their basic needs and to stimulate agricultural production; and where, at the same time, investment, development and infrastructural projects and large-scale agriculture can flourish.

Before considering the question of the consolidation of the present process we need to look first at the 'organic crisis' in South Africa and some of its major ramifications.

SOUTH AFRICA'S 'TOTAL NATIONAL STRATEGY' AND THE NKOMATI ACCORD

The study by Saul and Gelb suggested that South Africa's 'organic crisis' and its attempts to manage and/or solve it had led inter alia to a realignment of forces. In the last few years it has become obvious that the proponents of a 'modernised apartheid capitalism' or the 'reform strategy', including the industrial and commercial (Afrikaner and non-Afrikaner) capital and the technocratic/bureaucratic wing of Afrikanerdom, have moved closer to Botha's National Party (NP), leaving in the wings a politically unimportant liberal party (Progressive Federal Party) and NP dissidents on the 'left' and the Conservative Party (CP) of Andries Treuernicht, also a NP dissident, on the 'right'.

Davis and O'Meara, taking this analysis a step further, suggest that the state's response to the organic crisis was the TNS which was designed to safeguard the survival of both apartheid and capitalism and, at the same time, adapt to modern conditions.[27] The major inter-dependent objectives of the TNS can be summarised as follows. Preservation of white minority rule and capitalism; full implementation of the policy of 'Grand Apartheid' (separate development) the creation of 'independent' Bantustans coupled with the de-nationalisation of Blacks; and finally the fostering of regional economic and military dominance. While those objectives are not at all new, the instruments for their achievement have been made more flexible. The TNS prescribes a 'carrot' and 'stick' approach with regard to both domestic and regional affairs.

Inside South Africa, the 'stick' is represented by ever-increasing repression, the continued policy of forced removals and the de-nationalisation of Black South Africans, continued oppression and intimidation of opposition movement and its leaders. The 'carrot' can be seen in a 'liberalised' labour dispensation, a new 'political dispensation' (allowing the Indians and Coloured communities constitutional 'reform'), the scrapping of certain apartheid laws (e.g. Mixed Marriages Act) and even an offer to talk to the ANC provided the movement renounces violence.

With regard to regional relations, it has been suggested by many authors[28] that the Nkomati Accord has been a conclusive success for the 'stick-approach' in regional affairs. The three inter-linked regional objectives of the TNS in regard to Mozambique can be summarised as (a) denial of operational, logistical and other support and facilities for the ANC (and the erection of a military *cordon sanitaire*) (b) the

institutionalisation of a South African dominated 'Constellation of
Southern African States' (CONSAS) and (c) the undermining of
alternative regional schemes such as SADCC especially through
attacks on its transport infrastructure. This judgement can be said to
have been partially achieved. The undeclared war ('stick') and support
for the MNR by South Africa and the subsequent signing of the
Nkomati agreement have led to an anti-subversion agreement with
Mozambique which had been a long-standing South African aim. At
the time of its signing, the Nkomati Accord had – in principle at least –
opened up desperately needed new possibilities also for South African
farmers, manufacturers, exporters and investors, who had been hit by
the worst economic crisis in decades, exacerbated by a prolonged
drought. The Accord therefore satisfied the interests of capitalist
factions of the ruling class-alliance, too. Hence, the Nkomati Accord
as an expression of both the 'organic crisis' and the TNS was a kind of
security valve which enabled the regime to partially escape from some
of the pressures generated by the crisis.[29] It marked on the one hand
the (preliminary) end of the policy of coercion and South Africa's
diplomatic isolation as well as the possibility of a new beginning of
greater cooperation between the republic and its neighbours; on the
other a re-affirmation of neo-apartheid. Only by understanding the
multi-functional nature of the Nkomati Accord can one explain the
satisfaction of the military and public enthusiasm as well as the
rocketing of stock market notations with which the Nkomati
agreement was greeted within South African business and *verligte
Afrikaner* circles. From their respective perspectives Nkomati marked
exactly the point, where for tactical reasons, the 'stick' against
Mozambique could be replaced by the 'carrot' without either
renouncing the 'stick' or the country's traditional objectives.[30]

Despite its short-term success, however, it remained doubtful from
the very beginning whether the Nkomati Accord would be able to yield
high returns for the ruling class-alliance in South Africa or whether the
TNS would continue to offer a useful political strategy for achieving its
stated objectives.

From the observation, that the principles of rationality and
negotiations – both scarce commodities in Afrikanerdom – prevailed at
Nkomati it could not necessarily be concluded, however, that the same
principles would continue to be applied in South Africa's dealings with
its neighbours – or with its own Black Majority. In fact, destabilisation
by proxy, i.e. in the case of Mozambique by the MNR was too efficient
an instrument for South Africa's military strategists to abandon

completely. There is evidence that South Africa has continued to re-supply the MNR since March 1984, although its strikes have lately been performed from bases in Malawi. Equally, the coercive 'stick' has again been wielded at Maputo, namely in the weeks preceding the crash of the presidential Tupolev 122, in which *inter alia* Pretoria announced the repatriation of some 60 000 migrant workers from Southern Mozambique. Shortly after the signing of the Nkomati Accord, it had been suggested by a number of observers including ex-President Nyerere of Tanzania that the more the struggle inside South Africa intensifies and the more the repressive features of white rule in South Africa fail to be managed by selective 'reforms', the more likely the conflict will again become externalised – despite 'non-aggression' agreements with its neighbours. Nyerere's prediction has since become true.

Thus, an assessment of the net-balance of the Nkomati Accord three years after its signing would suggest that it has only partially achieved South Africa's strategic and economic objectives. Its primary objective, the expulsion of ANC militants from Mozambique and the cutting of infiltration routes has been achieved. But the expected decrease in armed activities of ANC combatants inside South Africa has not materialised. In fact, official South African sources noted an increase of such activities in the years after Nkomati as compacted to the same period the previous year. Nor has the envisaged economic cooperation with Mozambique materialised despite the broad range of bi-lateral agreements which have been signed in the wake of Nkomati. Even the Casbora–Bassa power supplies could not be resumed.

Finally, the Nkomati Accord has contributed to an increased internalisation and sharpening of the conflict, while at the same time, at least politically, it has deprived Pretoria – in the months after Nkomati – of the option of externalising the conflict again. Nkomati had become a point of reference for Western policy towards Southern Africa. In other words, the 'stick' formerly used against Mozambique was being increasingly applied at home and the threshold which Pretoria had to cross in order to reapply the 'stick' again had voluntarily been increased by signing a non-aggression agreement with Mozambique.[31] It even can be argued that the Nkomati Accord has had a direct bearing on the intensification of the liberation struggle inside South Africa in that it has forced the ANC and other organisations of the liberation movement, such as the United Democratic Front (UDF) to readjust their strategy and tactics, with a new emphasis on coordinated internal mass mobilisation and struggle.[32] It is not accidental that the post-Nkomati era has seen the most widespread and effective 'unrest' in South Africa's history as well as the first 'consultative' conference of the ANC in more than 15 years.[33] This is, of course, related to the fact that the Nkomati Accord, although initially a 'bitter pill' for the liberation movement, has, in an analogy with medicine, strengthened its resistance, both spiritually and physically. After Nkomati, the degree of coordinated action has been much higher and more effective than in previous campaigns. Most analysts agree, that mass actions such as strikes, consumer boycotts, students boycotts, sabotage and stay-aways coupled with the most serious economic crisis in half a century and mounting international pressure (e.g. disinvestment, sanctions) have combined to create a potentially explosive situation, the worst in recent history.[34] Highly organised and coordinated actions by Black organisations have led some South African government officials to suggest, that South Africa is 'at the beginning of (a period of) revolutionary warfare'.[35]

With the vicious circles of violence and oppression and the 'organic crisis' remaining the most important feature of contemporary South Africa what is the future for the Nkomati Accord? What are the chances of peace in Mozambique? What will this country's external relations look like in the future and will its recent policy shifts be irreversible? Or will, as Hanlon suggests, the Mozambican Revolution 'still come under fire'[36] even if the shooting were to stop and peace and stability return? I shall attempt to answer these questions with the following conflict scenarios.

TWO CONFLICT SCENARIOS

Optimistic scenario

Given the on-going MNR campaign in Mozambique as well as the unresolved problem of apartheid in South Africa and the denial of independence of Namibia, regional instability and violence will continue to be an important parameter of FRELIMO policy making, even if, in the long run, the 'rescue operations' for the Nkomati Accord yield positive results. This would still be the case were Mozambique's endeavours to eliminate the MNR either militarily and/or politically (by amnesty and re-integration) to be supported by corresponding initiatives by the West (both with regard to increased assistance to Mozambique and pressure on South Africa, the MNR and its leaders).

Under the assumption that (a) the 'spirit of Nkomati' can be kept alive and the MNR neutralised and (b) Western initiatives do not interfere with FRELIMO objectives of non-alignment Maputo might be able to resolve the security and economic crisis and build a structurally more balanced, more liberal mixed economy, even in the medium term at the cost of a higher degree of dependence on South Africa. A more stable Mozambique would equally affect SADCC as well as South Africa – the latter, however, in economic terms only. Under conditions of partial stability Mozambique's foreign policy would continue to look both east and west, thus being one of 'straddling' as it would involve the participation in 'projects' of an inherently antagonistic nature (SADCC and FLS vs. bi-lateral projects with South Africa; possibly military aid from both Superpowers). Given the recent policy shifts the 'policy of straddling' would certainly involve a strong and increasing bias towards the West. It would, however, neither exclude increasing economic cooperation with CMEA-countries nor – largely symbolic perhaps – political statements in favour of the 'socialist community' (such as the diplomatic recognition of the regime in Afghanistan). Such cooperation and statements are necessary to counter-balance Mozambique's economic and diplomatic bias to the West and to emphasise its commitment to non-alignment. In the process the role of the socialist community for Mozambique would shift from that of 'natural ally' to a 'historical ally' (Schoeller). Thus, despite a policy of 'straddling' Mozambique would be able to strengthen its economic and political self-reliance, or non-alignment thereby helping it to make a significant contribution to regional security and economic development.

Pessimistic scenario

This is based on the assumption that the MNR will continue to receive aid from its backers in South Africa, Portugal and elsewhere to 'recolonise' Mozambique either by forcing a 'coalition' government upon FRELIMO or toppling the regime altogether.[37] Continued and possibly increasing MNR activities would not only accelerate the economic and political paralysis of Mozambique, but would equally jeopardise and even halt all foreign assistance, including aid from South Africa. This already severely damaged economic base of the country would be completely destroyed, since one can expect FRELIMO to defend Mozambique's hard-won independence by every means in its power. To defeat the MNR militarily and avoid a 'coalition' government FRELIMO in a last resort and against its own outspoken will might be forced to invoke the treaties of friendship and cooperation with the USSR and Cuba and request military assistance, including the deployment of combat troops. In the absence of sufficient hard cash FRELIMO would have to pay for such assistance by providing military bases to the Warsaw Pact. Even if the latter could be avoided, South Africa and the United States would not tolerate this 'internationalisation' of the conflict. At worst, a Superpower confrontation, at best an Angola-type of stalemate situation would ensue. In case the FRELIMO regime were completely replaced by an MNR regime, the latter would have to be kept in power by its backers. With 20 years of experience in armed struggle FRELIMO would certainly go underground and conduct a guerilla war, presumably supported by the large majority of the Mozambican people, the Frontline States (Tanzania, Zambia, Zimbabwe) the South African liberation movements and of course the Soviet Bloc. Needless to say any over-escalation could only adversely affect South Africa.[38] Any success for the proponents of a re-colonisation strategy would represent only pyrrhic victory at best.

Many analysts tend to subscribe to a pessimistic rather than optimistic view about the future of Southern Africa.[39] What foreign policy will evolve therefore in Mozambique in future is not only a function of the power struggle in Mozambique and of the continuity of the present regime and its set of national objectives, but also a question of the dynamism of the struggle for liberation in South Africa. In these circumstances what should the West's policy be?

In my view the West has in principle the following four options:

(1) *Support for the* status quo *or 'constructive fence-sitting'.*

This option of doing nothing would boil down to the tacit support for President Botha's position of non-negotiation with the organisations of the black majority (ANC, UDF etc.) and his destabilisation policies in the region. This would be quite unrealistic, since the West has already committed itself to the principle of negotiations for 'peaceful change' and the release of Nelson Mandela as well as to the support for SADCC, the real and potential victim of South African destabilisation.

(2) *Comprehensive support for SADCC.*

This option, although highly desirable from a development perspective, is equally unrealistic because it does not take into

account the regional core-problem, namely the crisis in South
Africa.
(3) *Comprehensive mandatory sanctions against South Africa.*
    This option would focus on the core problem, but would
certainly have serious repercussions for some of the SADCC-
states.[40] It is also unrealistic, because the Western members of the
Security Council are unlikely in the forseeable future to vote for
and implement such an option.
(4) *Mix of options (2) and (3).*
    Under the present circumstances, and given the post-Nkomati
experience, I assume that the West's most likely policy towards
Southern Africa will be a mix of elements of both (2) and (3) under
the motto: increasing sanctions and increasing support for
SADCC.

What could scenario (4) mean for Mozambique? What Western
policies are specifically required for this country?

WHAT ROLE FOR THE WEST? THE ARGUMENT FOR A WESTERN 'MOZAMBIQUE OPTION'

The Nkomati Accord, whatever its future, has undoubtedly opened
up a new chapter in the relations between Mozambique and South
Africa, which together with the Lusaka Accord between Angola and
South Africa marked something of a breakthrough in diplomatic
negotiations after years of stalemate. The new initiatives were
welcomed by the West, notably the United States (which assisted
diplomatically) and the countries of the EEC (which sent messages of
approval). The signatories of both the Nkomati Accord and the
Lusaka Agreement (between Angola and South Africa in February
1984) struck a theme for which the West have been calling for some
time: peaceful change, negotiations instead of violence, a constructive
relationship, mutual interests, etc. Merely on those grounds the West
must have vested interest in the maintenance of the momentum, which
both agreements have generated. As far as Mozambique is concerned,
the country has, for the first time since independence chosen to pursue
a policy linking internal capitalist transformation of key economic
sectors with a realignment of its international relations (closer
cooperation with the West) and a similar realignment of its regional
relations (closer cooperation with South Africa and Malawi), without

abandoning its overall principles (anti-racism, anti-colonialism, good neighbourliness, non-alignment etc.) and its political priorities (national reconstruction and reconciliation, regional cooperation). But because of its own weaknesses as an underdeveloped, structurally deficient country and its vulnerability vis-a-vis South African destabilisation, Mozambique will remain dependent on support and assistance from the West. This is likely to be so not only because of the logic of Mozambique's present policy but also because the country itself has proved somewhat painfully that the 'socialist option' did not work.

The success of Mozambique's present policy of national as well as regional *détente*, peace and reconstruction therefore depends to a very large degree on whether or not the West will design and pursue a 'Mozambique option',[41] which would complement its policy of 'active constructive engagement' (US) and of 'critical dialogue' (EEC) with South Africa which includes and will continue to include elements of coercion, unless Pretoria meets the conditions stipulated by the sanctions legislation of Western countries.

At the core of the Western 'Mozambique option' could be a special assistance programme, a support and aid package with an emphasis on economic and political cooperation. This package might include the following components:

— large-scale emergency food aid ('Operation Hunger'), supplies of medical items and clothes for some 6 million Mozambicans at risk. This project has been started in May 1987 following Mozambique's appeal for international assistance to combat the consequences of drought and armed banditry;
— a special support programme for the hundreds of thousands of Mozambican refugees in Zimbabwe, Malawi and Zambia;
— contingency employment and integration programmes for Mozambican migrant labourers who have already fallen or may fall victim to South Africa's repatriation plans;
— a special support programme for the rehabilitation and extension of Mozambique's railways and harbours, which are of strategic importance to the SADCC as a whole. Concerning the procurement of funds and the implementation of projects, significant progress has been made on the Beira and Nacala Corridors, where Western donors are the major cooperation partners. Can these projects be extended to include the Maputo Corridor, as well as the Chicualacuala (Limpopo) Line?

— development assistance programmes dovetailed to Mozambique's economic reform programme and aimed at boosting agricultural production (both for the domestic and world market);
— budget and balance of payments support; remission of debts, supportive investment policies.

Given the pessimistic evaluation of developments in Southern Africa, such a package would have to be qualified as a 'high risk' option. It could be argued, however, that 'a prudent foreign policy must be willing in certain situations to implement stabilisation programmes even in endangered regions, i.e. even at great risk'.[42] I would further contend that the suggested support and aid package would significantly increase intra-state as well as inter-state (regional) stability.

In the medium term, the success of such a stabilisation programme will hinge on the accomplishment of three inter-related security conditions, the first two being of a short and medium term nature, the third of a long term:

(a) ending of armed banditry and the restoration of peace;
(b) ending of external support for the MNR either from South Africa or other 'connections';
(c) the prevention of any resumption of South African aggression against Mozambique.

Precisely because security remains the area of highest priority in Mozambique and its importance as a condition for the success or failure of a western economic stabilisation programme, a security component as part of a cooperation package is really mandatory. The following section includes some observations on the possible scope of such cooperation.

Elements and conditions of western security cooperation with Mozambique

It is certainly debatable whether Mozambique can be considered a 'small state' according to the criteria advanced by Jonathan Alford in a recent article.[43] But there can be no doubt that Alford's observations and conclusions bear some relevance to the security situation in Mozambique, even if his rather general observations differ from the specific situation with regard to the clear-cut distinction between internal and external threat. The MNR, from its very outset, has always included an internal as well as an external wing, irrespective of conflicts within and between these wings.[44]

Despite the blurred dividing lines between the various components of the movement and its backers I shall maintain the distinction: internal/external for reasons of analysis.

What elements could or should western security assistance to Mozambique consist of in the short and respectively long term?

Short-term crisis assistance

In the short term the elimination of MNR activities by military means will depend on the efficacy of the countermeasures, which are jointly executed by the Mozambican Army and its Zimbabwean and Tanzanian allies. The better its organisation and mobility, its supplies and logistical back-up, its motivation and morale, the higher will be the chance of successfully pre-empting or countering MNR operations. Hence, all measures which increase the efficiency of the army, the Popular Mozambican Liberation Forces (FPLM), such as the supply of military and non-military items (light arms, ammunition, vehicles, helicopters, communication equipment, spare parts, food, fuel, etc.) would help to improve its performance.[45] There are indications that programmes along these lines are being considered in Washington and other Western capitals. The same is true for the setting-up of highly mobile counter insurgency units, assistance for which is being negotiated with Portugal and Britain.

In the non-military field of internal security, western nations could play an important role in financing and supplying the reintegration camps, which Maputo would like to establish for those 'bandidos armados' who respond to FRELIMO's amnesty offer. The Federal Republic of Germany has already expressed an interest in such projects.

The deployment of a peacekeeping or policing force (or elements thereof), considered by Alford as a useful component of crisis assistance, would – in present circumstances – neither be advisable nor be welcomed by Mozambique's government. President Chissano recently pointed out that the war in Mozambique was one 'without battle lines', making it extremely difficult to deploy conventional forces. However, if an armistice between the MNR and FPLM were to be worked out as envisaged by the 'Pretoria Declaration' of 4 October 1984, limited participation in and support for a monitoring force might be both useful and welcome.

One important way of indirectly assisting Mozambique in the field of defence would be to increase Western military cooperation with other Frontline states, taking into account that 'all of the Frontline States are cooperating with us [in defence matters], but to varying degrees of course'.[46] Apart from their specific support for Mozambique, there are three areas in which the Frontline states' efforts to coordinate their defence activities could be supported externally: military intelligence, military staff exchange and joint defence procurement and weapons systems studies.[47]

With regard to the curbing of the external support for the MNR the United States and Europe cannot offer much in military terms. They might be able to exchange intelligence information with Maputo concerning MNR activities and supply lines outside Mozambique. But their major contribution to an isolation of the external MNR wings could be in the field of diplomacy – for example in their own relations with Pretoria, Lisbon and some of the Arab states (e.g. Oman, Comoros) – even in those capitals of Western Europe where the MNR has its backers.

Given the assumption that western security assistance might play a significant role in the containment of MNR activities and the easing of the security crisis in Mozambique, there is a fair chance that events might move from the pessimistic to the optimistic scenario. How could western security assistance in the long run contribute to the stabilisation of conditions of peace and to a climate of national reintegration and reconstruction? How could a fragile peace be preserved and extended by means of military assistance?

Long-term non-crisis assistance

For this purpose a delicate balance would need to be struck between Mozambique's need to deter a South African incursion on the one hand and to be able to conduct a proper counter-guerilla strategy on the other.[48] With regard to the internal aspect, Alford's exemplary breakdown of an assistance programme[49] could be useful for Mozambique, too:

— training security forces (on governmental or non-governmental basis);
— providing of arms and specific technical training in their use and maintenance;
— managing, surveying and protecting important economic zones and installations;

— information and intelligence gathering and processing, relevant for regime security;
— contingency planning.

It is remarkable that so far Britain is the only Western country which appears to have systematically pursued a security cooperation strategy with Mozambique which takes account of these long-term objectives. According to President Chissano, Britain has realised 'that the country's own interests [in the region] lie in helping Mozambique defend itself from foreign threats, even if they come from armed bandits'.[50] Without doubt, herein lies one of the major reasons for the excellent bilateral relations which exist, despite – or because of? – Margaret Thatcher's strong anti-sanctions stance.

With regard to external forces of destabilisation and insecurity, the West must not allow itself to be used by organisations such as the MNR which claim to be 'pro-Western', and act in the West's interest, but serve the opposite purpose. A long-term security perspective with regard to Mozambique must entail ending future prevention of any kind of support (financial, political and otherwise) to the MNR. At the same time, South Africa must continually be monitored to check its policy of direct and indirect destabilisation. An enforced arms embargo and the implementation of economic sanctions were South Africa to violate the principles of the Nkomati Accord might serve this purpose.

Ramifications for Mozambique's relations with the Warsaw Pact

How would significantly increased economic and military cooperation between NATO countries and the People's Republic of Mozambique affect the latter's relations with the Soviet Union and the other countries of the Warsaw Pact?

My hypothesis is that the relative importance of the Warsaw Pact as hitherto major arms supplier and military cooperation partner would decline, provided the Warsaw Pact would not react to an increased cooperation with Western suppliers by offering adequate, military equipment, appropriate to Mozambique's security needs at comparatively cheap (dumping) prices taking advantage of the country's foreign exchange shortage. In the past this was not the case: neither was Maputo treated as a preferential customer, nor did it receive the (sophisticated) hardware it needed (see below). On the other hand, the West is unlikely to completely replace the Warsaw Pact as a major source of arms however cheap and favourable their conditions of supply would be. If it did, this would run counter to the Government's professed objective of 'reducing old dependencies while avoiding new ones'.

In other words, while Maputo is interested in acquiring appropriate military equipment and training (especially for anti-MNR operations) at an economically favourable as well as politically agreeable cost, it does not wish to translate its military dependency on the East into dependency on the West. Thus, as far as military cooperation is concerned, Maputo is bound to continue to diversify its relations in a manner similar to India, albeit on a much lower (quantitative and qualitative) level. A look at Mozambique's past options underlines this point.

Under the 'socialist option' Mozambique strengthened military relations with CMEA countries with the dual objective of safeguarding the Mozambican revolution against (external) imperialist aggression (namely South Africa and Rhodesia) and (internal) counter-revolution. To these ends the treaties of friendship and cooperation with the Soviet Union and Cuba, including stipulations concerning security cooperation. These were supplemented by military cooperation programmes, specific protocols and agreements. In effect, these programmes extended the military cooperation which had existed before independence, when first China, and later Cuba, the Soviet Union and Eastern Europe had become FRELIMO's primary suppliers of arms. However, the quantity and quality of FRELIMO's arms procurement changed significantly after independence. The transformation of the ancient FRELIMO guerrillas into a permanent 'Peoples Liberation Army' of conscripts (FPLM), the defence against anti-insurgency operation (e.g. air raids, commando attacks) by the Rhodesian Army on Mozambican territory as well as the conventional threat posed by a highly militarised South Africa obviously required a heavy emphasis on military hardware: air reconnaissance and defence equipment; fighter aircraft, transport planes and helicopters; troop carriers. This period saw the introduction of the 'Warsaw Pact rule book' at the FPLM military academy at Nampula, coupled with the secondment of Soviet and Cuban military advisers and instructors provided the corresponding 'software', replacing the former FRELIMO guerilla warfare doctrine.

However, in the early 1980s it became apparent that military cooperation with the socialist states had not lived up to mutual expectations. Mozambique consistently refused to provide naval and other military bases to the Soviet Union which obviously it would have liked to obtain in exchange for preferential treatment of Mozambique with regard to arms sales. As a consequence, Mozambique's military 'shopping list' was not satisfied by Soviet supplies and it was reported that Mozambican leaders complained about the delivery of outdated and inappropriate weaponry by their 'natural allies'.[51] After all, the latter considered military assistance primarily as a commercial transaction to be paid for in foreign exchange, thus adding a further strain on Mozambique's deteriorating balance of payments.

Also in 1981 it became apparent that the quality of both the military 'hard-' and 'software' provided by the Eastern Bloc was inadequate to defend the country against a new phase of MNR operations. In terms of hardware, Mozambique particularly lacked helicopters, highly effective in anti-guerrilla operations in the bush. With regard to software, the 'Warsaw Pact rule book' proved so inadequate for the conduct of such operations, the FRELIMO had to revitalise the virtues of its guerrilla struggle, namely popular vigilance, people's militia, decentralised operations, etc. Also in 1981, extensive abuse of power and violations of the constitution became known, notably in the security apparatus. This caused President Machel to announce in November 1981 a legal 'offensive' which was directed against the security forces, and by implication was critical of the 'natural allies', their major suppliers, instructors and advisers.

Taken together, these measures led to a policy of diversification of military and security cooperation as part and parcel of FRELIMO's 'double track option' in the period 1981–2. In the wake of the visit of Portugal's president, Eanes, (November 1981), the Peoples Republic of Mozambique signed an agreement with NATO member Portugal in April 1982 in the field of military cooperation.[52] Whether prompted or not by the agreement with Portugal, the Soviet Union availed itself to upgrade substantially its arms sales to Maputo, both quantitatively and qualitatively. An agreement to this effect was entered into in May 1982.[53] But this did not stop Maputo from continuing its diversification policy. A number of protocols and agreements with African and other non-aligned countries were signed (e.g. Libya, Yugoslavia, North Korea) and Zimbabwean troops were deployed on Mozambican territory for the protection of the Beira–Mutare transport corridor. And in 1983, during Samora Machel's visit to Western Europe, security issues and potential military cooperation featured prominently in his talks with Margaret Thatcher and François

Mitterrand. In the same year it was even reported that the United States had been approached with a request for economic and military assistance.[54]

With regard to military assistance the rationale behind FRELIMO's 'opening to NATO' is obvious. On the one hand, South Africa's direct and indirect aggression required increased and more appropriate defence capabilities, both in terms of hardware (e.g. helicopters) and anti-guerilla strategies. In both regards, the military assistance rendered by the Warsaw Pact appeared to be inadequate. Machel's meeting Andropov in Moscow in March 1983 apparently did not result in a new commitment by the Soviet Union to increase the supply of military hardware.[55] Thus, the turn to Portugal and Britain, with their decade-long African experiences in counter-insurgency operations, for training and logistical assistance, and to France as a potential supplier of helicopters was not an unrealistic choice. At the same time, Maputo sought a stronger commitment by the West to pressurise South Africa into renouncing its aggressive regional policy. To this end, Maputo made it known that it was only willing to increase its demand for Eastern Bloc, and possibly Cuban, assistance (and possibly in the absence of enough foreign exchange to meet the cost to accept the provision of military bases of some sort to the USSR as part of the remuneration for such assistance), 'if international measures are not taken to stop Pretoria from escalating its aggression'.[56] As pointed out in the pessimistic scenario above, this outcome still cannot be ruled out.

CONCLUSION

How can the cost for a Western military assistance programme to Mozambique be met, given the lack of foreign exchange in Mozambique on the one hand, and the commercial interests of the arms suppliers on the other?

Increased overall assistance to Mozambique could provide the answer if one takes Alford's contention into account that security assistance, if sought by a legitimate regime is 'just as much part of developing assistance as is aid and trade'.[57] There can be no doubt whatever that historically, legally and politically FRELIMO is the legitimate government of Mozambique and that military assistance would be highly appropriate and welcome in the present circumstances. On the other hand, it is equally clear that military assistance is of highest priority in the short term only. In the long term, a switch in emphasis from military to economic assistance is absolutely necessary. Like the 'Zimbabwe Conference on Reconstruction and Development' (ZIMCORD) an internationally sponsored 'Mozambique Conference on Reconstruction and Development' (MOCORD) could mark the turning point from a situation of war and underdevelopment to an era of peaceful transformation and development. In the final analysis the economic and social welfare of the entire population; national integration and reconciliation; and increased regional economic cooperation are better guarantors of internal as well as regional peace and stability than weapons and soldiers.

Whatever 'high risk' option western security assistance to Mozambique might be in the short term, it might, if complemented and followed up by economic assistance, become a valuable and powerful contribution to, and investment in, a peaceful Southern Africa.

Notes and References

CHAPTER 1   EAST OF SUEZ REVISITED: THE
STRATEGIC RECOUPLING OF WESTERN EUROPE
AND THE THIRD WORLD

1. Cited Christopher Mayhew, *Britain's Role Tomorrow* (London: Hutchinson, 1967) p. 19.
2. See Anthony Clayton, 'The military relations between Britain and the Commonwealth countries', in W. H. Morris-Jones, *Decolonisation and After: the British and French Experience* (London: Frank Cass, 1980) pp. 193–224.
3. Andrew Schonfield, *Europe: journey to an unknown destination* (London: Penguin, 1974) p. 44.
4. Cited Brian Urquhart, *Hammarskjöld* (London: 1973) p 397.
5. Michael Howard, *Studies in war and peace* (London: 1970) p. 124.
6. For the latter see Robert Elsworth, 'New imperatives for the old Alliance', *Atlantic Community Quarterly* 16:4, Winter 1978–9, pp. 421–2.
7. Lawrence Martin, 'British defence policy: the long recessional', *Adelphi Paper* 61 (IISS: 1969).
8. *Department of State Bulletin*, 22 June 1950, pp. 999–1002.
9. Lecture delivered to the Institut des Hauts Etudes de Defense Nationale, 25 June 1970, reprinted *Revue de Defense Nationale*, August–September 1970, pp. 1245–58.
10. *Africa Confidential* 3:20, 1972.
11. *Le Monde*, 4 June 1976.
12. Herman Fransell, 'Patterns of change in OECD: energy developments and their implications for the world oil market', *Middle East Economic Survey*, 6 April 1984.
13. Shahram Chubin, 'Oil and the Persian Gulf: a continuing problem', *Atlantic Quarterly* 2:4, Winter 1984, p. 322.
14. Although the sale did not go ahead the new guidelines introduced in May 1982 abandoned the negative constraint of 'areas of tension' in favour of the positive incentive of a 'vital security interest'.
15. *Le Monde*, 14 February 1984.
16. John K. Galbraith, *The Age of Uncertainty* (Boston: 1977) pp. 77, 225.
17. Oden Aburdene, 'Falling oil prices and the world economy', *American-Arab Affairs*, No. 4 (Spring 1983) pp. 46–53.
18. Cited Anthony Cordesman, *The Gulf and the search for strategic stability* (New York: Westview, 1984) p. 25.
19. Cited Françoise de la Serre 'France: A penchant for leadership', in

Christopher Hill (ed.), *National Foreign Policies and European political co-operation* (London: Allen and Unwin, 1983) p. 68.

20. *Le Monde*, 26 December 1983.
21. *Guardian*, 9 April 1984.
22. See Ali Mazrui, 'Third World security: a cultural perspective', *International Affairs*, Winter 1980–81, pp. 1–21.
23. Cited Nicholas Bethell, *The Palestine Triangle: the struggle between the British, the Jews and the Arabs 1935–48* (London: 1979) p. 358.
24. Gerard Chaliand, *The Struggle for Africa* (London: Macmillan, 1982) p. 16.
25. Paul Johnson, *A History of the Modern World from 1917 to the 1980s* (London: Weidenfeld and Nicolson, 1983) p. 543.
26. Cited Elenga M'buyinga, *Pan Africanism or Neo-colonialism* (London: Zed Press, 1982).
27. Patrick Marnham, *Fantastic Invasion: dispatches from contemporary Africa* (London: Jonathan Cape, 1980) p. 196.
28. See Christopher Coker, 'L'Afrique du Sud et l'Afrique australe', *Politique Etrangere*, 2/84 (1984) p. 294.
29. Ibid.
30. Cited Yanis Valinakis, 'Italian security concerns and policy', *International Spectator*, April– June 1984, p. 111.
31. *Guardian*, 21 January 1978.
32. Cited Ali Mazrui, *The African condition: a political diagnosis* (London: Heinemann, 1980) p. x.
33. Charles Hernu, 'Repondre aux defis d'un monde dangereux', *Defense Nationale*, December 1981, p. 9.
34. Charles Hernu, 'Securité internationale et development, La France et l'Afrique', *Revue des Deux Mondes*, August 1982, p. 265.
35. John Hargreaves, 'The Berlin West Africa Conference: a timely centenary', *History Today*, 34:11, November 1984, pp. 21–2. In creating a specifically European free trade regime for Africa, Lome, like the Yaounde convention before it, actually comes near in conception to a memorandum drafted by the British Colonial Office in 1918 which had called for more open economic access, the continent's military neutrality (in today's diplomatic vernacular – its non-alignment) and 'fair treatment' of the Africans' objectives which the paper vouchsafed could best be served by extending the Berlin Act from the Congo basin to the whole of sub-Saharan Africa north of the Zambezi.
36. *Africa Now*, March 1982.
37. Cited James Wyllie, *The influence of British arms* (London: Allen and Unwin, 1984) pp. 105–6.
38. Cited Luigi Caligaris, 'Italian defence policy: problems and prospects', *Survival*, March/April 1983, p. 70.
39. Cited Valinakis, 'Italian security concerns', *op. cit.*, p. 111.
40. *The Times*, 23 November 1984.
41. Gianni Bonvicini, 'Italy: an integrationist perspective', in Hill, *National Foreign Policies*, p. 80.
42. *Africa 78*, February 1978.
43. *International Herald Tribune*, 6 July 1978.

44. F. Otto de Miksche, 'La securité de l'Europe Occidentale', *Defense Nationale*, February 1981.
45. *Le Monde*, 2 November 1982.
46. de Miksche, 'La securité de l'Europe'.
47. Paul Gallis, 'The NATO allies, Japan and the Persian Gulf', *Congressional Research Service*, 37 (1984).
48. See David Yost, 'French policy in Chad and the Libyan challenge', *Orbis* 26:4 Winter 1983, p. 980.
49. Dominique Moisi, 'Europe and the United States: the Middle East conundrum', *Atlantic Quarterly* 2:2, Summer 1984, p. 163.
50. *The Times*, 29 March 1984.
51. Moisi, 'Europe and the United States', p. 169.
52. *The Times*, 20 August 1983.
53. James Goldsborough, 'Dateline Paris: Africa's policeman', *Foreign Policy*, Winter 1978/9, pp. 174–90.
54. Bruce Palmer, 'US security interests in Africa South of the Sahara', *American Enterprise Institute Defense Review* 2:6, 1978, pp. 39–40.
55. *Operation MANTA: Tchad 1983–4* by 'Colonel Spartacus' (Paris: Plon, 1985).
56. *Africa 83* (July 1978).
57. *Le Monde*, 2 November 1982. For a discussion of Britain's imperial re-entry in 1939, see John Gallagher, *The decline, revival and fall of the British Empire* (Cambridge University Press, 1982) pp. 136–7.
58. General Report on Alliance Security issues (North Atlantic Assembly Military Committee 1980) x 200 MC(80) 8 para 13.

CHAPTER 2   THE UNITED STATES, BRITAIN AND OUT-OF-AREA PROBLEMS

1. P. Darby, 'East of Suez Reassessed' in J. Baylis (ed.), *British Defence Policy in a Changing World* (London: Croom Helm, 1977) p. 61.
2. The phrase was initially used by Harlan Cleveland and also figures in a forthcoming study, S. Sloan, *NATO's Future: Toward a New Transatlantic Bargain* (London: Macmillan, 1985).
3. This is developed more fully in P. Williams, *The Senate and U.S. Troops in Europe* (London: Macmillan, 1985).
4. R. Neustadt, *Alliance Politics* (New York: Columbia University Press, 1970) p. 13.
5. J. Baylis, 'The Anglo-American Relationship in Defence' in Baylis, *British Defence Policy*, p. 77.
6. See 'NATO Today: The Alliance in Evolution', a report to the Committee on Foreign Relations, United States Senate (April 1982) p. 36.
7. Quoted in S. Sloan, 'Crisis in the Atlantic Alliance: Origins and Implications', prepared for the Committee on Foreign Relations, United States Senate by the Foreign Affairs and National Defense Division, Library of Congress (March 1982) p. 18.

CHAPTER 3 THE NATO ALLIES AND THE PERSIAN GULF

1. US Library of Congress, Congressional Research Service, 'Oil Supply Disruptions and the U.S. Economy', by Robert L. Bamberger *et al.* (Washington, DC, 1984).
2. This point is discussed in Nicolas Mosar, 'Interim Report of the Sub-Committee on Out-of-Area Security Challenges to the Alliance', North Atlantic Assembly, Luxembourg: November 1983, pp. 2–4.
3. Final Communique of the North Atlantic Council, Washington, DC, 31 May 1984, p. 1.
4. Commission of the European Communities, 'Community Energy Strategy to 1990', Brussels, 1984, pp. 1–3.
5. John Law, *Arab Investors: Who They Are, What They Buy, and Where*, vol. I (Chase World Information Center, New York, 1980) pp. 41–2, 81–4.
6. US Library of Congress, Congressional Research Service, 'U.S., U.K. and French naval force levels in the Persian Gulf/Arabian Sea/Indian Ocean region over last six months', CRS Memorandum to House Merchant Marine and Fisheries Committee, by Ronald O'Rourke, 22 June 1984, Washington, DC, 1984, pp. 4–5.
7. 'A Closing of French Ranks Short of a Withdrawal', *Le Monde*, 26 Dec. 1983, p. 3.
8. *Defense and Foreign Affairs Daily*, 8 Feb. 1984, p. 1; 'France and the Middle East', *Middle East Economic Digest*, April 1984, pp. 6–13, 'News and Comments from France', Embassy of France Press and Information Service, 27 Sept. 1984, p. 4.
9. 'French, British showing caution on issue of intervention in Gulf', *Washington Post*, 31 May 1984, p. A28; 'Europe plays down Gulf Crisis', *International Herald Tribune*, 1 June 1984, p. 2.
10. Ibid.
11. 'Baghdad proposes to reimburse Paris in oil for a part of its debt', *Le Monde*, 14 May 1983, p. 3.
12. CIA, *International Energy Statistical Review*, Washington, CIA, 26 March 1985, p. 7.
13. 'French Nervousness Apparent', *The Middle East Economic Digest*, 11 June 1982, pp. 36, 41; 'France and the Middle East', *Middle East Economic Journal Special Report*, April 1984; 'French–Iraqi ties get closer, threaten to widen war in Gulf', *Wall Street Journal*, 19 Aug. 1983, p. 1; 'Paris offers to reschedule Iraq's debt', *Le Monde*, 18 Aug. 1983, p. 20.
14. 'Baghdad proposes to Paris . . .', *Le Monde*, 14 May 1983, p. 4.
15. CIA, *Energy Statistical Review*, 26 March 1985, p. 7.
16. Commission of the European Communities, 'Review of Member States' Energy Policies', Brussels, 29 Feb. 1980, p. 80; Benson, Sumner, 'Soviet Gas, Arab Oil, Western Security', *Washington Quarterly* vol. 7, Winter 1984, p. 134.
17. CIA, *Energy Statistical Review*, 26 March 1985, p. 8.

18. US Congress, House, Committee on Foreign Affairs, Subcommittee on Europe and the Middle East, Developments in Europe, p. 29.
19. FBIS, *Western Europe*, 1 June 1984, p. T2 and 6 June 1984, p. T3.
20. Turkey reportedly rejects Iranian deal to shut Iraqi pipeline. *Christian Science Monitor*, 22 June 1984, p. 1.
21. FBIS, *Western Europe*, 2 Aug. 1984, pp. T1–T2; 'Iran and Turkey sign $3 Billion Barter Accord', *Wall Street Journal*, 23 Jan. 1985, p. 6.
22. CIA, *Energy Statistical Review*, 26 March 1985, p. 6.
23. 'The Gulf War and its repercussions', *Le Monde*, 24 May 1984, p. 4; 'A British Tanker struck by two missiles', *Le Monde*, 12 July 1984, p. 28.
24. See US Congress, Senate Foreign Relations Committee, 'War in the Gulf', Aug. 1984, Washington, 1984, pp. 12–13.
25. Farley, Jonathan, 'The Gulf War and the Littoral States', *The World Today*, July 1984, pp. 273–5. For a less pessimistic view of the military capabilities of the GCC, see Senate Foreign Relations Committee Report, 'War in the Gulf', p. 17.
26. 'Paris discreetly keeps its distance', *Le Monde*, 10 Feb. 1984, p. 2.
27. 'The Multinational Force at issue', *Le Monde*, 26 Dec. 1983, p. 1.
28. 'Mr. Mitterrand . . . the life of our soldiers in Lebanon', *Le Monde*, 14 Feb. 1984, p. 10.
29. For a description of the workings of the IEP and the hypothetical effects upon the petroleum market of differing levels of disruptions of the flow of oil, see US Library of Congress, Congressional Research Service; 'U.S. Participation in the Emergency Sharing Program of the IEA: The Role of Fair-Sharing', typed report by Robert Bamberger and David J. Cantor, 10 Nov. 1983, Washington, 1980; 'Oil Supply Disruptions and the U.S. Economy', CRS Report by Robert Bamberger *et al.*, July 1984; 'Escalation of the Conflict in the Persian Gulf', CRS White Paper by Robert Bamberger and Clyde R. Mark, 30 May 1984, Washington, pp. 31–8.
30. 'Preparing for the Next Energy Crisis', US Congress, House, Committee on Government Operations, Washington, US Govt. Print. Off., 17 May 1984, pp. 14–20, 26.
31. See Bamberger, Robert and Mark, Clyde, *Escalation of the Conflict in the Persian Gulf*, Congressional Research Service, 30 May 1986 (Washington DC 1986), pp. 26–31, for discussion of the elemental importance of Saudi production capacity. For a more complete description of the functions and vulnerabilities of the pumping stations, separator plants, and port and storage facilities, see US Congress, House Committee on International Relations, Special Subcommittee on Investigations, 'Oil Fields as Military Objectives', Committee Print, Washington, 1975, pp. 45–6.
32. For a discussion of the pressures on Japan in 1979, see Fuji Kamija, 'U.S.–Japan Relations in Retrospect and Future Challenges', in *The Common Security Interests of Japan, the United States and NATO* (Cambridge, Mass., 1981) pp. 139–40.
33. *The Times*, 1 June 1984.
34. 'If the Gulf is closed', *Foreign Report*, 12 July 1984, p. 4.
35. 'Mitterrand in Jordan', *Le Monde*, 10 July 1984, p. 3.

36. 'The visit to Jordan of the President of the Republic', *Le Monde*, 11 July 1984, p. 3.
37. 'French, British showing caution', *Washington Post*; 'Europe plays down Gulf crisis', *International Herald Tribune*; 'Italian ships join Red Sea mine hunt', *The Washington Post*, 29 August 1984, p. A1.
38. The President's News Conference of 22 May 1984, Presidential Documents, Washington, Office of the Federal Register of the National Archives, vol. 20, no. 21, p. 747.
39. See, for example, 'Turks turn down U.S. on Facility for Intervention Force', *International Herald Tribune*, 17 April 1984, p. 1.
40. For facilities which might be available to American forces and descriptions of American forces likely to be committed, see US Library of Congress, Congressional Research Service. Regional Support Facilities for the Rapid Deployment Force, report no. 82–53F, by James P. Wootten, 25 March 1982; for a description of the specific nature of possible American responses, see Bamberger and Mark, *Escalation of the Conflict*, pp. 8–10, 15–20.
41. 'Some alarmed by scenario on Iran–Iraq War', *Washington Post*, 25 Aug. 1984, p. G12.
42. FBIS, *Western Europe*, 15 Aug. 1984, pp. L4–L5.
43. See US Congress, Joint Economic Committee, Subcommittee on International Trade, Finance, and Security Economics, 'Allocation of Resources in the Soviet Union and China – 1983', Appendix; CIA Study, 'USSR: Economic Trends and Policy Developments', 28 June and 20 Sept. 1983, Washington, 1983.

CHAPTER 4   NATO AND THE SOUTH ATLANTIC: A CASE STUDY IN THE COMPLEXITIES OF OUT-OF-AREA OPERATIONS

1. For the purpose of this discussion the South Atlantic can be defined as that part of the Atlantic Ocean south of the Tropic of Cancer, the southern limit of the NATO area.
2. It is true that the Cuban crisis increased Washington's concern over possible Communist advances in Latin America; yet the Cuban crisis – together with the Congo crisis on the other side of the Atlantic – also demonstrated the inability of the Soviet Union to project its power over long distances.
3. During the Second World War the north-east of Brazil and the Atlantic narrows had been included within the US strategic defence perimeter, the so-called 'Quarter-Sphere Defense'. Following the end of the war, however, the Latin American region was effectively demoted in strategic terms. See John Child, 'Strategic Concepts in Latin America: An Update', *Inter-American Economic Affairs*, no. 34, Summer 1980, pp. 61–82.
4. For a history of the IAMS, see John Child, *Unequal Alliance: The*

172   *Notes and References*

Inter-American Military System, 1938–1978 (Boulder: Westview Press, 1980).

5. Gorden Connell Smith, *The Inter-American System* (New York: Oxford University Press, 1966) p. 122.
6. For details of the evolution of UNITAS, see Child, p. 163.
7. Ibid., p. 236.
8. For a typical statement of the strategic importance of the South Atlantic, see Robert J. Hanks, *The Cape Route: Imperilled Western Lifeline* (Cambridge, Mass., Institute for Foreign Policy Analysis, 1981) and Stewart Menaul, 'The Security of the Southern Oceans: Southern Africa the Key', *NATO's Fifteen Nations*, April–May, 1972.
9. A. L. Roberts, 'Peace Beyond NATO – The Challenge to Europe', *Seaford House Papers*, 1983, p. 112.
10. See Larry W. Bowman, 'The Strategic Importance of South Africa to the United States: An Appraisal and Policy Analysis', *African Affairs*, 81, 323 (April 1982) p. 161.
11. On this point see Hervé Coutau-Bégarie, 'L'Atlantique Sud, Nouveau Point Chaud', *Politique Internationale*, no. 19, 1983, pp. 211–12.
12. For a view of the increased importance placed on strategic seabed resources by the US Department of Defence, see Leigh S. Ratiner, 'The Law of the Sea: Crossroads for US Policy', *Foreign Affairs*, 60, 5 (Summer 1982): 1006–1021. For an assessment of fishing potential, see Alberto Miguez and Antonio Sanchez-Gijon, *El Atlantico Sud* (Instituto de Cuestiones Internacionales, Madrid, 1985) pp. 19–21.
13. On this subject, see for example, M. McGwire and J. McDonnell, eds, *Soviet Naval Influence: Domestic and Foreign Dimensions* (New York: Praeger, 1977); Bradford Dismukes and James McConnell, eds, *Soviet Naval Diplomacy* (New York: Pergamon, 1979); US Senate, Committee on Commerce, *Soviet Oceans Development* (Washington, DC: US Government Printing Office, 1976).
14. See David K. Hall, 'Naval Diplomacy in West African Waters', in Stephen S. Kaplan, *Diplomacy of Power: Soviet Armed Forces as a Political Instrument* (Washington, DC: The Brookings Institution, 1981) and Robert Harkavy, *Great Power Competition for Overseas Bases: The Geopolitics of Access Diplomacy* (London: Pergamon, 1982) pp. 195–203.
15. See Coutau–Begarie, 'L'Atlantique Sud', p. 211.
16. See Jorge I. Domínguez, 'The United states and its Regional Security Interests: The Caribbean, Central and South America', *Daedalus*, vol. 109, no. 4, Fall 1980, p. 199.
17. See Miguez and Sanchez-Gijon, *El Atlantico Sur*, p. 20 and Michael B. Davidchik and Robert B. Mahoney, 'Soviet Civil Fleets and the Third World' in Dismukes and McConnell (eds), *Soviet Naval Diplomacy*.
18. See Bowman, 'The Strategic Importance of South Africa', pp. 177–8.
19. Leonard Sullivan, Paul Nitze and the Atlantic Council's Working Group on Securing the Seas, *Securing the Seas: The Soviet Challenge and Western Alliance Options* (Boulder, Westview: 1979). It is worth pointing out, however, that the priority given to sea-lane interdiction in Soviet planning may well be increasing. See James M. McConnell, 'The Soviet Anti-

SLOC Mission in the Context of Soviet Doctrine'. Conference paper May 1982, in *Conference on the Protection of Shipping in the North Atlantic* (Washington DC: Center for Naval Analysis, 1982) pp. 11–23.

20. *Texts Adopted by the North Atlantic Assembly at its Eighteenth Session* (Bonn, November 1972) p. 14. Quoted in Bowman, 'The Strategic Importance of South Africa', p. 176.

21. *Twenty-second Meeting of the North Atlantic Assembly*, p. 7, quoted in Bowman, p. 177.

22. *Diligent Report on Surveillance and Protection of Shipping Routes for Supplies of Energy and Strategic Minerals to the Countries of the European Community*, European Parliament Document 1–697–80, 7 January 1981, p. 5.

23. Coutau-Bégarie, 'L'Atlantique Sud', p. 218.

24. *Atlantic News*, no. 1497, 24 Feb. 1983.

25. See Christopher Coker, 'The Western Alliance and Africa', *African Affairs*, 81, 324, July 1982, pp. 328–31.

26. *The Cape Times*, 17 Dec. 1980 and the *South African Digest*, 21 Sept. 1984.

27. Harry D. Train, 'NATO – Global Outlook?' *Navy International* 86 (Jan. 1981) p. 11.

28. In addition Annex II of Protocol III of the WEU Treaty limits Germany to 8 destroyers; other surface vessels must be under 3000 tons and submarines no more than 15 000 tons.

29. On this question see Gregory Treverton, 'Defence Beyond Europe', *Survival* xxv, no. 5, Sept./Oct. 1983 and Douglas Stuart, 'From the Washington Talks to the RDF', *Atlantic Quarterly*, 2, 1, Spring 1984.

30. Miles Kahler, 'The United States and Western Europe: The Diplomatic Consequences of Mr. Reagan' in Oye, Lieber and Rothchild (eds) *Eagle Defiant: United States Foreign Policy in the 1890s* (Boston: Little Brown, 1983) pp. 295–9.

31. This becomes very clear from the debates in the European Parliament on the Diligent Report, Sitting of 18 November 1981, Document Nr. 1–277/155, p. 156ff.

32. Mr Nicholas Mosar, rapporteur, *Interim Report of the Sub-Committee the Out of Area Security Challenges to the Alliance*, North Atlantic Assembly, Political Committee, November 1984, p. 8.

33. See A. L. Roberts, 'Peace Beyond NATO', p. 122. As Roberts points out, possible channels for consultation and coordination include the WEU and the various mechanisms of European Political Cooperation. See also the Diligent Report p. 5.

34. Dov S. Zakheim, 'The South Atlantic Conflict: Strategic, Military and Technological Lessons' in Alberto R. Coll and Anthony C. Arend (eds), *The Falklands War. Lessons for Strategy, Diplomacy and International Law* (London: Allen and Unwin, 1985) p. 167.

35. It does not, however, completely remove the problem as Washington's dilemma over how to respond to the Falklands crisis graphically illustrated.

36. See the Mosar Report, pp. 9–11.

37. Michael O. McCune, 'The Case for NATO – Prospectus for an Atlantic Treaty Organisation', unpublished paper, November 1980, p. 12.
38. See *Securing the Seas*, pp. 108–16.
39. As the House of Commons Defence Committee concluded: 'Since the deployment of forces to the South Atlantic is in addition to the United Kingdom's established NATO roles, it is inevitable that in some respects this diversion of resources will have a detrimental effect on the essential commitments in the North Atlantic and European theatres.' *Third Report from the Defence Committee of the House of Commons*, Session 1982–3 p. xviii.
40. The only formal ties between NATO and the regional powers have been participation of Latin American navies as observers in US Atlantic Fleet and NATO readiness exercises in the Caribbean (READEX, CARIBEX).
41. Patrick Wall, 'The Southern African Background' in Wall (ed.), *The Southern Oceans and the Security of the Free World* (London: Stacey International, 1977) p. 32.
42. *Le Monde*, 24 July 1981.
43. For a more detailed survey see Andrew Hurrell, 'The Politics of South Atlantic Security. A Survey of Proposals for a South Atlantic Treaty Organisation', *International Affairs*, 59, 2 (Spring 1983). Moscow has frequently sought to fuel such speculation in order to embarrass Washington. For a recent example of this see Victor Lunin 'La Crísis en el Atlantico Sur y sus Consecuencias', *America Latina* (Moscow), 11, Nov. 1982, p. 23.
44. *Süddeutsche Zeitung*, 22 May 1957.
45. *New York Times*, 12, 14 May 1957.
46. 'Argentina and South Africa plan stronger trade and defence ties', *Christian Science Monitor*, 18 January 1968.
47. 'Red peril seen in South Atlantic', *Christian Science Monitor*, 12 April 1969.
48. *Frankfurter Allgemeine Zeitung*, 15 April 1969.
49. 'Red flag off the Cape of Good Hope', *Daily Telegraph*, 16 May 1969.
50. For a detailed discussion of the Luso-Brazilian Community, see Wayne Selcher, *The Afro-Asian Dimension of Brazilian Foreign Policy* (Gainesville: University of Florida Press, 1974) pp. 61–5.
51. It is worth pointing out that these moves coincided with Portugal's efforts to draw NATO into its colonial war as part of wider proposals to improve the security of the South Atlantic. See Christopher Coker, 'The Western Alliance and Africa', *African Affairs*, vol. 81, no. 324, July 1982, pp. 324–8.
52. See *New York Times*, 14 July 1969; *Le Monde*, 13 July 1969.
53. 'Talk grows of South Atlantic pact aimed at Russia', *International Herald Tribune*, 30 November 1976.
54. 'SATO is revived', *Observer Foreign News Service*, 1 December 1976.
55. *La Nación*, 8 April 1976. Quoted in Margaret Daly Hayes, 'Der Südatlantik: Interessen der Grossmächte und der Anlieger', *Europa Archiv*, Folge 18; 1978, p. 592.

56. Quoted in Robert S. Leiken, 'Eastern Winds in Latin America', *Foreign Policy* no. 42 (Spring 1981) p. 96.
57. *New York Times*, 20 April 1980.
58. *Le Monde*, 24 July 1981.
59. *Le Monde*, 19 August 1981.
60. 'Bündnisstrategien im südlichen Lateinamerika: Ansätze zu einem Sudatlantikpakt', *Neue Züricher Zeitung*, 14 September 1980.
61. 'Pact meeting: Mystery over South African delegates', *Rand Daily Mail*, 26 May 1981; 'South Atlantic pact takes shape in Argentina', *Financial Times*, 26 May 1981.
62. The Silvermine intelligence complex is usually pointed to in this respect – a bomb-proof, fully computerised communications centre equipped to monitor 25 million square miles of ocean from Venezuela to India.
63. South African literature on its own strategic importance is voluminous, see Bowman, 'The strategic importance of South Africa', pp. 161–71. It has even taken out advertisements in western press stressing its pivotal role in the defence of the West, e.g. *New York Times*, 17 April 1975. For a specifically South African view of SATO, see Institute of Strategic Studies, Pretoria, 'A South Atlantic Treaty Organisation?', *South African Digest*, 5 June 1981, p. 2.
64. On economic ties, see David Fig, 'The Atlantic Connection: Growing Links Between South Africa and Latin America' in *Britain and Latin America* (London: Latin America Bureau, 1979) pp. 92–102.
65. See Coker, 'The Western Alliance and Africa' p. 329. It is worth quoting Coker's conclusion regarding the NATO debates over the Cape Route in the early 1970s. 'What the SACLANT story illustrates is how little South Africa itself has figured in NATO planning, how little allied planning in recent years has actually focussed on Southern Africa', ibid., p. 331.
66. Despite these changes the arguments within South Africa for a wider naval role have continued, see for example, R. K. Campbell 'Sea Power and South Africa', Institute of Stategic Studies, Pretoria, Publication no. 18, 1984.
67. See *Financial Times*, 18 June 1981 and 1 March 1982.
68. See Michael Clough, 'United States Policy in Southern Africa', *Current History* 83, 491 (March 1984) and Gerald Bender, 'The Reagan Administration and Southern Africa', *Atlantic Quarterly* 2, 3 (Autumn 1984).
69. See for instance *Sunday Times*, 16 Dec. 1984.
70. See John Child, 'Geopolitical Thinking in Latin America', *Latin American Research Review*, 1979, vol. xiv, no. 2, pp.89–111.
71. For details of Argentina's claims in Antarctica see Eduardo M. de la Cruz, 'Derechos Argentinos sobre la Antártica y las pretensiones ajenas', *Estrategia*, 43/44, 1976–7, pp. 60–71; and Edward Milenky and Steven Schwab, 'Latin America and Antarctica', *Current History* 82, 481 (Feb. 1983).
72. See Juan E. Guglialmelli, 'Argentina. Política Nacional y Política de Fronteras', *Estrategia*, 37/38, 1975–6, pp. 5–21.
73. For a survey of Argentina's foreign policy see Edward S. Milenky,

Argentina's Foreign Policies (Boulder, Colorado: Westview, 1978); John Finan, 'Argentina' in Harold Davis and Larman C. Wilson (eds), *Latin American Foreign Policies: An Analysis* (London: Johns Hopkins University Press, 1975); and Juan Archibaldo Lanús, *De Chapultepec al Beagle, Política Exterior Argentina 1945–1980* (Buenos Aires: Emencé Editores, 1984).

74. Milenky, *Argentina's Foreign Policies*, pp. 1–20.
75. For an overview of recent foreign policy see Dennis R. Gordon, 'Argentina's Foreign Policy in the Post-Malvinas Era' in Elizabeth Ferris and Jennie Lincoln, *Dynamics of Latin American Foreign Policies: Challenges for the 1980s* (Boulder, Westview, 1985); and Wolf Grabendorf, 'Argentiniens neue Aussenpolitik: Demokratisierung und Verschuldung', *Europa Archiv*, Folge 19, October 1984.
76. Although the government has stated that it would like to cut back arms expenditure by one third in the interests of economic recovery, the country does appear to have made good the losses sustained in the Falklands War, see University of Bradford, 'Assessment of Argentinian Rearmament', *Peace Studies Brief*, no. 19, 14 January 1985 and *Jane's Defence Weekly*, 7 April 1984.
77. See 'Agreement package with Algeria', *Latin American Weekly*, 4 January 1985 and *The Hindu*, 2 February 1985. See also 'Non-Aligned Quest now Confirmed', *L.A.W.R.*, 9 November 1984.
78. Foreign Ministry press release, 28 March 1984. Quoted in Grabendorff, 'Argentiens neue Aussenpolitik,' p. 604.
79. See Milenky, *Argentina's Foreign Policies*, pp. 153–7.
80. For a survey of this issue see Nikki Miller and Laurence Whitehead, 'The Soviet Interest in Latin America: An Economic Perspective', in Robert Cassen (ed.), *The Soviet Union and the Third World* (London: Chatham House).
81. Robert Leiken, 'Soviet Strategy in Latin America', *Washington Papers*, vol. x, no. 93, 1982, pp. 21–2.
82. 'The best guarantee for stability would be to bring Argentina, Chile, South Africa, and other riparian States, with the backing of the USA and the European Community into a new South Atlantic community. One task of this community would be to assure the security of the South Atlantic sea lanes and air routes, another could be the development of Antarctica,' Julian Amery, 'A Look to the Future', *Encounter*, April 1985, pp. 77fl. However, Amery ignores not only Argentina's basic attitude toward the Falklands but also the whole context of Argentinian foreign policy outlined above.
83. See Michael Morris, *International Politics and the Sea: The Case of Brazil* (Boulder, Colorado: Westview, 1979) p. 276.
84. Michael Morris, *International Politics and the Sea*, pp. 25–6.
85. For a discussion of Brazil's position on Antarctica see Therezinha de Castro, *Rumo á Antártica* (Rio de Janeiro: Livraria Freitas Bastos, 1976); also Carlos J. Moneta, 'Antarctica, Latin America and the International System in the 1980s: Towards a New Antarctic Order', *Journal of Inter-American Studies and World Affairs*, vol. 33, no. 1, February 1981,

pp. 29–68, and M. J. Paterson, 'Antarctica: The Last Great Land Rush', *International Organisation*, vol. 34, no. 3, Summer 1980, pp. 377–403.

86. Golbery do Couto y Silva, *Aspectos Geopoliticos do Brasil* (Rio de Janeiro: Jose Olympio, 1957) pp. 27–8.

87. Hilton Berutti Augusto Moreira, 'O Brasil e suas responsibilidades no Atlántico Sul', *Segurança e Desenvolvimento*, no. 169, 1972, p. 103.

88. Carlos de Meira Mattos, *A Geopolitica e as Projectoes do Poder* (Rio de Janeiro: Jose Olympio, 1977) esp. chs VIII and IX.

89. *Veja*, 31 December 1975.

90. 'Atlantico Sul: Tes Visoes de Una Estrategia', *Segurança e Desenvolvimento*, no. 104, 1976, p. 136.

91. See, for instance, *O Estado de Sao Paulo*, 24 September 1976 and *Jornal do Brasil*, 28 September 1976.

92. Quoted in Hayes, *Der Südatlantik*, p. 593. Brazil's pragmatic approach to diplomacy has meant that, despite the official switch in its African policy, discreet although highly profitable ties with South Africa have continued and in 1978–9 South African exports to Brazil were larger than those of any other African country.

93. *Jornal do Brasil*, 6/7 October 1977.

94. 'Nao é preciso um pacto no Atlântico Sul', *Veja*, 25 April 1979.

95. Reported in *Le Monde*, 19 August 1981.

96. At the San Jose de Costa Rica Conference in 1975, the eastern security limit of the Inter-American Treaty of Reciprocal Assistance (the Rio Treaty) was fixed at 20 degrees West of Greenwich.

97. For Brazilian criticism of the intrusion of Superpower rivalry into the region and Brazil's antipathy to any form of security pact, see 'Figueiredo on need to Safeguard South Atlantic', *FBIS*, 8 July 1982.

98. See Tom Forrest, 'Brazil and Africa: Geopolitics, Trade and Technology in the South Atlantic', *African Affairs*, vol. 81, no. 322, January 1982, pp. 3–20. For a Nigerian view of the 'SATO' question, see A. Bolaji Akinyemi, 'The Need for an African South Atlantic Organisation', *Nigerian Forum*, vol. I 1981, pp. 125–30, quoted in Wayne Selcher, 'Dilemas de Politica en las Relaciones de Brasil con Africa: Ejemplo de Obstáculos en las Relaciones Sur-Sur', *Foro Internacional*, vol. XXIII, no. 1, jul-set 1982, p. 36.

99. For details of this agreement see Jim Brooke, 'Dateline Brazil: Southern Superpower', *Foreign Policy*, Fall 1981, p. 178.

100. For a survey of recent US–Brazilian relations see Andrew Hurrell, 'Brazil, the United States and the Debt', *The World Today*, March 1985.

101. *Jane's Defence Weekly*, 8 December 1984.

102. See Robert J. Branco, 'The United States and Brazil', National Security Affairs Monograph Series 84–1, 1984 [National Defense University, Washington] p. 79.

103. See Luiz Paul Macedo Carvalho, 'Atlantico Sul', *A Defesa Nacional*, 710, Nov/Dez 1983 and his 'Interesses e responsibilidades do Brasil no Atlantico Sul', ibid., 711, Jan./Fev. 1984.

104. See for instance 'O Choque da Guerra' *Veja*, 30 June 1982.

105. See *Estado de Sao Paulo*, 7 August 1983 and *O Globo*, 29 May 1982.

106. For details of the base on Trinidad, see *The Times*, 5 June 1982. Plans were subsequently shelved because of financial constraints.
107. Domingos P. C. B. Ferreira, 'The Navy of Brazil: An Emerging Power at Sea', National Security Affairs Issue Paper, no. 83–1. National Defense University, Washington, 1983, pp. 36–7.

CHAPTER 5   AFRICA AS AN OUT-OF-AREA PROBLEM FOR NATO

1. See the author's more general discussion of these four types of situations in 'NATO Out-of-Area Disputes: From the Washington Talks to the RDF', *Atlantic Quarterly*, Spring 1984, pp. 50–66.
2. Quoted in Guy de Carmoy, *The Foreign Policies of France: 1944–1968* (Chicago: Chicago University Press, 1970), p. 19.
3. Minutes of the 10th meeting of the Washington Exploratory Talks, 22 December 1948, 3 p.m., 'Foreign Relations of the United States' (hereinafter cited as *FRUS*), III, 1948, pp. 325–6.
4. Ibid. For a more extensive discussion of the Washington Talks and the issue of Algerian inclusion, see Douglas Stuart and William Tow, *The Limits of Alliance: NATO Out-of-Areas Problems Since 1949* (forthcoming).
5. Memorandum on French North Africa by Policy Planning Staff, Washington, 22 March 1948, *FRUS*, III, 1948, pp. 683–4.
6. It is worth mentioning, however, that the public attention accorded to the possibility of a Soviet conventional offensive against Western Europe in the late 1940s was encouraged by a leadership in Washington that had ample evidence of the unlikelihood of such an occurrence. See, in particular, Matthew Evangelista, 'Stalin's Postwar Army Reappraised', *International Security*, vol. 7, no. 3, Winter 1982/83, pp. 110–38. Regarding Operation Torch, see in particular Luis Pasqual Sanchez-Gijon, *La Planificacion Militar Britanica y Espana* (Madrid: Instituto de Cuestiones Internacionales, 1983).
7. The colonialist geo-strategic perspective was reflected in a number of French journals in the 1950s of which *Revue de Défense National* is the most well known. For a survey of these writings, see Raoul Girardet, *L'Idee Coloniale in France: 1871–1962* (Paris: Le Table Ronde, 1972). Regarding the *guerre revolutionnaire*, see, in particular, L. M. Chassim, 'Vers un encerclement de l'occident', *Revue du Défense Nationale*, May 1956, pp. 531–52.
8. Message from John Ohly, Deputy Director, Mutual Defense Assistance Program, to Dean Rusk, Assistant Secretary of State for Far Eastern Affairs, Washington, 20 November 1950, *FRUS*, VI, 1950, pp. 924–5.
9. Dean Acheson, *Present at the Creation* (New York: Norton, 1969), p. 638.
10. Edgar Furniss, *De Gaulle and the French Army* (New York: 20th Century Fund, 1964), pp. 182–3.
11. *FRUS*, vol. II, 1952–4, p. 148.

Notes and References

Notes and References 179

12. Quoted in Donald Neff, *Warriors at Suez* (New York: Simon & Schuster, 1981), p. 390.
13. The French reaction to JFK's speech is discussed by Arthur Schlesinger, *A Thousand Days* (New York: Houghton-Mifflin, 1965), pp. 510–12. See also Chester Bowles' study of *Africa's Challenge to America* (Berkeley: University of California Press, 1956).
14. Quoted in Alistair Horne, *A Savage War of Peace* (New York: Penguin, 1977), p. 243.
15. Jacques Soustelle, 'France Looks at Her Alliances', *Foreign Affairs*, October 1956, pp. 116–30.
16. Regarding De Gaulle's new policies for security in Africa, see, in particular, Pierre Dabezies, 'La Politique Militaire de la France en Afrique Noire sous le General de Gaulle', in *La Politique Africaine du General de Gaulle (1958–1969)* (Paris: Pedone, 1980), pp. 229–62.
17. Dulles Telegram to Eisenhower, 6 February 1959, reprinted in Bernard Ledwidge, *De Gaulle et les Americains* (Paris: Flammarion, 1984), p. 70.
18. Kennan, George, *Memoirs* (Boston: Little, Brown, 1967), p. 150. See also Hugh Kay, *Salazar and Modern Portugal* (New York: Hawthorne Books, 1970), pp. 151–70.
19. Hickerson to Marshall, *FRUS*, vol. iii, 1948, p. 999.
20. Hickerson to MacVeagh, *FRUS*, iii, 1948, pp. 1005–7. It is worth mentioning that the geo-political arguments in favour of Portuguese membership were enhanced by the very positive image that the Salazar government had acquired in Washington because of its management of the wartime and post-war Portuguese economy. In 1948 Hickerson reminded Marshall that 'Portugal's financial situation is sound; its budget has been balanced for the past 15 years and the escudo is one of the firmest currencies in Europe. Portugal is participating in the ERP (European Recovery Program) but is receiving no financial assistance. Portugal has offered to make loans to other countries to assist in the purchase of Portuguese goods.' (*FRUS*, iii, 1948), p. 999.
21. Acheson, *Present . . .* , p. 628.
22. See the chronology regarding base usage in Giles Binney, 'The "Portuguese Platform" – Reflexions About its Usefulness in the Context of the East/West Confrontation', in *The Seaford House Papers: 1983* (London: Royal College of Defense Studies, 1983), p. 97.
23. Between 1949 and 1961 total US economic and military assistance to Portugal was $370 million. Data are provided in S. J. Bosgra and C. Van Krimpen, 'Portugal and NATO', reprinted in *Africa, Contemporary Record, 1969–70* (London: Rex Collings, 1970), page C-131.
24. The distinction between Eurocentric and Afrocentric approaches in US foreign policy is developed in an interesting article by Steven Metz entitled 'American Attitudes Towards Decolonization in Africa', *Political Science Quarterly*, Fall 1984, pp. 515–33.
25. James Penfield, 'The Role of the United States in Africa: Our Interests and Operations', *Department of State Bulletin*, 8 June 1959, p. 842. Quoted in Stephen Weissman, *American Foreign Policy in the Congo: 1960–1964* (Ithaca: Cornell University Press, 1974), p. 51.

26. George Ball, *The Past Has Another Pattern* (New York: Norton, 1982), p. 181.
27. Ball, p. 277.
28. Roger Hilsman, *To Move a Nation* (New York: Doubleday, 1967), p. 249.
29. Bowles, pp. 89–90.
30. Schlesinger, p. 517.
31. Cited in Luc Crollen, *Portugal, the US and NATO* (Leuven: Leuven University Press, 1973), p. 127.
32. Regarding the relativisation of NATO in contemporary US foreign policy, see Pierre Hassner, 'Intra-Alliance Diversities and Challenges: NATO in an Age of Hot Peace', in Kenneth Myers (ed.), *NATO: The Next 30 Years* (Boulder: Westview, 1980), p. 384.
33. *New York Times*, 4 June 1961.
34. Crollen, p. 43.
35. Great Britain, Portugal's traditional ally and chief sponsor at the time of NATO's formation became increasingly disenchanted with Lisbon in the wake of the Portuguese government's violent repressions of the 1961 Angola revolt. Domestic criticism of Portugal was coordinated by Protestant groups in Britain, against what was seen as an anti-Protestant repression in Angola. According to one Protestant fact-finding mission in 1961, 'a review of Portugal's membership [in] the NATO alliance is long overdue in view of her denial of the Christian and democratic principles which are supposed to form the basis of the NATO alliance'. Quoted in John Marcum, *The Angolan Revolution, Vol. 1 (1950–1962)* (Cambridge: MIT Press, 1969), p. 148.
36. *Survey of International Affairs: 1961* (London: Oxford University Press, 1965), p. 77.
37. See, in particular, *The Arms Trade with the Third World* (Stockholm: Stockholm International Peace Research Institute, 1971), pp. 668–74; and Bosgra and Van Krimpen, pp. C-117–C-139. In 1962 the US was to admit in the United Nations that it recognised that some of the arms supplied to Portugal under NATO auspices were being transhipped to Angola. In 1966 at the time of a West German sale of surplus aircraft to Lisbon, a Portuguese Foreign Ministry spokesman asserted that 'the transaction was agreed within the spirit of the North Atlantic Pact. It was agreed that the planes would be used only for defensive purposes within Portuguese territory, Portuguese territory extends to Africa . . .' (Bosgra and Van Krimpen, C-132 and C-122).
38. Schlesinger, pp. 480–1.
39. Bosgra and Van Krimpen, page C-133.
40. Crollen, p. 127.
41. Bosgra and Van Krimpen, page C-133.
42. Quoted in *Africa Contemporary Record: 1968–69*, p. 401.
43. Weissmann, *American Foreign Policy in Congo*, p. 44.
44. Weissmann, p. 54.
45. Text of a Note from Foreign Minister Gromyko to the Belgian Ambassador in Moscow, 13 July 1960. Reprinted in W. J. Ganslof Van der Meersch, *Fin de la Souveraneté Belge au Congo* (The Hague: Nijhoff, 1963), p. 480.

46. See Jules Gerard-Libois, *Katanga Secession* (Madison: University of Wisconsin Press, 1966), p. 112.
47. P. H. Spaak, *Combats Inacheves Vol. II* (Paris: Fayard, 1969), p. 239.
48. Weissman, p. 76.
49. Discussed in Madeleine Kalb, *The Congo Cables* (New York: Macmillan, 1982), pp. 204–5.
50. See *Survey . . . 1961*, pp. 478–9.
51. Kalb, p. 220.
52. P. H. Spaak, pp. 221–2.
53. *Survey . . .* , p. 462.
54. *New York Times*, 25 March 1961.
55. John Newhouse, *De Gaulle and the Anglo Saxons* (London: Andre Deutsch, 1970), p. 130.
56. The out-of-area aspects of the Directorate scheme are discussed in D. Stuart and W. Tow, *The Limits of Alliance: NATO Out-of-Area Problems Since 1949* (forthcoming).
57. Regarding the differences between Spaak and De Gaulle, see *Survey . . . 1961*, pp. 54–64.
58. Kalb, p. 316.
59. *The Observer*, 17 December 1961, cited in *Survey . . . 1961*, p. 85.
60. Macmillan takes some credit for convincing JFK and Rusk to take control of the UN situation 'instead of leaving the direction to the Adlai Stevensons and other half-baked "liberals"', *Pointing the Way: 1959–61* (London: Macmillan, 1972), pp. 451 and 456–7.
61. Weissman, p. 188.
62. Gerard-Libois, p. 276.
63. 'Europe Still Needs the US – "The Most Powerful Nation"', *US News & World Report*, 17 May 1976, pp. 50–51.
64. For reports of US/French consultation in 1977, see *Washington Post*, 25 March 1977.
65. Quoted in Oye Ogunbadejo, 'Conflict in Africa: A Case Study of the Shaba Crisis, 1977', *World Affairs*, Winter 1979, p. 233.
66. Regarding the factional struggles within the Carter administration, see Gerald Bender, 'Angola, the Cubans, and American Anxieties', *Foreign Policy*, Summer 1978, pp. 3–30.
67. See, in particular, Crawford Young, 'Zaire: The Unending Crises', *Foreign Affairs*, Fall 1978, pp. 169–85.
68. This, acording to Cyrus Vance, *Hard Choices* (New York: Simon & Schuster, 1983), pp. 70–71.
69. Robert Turner, *The War Powers Resolution: Its Implementation in Theory and Practice* (Philadelphia: Philadelphia Policy Papers, Foreign Policy Research Institute, 1983), pp. 68–9.
70. See comments by Tanzanian and Nigerian heads of state, cited in Christopher Coker, *NATO, the Warsaw Pact and Africa* (London: Macmillan, 1985) pp. 1–2.
71. Quoted in *Africa Contemporary Record, 1977/78* (London: Holmes & Meier, 1979), B594.
72. *L'Année Politique, 1978* (Paris: Editions du Grand Siècle, 1978), p. 210.
73. *New York Times*, 31 May 1978. For a chronology of the second Shaba

crisis, and a sampling of comments by other governments, see *Le Monde*, 24 May 1978.
74. *New York Times*, 31 May 1978.
75. Guy Méry, quoted in Pierre Lellouche and Dominique Moisi, 'French Policy in Africa: A Lonely Battle Against Destabilization', *International Security*, Spring 1978, p. 130.
76. Peter Mangold, 'Shaba I and Shaba II', *Survival*, May/June 1979, p. 107.
77. Alfred Grosser, 'General De Gaulle and the Foreign Policy of the Fifth Republic', *International Affairs* (London), April 1963, p. 199. Cited in Michael Harrison, *The Reluctant Ally* (Baltimore: The Johns Hopkins University Press, 1981), pp. 47–8.
78. Ball, p. 278.
79. Henri Grimal, *Decolonization* (London: Routledge & Kegan Paul, 1978), p. 322.
80. Giscard press conference, quoted in Mangold, p. 110.
81. *New York Times*, 1 June 1978.
82. Pierre Lellouche and Dominique Moisi, 'French Policy in Africa . . .', pp. 108–33.

CHAPTER 6   FRANCE, NATO AND REGIONAL CONFLICT IN AFRICA

1. Jacques Frémaux and André Martel, 'French Defence Policy 1947–1949', in Olav Riste (ed.), *Western Security: The Formative Years* (Norwegian University Press, Oslo, 1985) p. 93.
2. Pierre Melandri, 'France and the Atlantic Alliance 1950–1953: Between Great Power Policy and European Integration,' in Riste, ibid., p. 268.
3. Marcel J. Jeanneney, *Rapport sur la Politique de Cooperation avec les Pays en voie de Developpement*, La Documentation Française, Paris, 1964, pp. 43–4.
4. Anne Kriegal, 'François Mitterrand Diplomate', *Politique Internationale*, Summer 1982, no. 16, p. 32.
5. Raoul Giradet, *L'Idée Coloniale en France (1871–1962)*, Paris, Table Ronde, 1972, p. 196.
6. For a recent report that explains how French aid to the Third World affects employment levels in France, see Yves Berthelot and Jacques de Bandt, *Impact des relations avec le Tiers Monde sur l'Economie Française*, La Documentation Française, Paris 1982.
7. Howard Schissel, 'Preserving the Economic Nexus,' *West Africa*, 27 June 1983.
8. For a complete breakdown of French African trade in 1982 see 'La Commerce de la France avec l'Afrique en 1982', *Marchés Tropicaux*, 16 September 1983.
9. See generally, François Charollais and Jean de Ribes, Le Défi de l'Outre Mer: L'Action Exterieure dans la Défense de la France, Paris, *Fondation pour les Etudes de Défense Nationale*, Cahier no. 26, 1983.

10. Press Conference of 12 April 1977 in *La Politique Etrangere de la France*, 2éieme trimestre, 1977, p. 16.
11. See for example, NATO Final Communiqué, Defence Planning Committee, June 1983, para 6.
12. Jean Pierre Cot, 'La France et l'Afrique: Quel Changement', *Politique Internationale*, Winter 1982/83, no. 18, p. 11.
13. 'Loi no. 83–606 du 8 juillet 1983 Portant Approbation de la Programmation Militaire pour les Années 1984–1988', published in *Journal Officiel*, 9 July 1983, *Assemblé Nationale*, pp. 2114–21.
14. Critias, 'Entre l'Europe et l'Outre Mer', *Le Monde*, 25 October 1983.
15. Jacques Isnard, 'La Force d'Action Rapide Française pourra Intervenir en Europe', *Le Monde*, 20–21 November 1983.
16. G. Moutard, 'La Programmation Militaire 1984–1988 et la Reorganisation de l'Armée de Terre', *L'Ancre d'Or Bazeilles*, January–February 1984.
17. Patrice Buffotot, 'La FAR et le 3ième Cercle', in CIRPES, *Paix et Conflits*, nouvelle serie, no. 6 1984.
18. *Le Monde*, 18 February 1984.
19. See 'Avis Presenté au nom de la Commission de la Défense Nationale et des Forces Armees sur la Projet de loi de Finances pour 1984', Tome 1, by Jacques Huygues des Etages, Annexe no. 1738 du P.V. de la Séance du 6 octobre, *Assemble Nationale*, p. 52.
20. Rapport de Luc Tinseau, deputé, Annexe no. 1485, au P.V. de la Séance de 11 mai 1983, *Assemblé Nationale*, 'Resumé des Travaux de la Commission de Défense et Conclusion', p. 68.
21. See, Anonymous, 'Le C.O.T.A.M.', *Freres d'Armes*, no. 129, July–August, 1984.
22. Antoine Sanguinetti, 'Aspects Maritimes et aériens de l'Intervention Exterieure', in CIRPES, op. cit. pp. 5–6.
23. Tinseau (quoted in n. 20).
24. John Chipman, 'France, Libya, and Chad, Note of the Month', *The World Today*, October 1983.
25. General Lacaze, 'La Politique de Défense de la France', *L'Armement*, March 1984.
26. Lt. Col. Paul Vallin, 'La Logistique', in 'Les Forces d'Action Rapide: Dossier du Mois', *Armées Aujourd'hui*, September 1983, no. 83.
27. A number of Quai d'Orsay departments are assigned to work on these problems and collaborate with the Bureau de Transports Maritimes, Aériens et de Surface (BTMAS) of the French Armed Forces.
28. Anonymous, Katcha et Mayumba 83, in *Frères d'Armes*, September–October, 1983.
29. The N'Diambour exercise involved 5000 French soldiers from the FAR and those stationed in Dakar.
30. Anonymous, 'Bandama 84, Exercise Bilateral Franco-Ivorien', *Frères d'Armes*, May–June 1984, p. 22.
31. George E. Moose, 'French Military Policy in Africa,' in William J. Foltz and Henry S. Bienen, *Arms and the African: Military Influences on Africa's International Relations*, Yale, 1985, p. 70.

32. Valery Giscard d'Estaing, 'New Opportunities and New Challenges', *Foreign Affairs*, Fall 1983, p. 192.
33. Allocution Prononcée par M. François Mitterrand, President de la République, Pour la Séance d'Ouverture de la 12eme Conference des Chefs d'Etat de France et d'Afrique, 12 Décembre 1985, French Press Service, 1985.

CHAPTER 7   SOUTHERN AFRICA AND THE WEST IN THE POST-NKOMATI PERIOD

1. John S. Saul, Stephen Gelb, 'The Crisis in South Africa: Class Defense, Class Revolution', in *Monthly Review*, vol. 33, no. 3 (July/Aug 1981), p. 3.
2. Ibid.
3. Stanley Uys on 'Apartheid's Crisis', *Guardian*, 17 June 1985, quoted in *ANC Weekly News Briefing*, vol. 9, no. 24, 16 June 1985, p. 19.
4. Many analysts agree that 'constructive engagement' has been a failure. See, for example, Martin Schümer, *Ende der Constructive Engagement Strategie? Wandel der amerikanischen Politik gegenüber dem Südlichen Afrika* (Bonn: Forschungsinstitut der Deutschen Gesellschaft für Auswärtige Politik, 1986).
5. The Frontline States (FLS) are Angola, Botswana, Mozambique, Tanzania, Zambia and Zimbabwe. Together with Lesotho, Malawi and Swaziland they constitute the countries of the 'Southern African Development Coordination Conference'.
6. Michael Howard, 'Europe, the Superpowers and Africa', in *Politikon*, vol. 9, no. 2, Dec. 1982, p. 12. It is noteworthy, though, that this feeling is presently 'more widespread' in certain European countries than in others.
7. See Bernhard Weimer, 'Europe, the United States and the Frontline States of Southern Africa: The case for closer cooperation', in *Atlantic Quarterly*, vol. 2, no. 1 (Spring 1984), pp. 67–87.
8. Michael Evans, *The Front-Line States, South Africa and Southern African Security. Military Prospects and Perspectives* (Harare: University of Zimbabwe, 1980), p. 14.
9. Lars Rudebeck, 'Development and Democracy'. Notes related to a study of people's power in Mozambique. Paper presented to the Conference on 'The formation of the nation in "the fire"' ' (African countries colonised by Portugal), Bissau, Guinea-Bissau, Jan. 1986.
10. People's Republic of Mozambique (National Planning Commission), Economic Report, Maputo, Jan. 1984, p. 41f.
11. Bernhard Weimer, *Mozambique's Foreign Policy 1975–1984: Junctions and Options* (unpublished draft).
12. This is particularly witnessed in the post-Machel era, in which there is a continuity of Mozambique's policies under the leadership of President Chissano, despite the loss of key-policy advisors and strategists. Professor Aquino de Bragança and Fernando Honwana, both eminent personalities in shaping Mozambican foreign policy, lost their lives

together with Samora Machel and other Mozambicans in the tragic Mbuzini plane crash.

13. Deon Geldenhuys, 'Recrossing the Matola Threshold: The "Terrorist Factor" in South Africa's Regional Relations', in *South Africa International*, vol. 13, no. 3 (Jan. 1983), pp. 152–71.

14. With regard to Mozambique's interests in the 'Nkomati-package', see Bernhard Weimer, 'Mozambique und der Nkomati-Akkord: Sicherheit, Wirtschaft, Politik', *Bericht über Gespräche in Mozambique* (Ebenhausen, Sept. 1984).

15. *Africa Research Bulletin* (Political Social Cultural Series), Aug. 1–31, 1984, p. 7334.

16. *Summary of World Broadcast* (SWB), ME/7783/B941, 25 Oct. 1984.

17. Abdul Rahman Mohamed Babu, 'Portugal's New Empire', in *Africa Now*, June 1984, pp. 42–3.

18. 'Africa do Sul, Portugal, Rhodesia'; see Stephen Louis Weigert, Alliances and Regional Integration: The Case of Southern Africa; 1964–74 (John Hopkins Unversity, Ph.D., 1978) Ann Arbor, 1978 (University Microfilms International, two volumes), pp. 170–5.

19. Ibid., pp. 436–61; Pretoria's 'Constellation of Southern African States' (CONSAS) scheme is an attempt to recreate an ASPRO-type of 'alliance for progress'.

20. Joseph Hanlon, *Mozambique: The Revolution under Fire* (London, 1984), especially part VI: 'The class-struggle continues', pp. 175–210.

21. 'Moçambique nunca envolveu o Governo português nas ligações come Renamo'. Interview with Aquino de Bragança, *Diário de Lisboa*, 22 March 1985, p. 7.

22. For scope and thrust of the economic reform programme see Prime Minister Machungo's speech to the People's Assembly on 14 January 1987; SWB/ME/W1425/A2/2–11, 27 January 1987.

23. According to the documents captured at the former MNR headquarters 'Casa Banana' in the Gorongoza Mountains as well as to other intelligence reports there is evidence of air drops and supplies by sea for the armed bandits from South African and Malawian territory in the post-Nkomati era. A key role in supporting MNR activities from South African territory is attributed to the South African Military Intelligence (SAMI) as well as to South Africa's special units for covert action, the Reconnaissance Commandos. The latter, from bases in Phalaborwa, Saldhana Bay and elsewhere, were involved in training, arming and communicating with MNR commandos as well as in illicit diamond trade for financing the covert activities in Mozambique.

24. *Financial Times*, 28 April 1987, p. 5.

25. Moçambique nunca envolveu, op. cit.

26. For Mozambique's agricultural potential as well as the failure of Frelimo's agricultural policies during previous policy options see Barry Munslow, 'State Intervention in Agriculture: the Mozambican Experience', in *Journal of Modern African Studies*, vol. 22, no. 2 (1984), pp. 199–221; Philip Raikes, 'Food Policy and Production in Mozambique since Independence', in *Review of African Political Economy*, no. 29 (July 1984), pp. 95–107.

186   *Notes and References*

27. Robert H. Davies, Dan O'Meara, 'The State of Analysis of the Southern African Region: Issues Raised by South African Strategy', in *Review of African Political Economy*, no. 29 (1984), pp. 64–76; see also Deon Geldenhuys, *Some Foreign Policy Implications of South Africa's 'Total National Strategy' with Particular Reference to the '12-Point-Plan'* (Braamfontein, 1981).

28. See for example Simon Jenkins, 'Regional Stability in Southern Africa', in *Optima*, vol. 32, no. 2 (1984), pp. 51–5; Klaus Freiherr von der Ropp, 'Afrikas Süden im Zeichen der Pax Pretoriana', in *Außenpolitik*, vol. 4 (1984), pp. 419–33.

29. As for Mozambique, it can be argued that this 'pressure' was extremely useful and welcome for bringing the economic machinery up-gear again. See interview with the former Mozambican Minister of Finance, Rui Baltazar, in Weimer, *Mozambique und der Nkomati Accord*.

30. That the 'stick' was not buried is evidenced during 1984 by the mounting South Africa pressure on Lesotho and Botswana aimed at the signing of a 'Caledon' and 'Notwane Accord' respectively, modelled after the Nkomati Accord. For 1985, the ill-fated 'recce' – operation 'Argon' – against Angola's oil installation at Cabinda and the SADF raid on ANC 'bases' in Gaborone/Botswana underpin the aggressive nature of South Africa's regional policies, as does the blockade of Lesotho in Jan. 1986, which toppled the Leabua Jonathan Regime.

31. A few months before the signing of the Nkomati Accord the author argued in favour of a raising of the threshold for South African 'stick' operations against Mozambique by suggesting European military (and economic) assistance to that country. He did not anticipate, however, that Pretoria itself, obviously by force of the 'organic crisis' and the logic of the TNS, would voluntarily take that step. Thus Pretoria's apparent desperation for a – presumably temporary – peace arrangement was then grossly underestimated. See Weimer, 'Europe, the United States . . .', op. cit.

32. See David Martin, Phyllis Johnson, 'Africa: The Old and the Unexpected', in *Foreign Affairs*, vol. 63, no. 3 (1985), p. 609.

33. This took place in Kabwe/Zambia from the 19 to 24 June 1985; see *SWB/Monitoring Report*, ME/7990/B/5, 29 June 1985.

34. *Sunday Express*, 11 Nov. 1984, quoted in *Weekly News Briefing* (ANC), vol. 8, no. 47, 18 November 1984, p. 1f.

35. This was said by the Deputy Minister of Defence and Law and Order, Mr Adrian Vlok. See SWB/ME/7931/B/5, 22 April 1985.

36. Hanlon, *Mozambique*, op. cit., p. 256.

37. In May 1985 President Nyerere warned of the danger of Mozambique's government being toppled and called on African countries to assist Mozambique; less than two years later this scenario has become reality and Tanzania was forced to deploy troops in northern Mozambique to protect its own southern flank. See SWB/ME/7947/B/4, 10 May 1985.

38. '. . . if the struggle [in Mozambique] started afresh it would bring together Southern African liberation movements and FRELIMO so as to bring the struggle for African liberation to a conclusion'. Ibid.

39. See, *inter alia*, Winrich Kühne, *Südafrika und seine Nachbarn: Durchbruch zum Frieden? Zur Bedeutung des Nichtangriffsvertrages mit*

Mozambique und der Waffenstillstandsvereinbarung mit Angola vom Frühjahr 1984. (Ebenhausen, 1984, SWP-S 312); Paul Goodison, Richard Levin, *The Nkomati Accord: The illusion of peace in Southern Africa* (Liverpool: University of Liverpool, Department of Political Theory and Institutions. Working Paper No. 11, 1984).

40. See Bernhard Weimer, *Südafrika gegen SADCC: Thesen zur regionalen Dynamik und zu den Auswirkungen von Sanktionen Südafrikas gegen seine Nachbarn* (Ebenhausen: Stiftung Wissenschaft und Politik, AP 2510, 1987).

41. Since Mozambique is an important member of the FLS and SADCC, and because of RSA's threat to other members of those groupings, an 'FLS' or 'SADCC' option is more appropriate. See Weimer, 'A case . . .' op. cit. as well as Bernhard Weimer, *Die Allianz der Frontlinien Staaten im Südlichen Afrika: vom "Mulungushi Club" (1974) zum "Nkomati Akkord" (1984)* (Ebenhausen, Bedingungen und Dynamik von Befreiung, Dialog und Integration in einer Krisen-region, 1985).

42. Winfried Veit, 'Political Stability and Political Risk', in *Vierteljahresberichte* no. 96, June 1984 (special issue: *Third World Stability and Political Risk: Trends and Scenarios*, edited by Winfried Veit), p. 117.

43. Jonathan Alford, 'Security Dilemmas of Small States', in *The World Today*, Aug./Sept. 1984, pp. 363–9.

44. See Paul Fauvet, 'Roots of Counter-Revolution: The Mozambique National Resistance', in *Review of African Political Economy*, no. 29, 1984, pp. 108–21.

45. From a strict military point of view, mobile air reconnaissance-cum-defence equipment would be highly efficient for the prevention of MNR supplies by air and the protection of economic and strategic key installations. Such equipment is, however, very expensive and complicated and, if supplied, would create the problem of adequate manning, i.e. the secondment of military personnel.

46. Interview with President Joaquim Chissano of Mozambique: 'A President in Search of Peace', in *Africa Asia*, no. 40 (April 1987), p. 10.

47. Evans, 'Front-Line States . . .', op. cit., p. 12ff.

48. See 'A "worst case" security scenario for Mozambique', in *Africa Now*, Dec. 1983, pp. 86–8.

49. Alford, 'Security Dilemmas . . .', op. cit., p. 365f.

50. Chissano, 'A President in Search of Peace', op. cit.

51. Allan Isaacman, Barbara Isaacman, *Mozambique. From Colonialism to Revolution, 1900–1982* (Aldershot: Boulder, 1983), p. 181.

52. This agreement reportedly covers the supply of uniforms, light weapons, ammunition, spare parts etc. to FPLM, the training of military personnel both in Portugal and Mozambique as well the repatriation of logistical data from the liberation war (maps etc.) to Mozambique. The programme covered by the agreement has not been fully implemented, largely due to the political unwillingness of Lisbon. Its resuscitation featured prominently on the occasion of the visit to Lisbon of Samora Machel's special envoy, Professor de Bragança (see footnote 18) as well as the 'private visit' to Maputo of Portugal's President Eanes in May 1985.

53. *Noticias*, 29 May 1982 and 2 June 1982, quoted in Isaacman/Isaacman, op. cit., p. 182.
54. *Frankfurter Rundschau*, 12 Nov. 1983, p. 6.
55. *Neue Zürcher Zeitung*, 8 March 1983, p. 3.
56. Joaquim Chissano, quoted in SWB/ME/7235/B/3, 19 Jan. 1983.
57. Alford, 'Security Dilemmas . . .', op. cit., p. 369.

Index